EATING
BESIDE
OURSELVES

eating beside ourselves

THRESHOLDS
OF FOODS
AND BODIES

Heather Paxson, editor

Duke University Press Durham and London 2023

This work is licensed under a Creative Commons Attribution-
NonCommercial-NoDerivatives 4.0 International License available
at https://creativecommons.org/licenses/by-nc-nd/4.0/.
Printed in the United States of America on acid-free paper ∞
Designed by Aimee Harrison
Typeset in Minion Pro and SangBleu Kingdom
by Westchester Publishing Services

Library of Congress Cataloging-in-Publication Data
Names: Paxson, Heather, [date] editor.
Title: Eating beside ourselves : thresholds of foods
and bodies / Heather Paxson, editor.
Description: Durham : Duke University Press, 2023. |
Includes bibliographical references and index.
Identifiers: LCCN 2022033907 (print)
LCCN 2022033908 (ebook)
ISBN 9781478016786 (hardcover)
ISBN 9781478019435 (paperback)
ISBN 9781478024064 (ebook)
ISBN 9781478093114 (ebook other)
Subjects: LCSH: Food—Social aspects. | Food habits—Social aspects. |
Nutrition policy. | BISAC: SOCIAL SCIENCE / Anthropology / Cultural
& Social | SOCIAL SCIENCE / Agriculture & Food (see also POLITICAL
SCIENCE / Public Policy / Agriculture & Food Policy)
Classification: LCC GT2850 .E34 2023 (print) | LCC GT2850 (ebook)
DDC 394.1/2—dc23/eng/20220830
LC record available at https://lccn.loc.gov/2022033907
LC ebook record available at https://lccn.loc.gov/2022033908

Cover art by Aimee C. Harrison

coral gardens and their metabolism

Conquistadors landing in the Caribbean used to note that the white sand beaches looked like sugar. But the sand they likened to sugar turned out to be dead coral, most grains having passed through the digestive system of a parrotfish. It was part of the fishes' metabolism.

In *Coral Gardens and Their Magic*—Bronislaw Malinowski's colonial account of agricultural practices as related to gardening techniques, ancestral meals, land fertility, and uses of coral from the nearby reef—Malinowski... observed people in the Trobriand Islands feeding their ancestors by burying food in the earth. He wrote, with more than a hint of judgment, "The Trobriander's misapprehension of the fundamentals of human procreation is here matched by his misunderstanding of the processes of nutrition and metabolism."... Of course, this interpretation reveals most of all Malinowski's own assumptions about what processes of nutrition and metabolism entail, informed by the sciences of his era: a single human body, processing intentionally eaten food.

Where does any one body's eating begin or end?

—AMY MORAN-THOMAS, *TRAVELING WITH SUGAR*

contents

FOREWORD · ix
WIM VAN DAELE

ACKNOWLEDGMENTS · xi

INTRODUCTION · **EATING BESIDE OURSELVES** · 1
HEATHER PAXSON

1 Sweetness across Thresholds at the Edge of the Sea · 29
AMY MORAN-THOMAS

2 The Food of Our Food: Medicated Feed and
the Industrialization of Metabolism · 56
HANNAH LANDECKER

INTERCALARY EXCHANGE · **PROCESSING** · 86
HANNAH LANDECKER / ALEX BLANCHETTE

3 The Politics of Palatability: Hog Viscera, Pet Food,
and the Trade in Industrial Sense Impressions · 89
ALEX BLANCHETTE

INTERCALARY EXCHANGE · **(IN)EDIBILITY** · 111
ALEX BLANCHETTE / MARIANNE ELISABETH LIEN

4 Becoming Food: Edibility as Threshold in Arctic Norway · 114
MARIANNE ELISABETH LIEN

INTERCALARY EXCHANGE · **GIVING** · 137
MARIANNE ELISABETH LIEN / HARRIS SOLOMON

5 On Life Support · 140
HARRIS SOLOMON

INTERCALARY EXCHANGE · **TRANSGRESSION** · 158
HARRIS SOLOMON / EMILY YATES-DOERR

6   The Placenta: An Ethnographic Account of Feeding Relations · 163
    EMILY YATES-DOERR

    INTERCALARY EXCHANGE · **NOURISHMENT** · 187
    EMILY YATES-DOERR / DEBORAH HEATH

7   Between Sky and Earth: Biodynamic Viticulture's Slow Science · 191
    DEBORAH HEATH

    CONTRIBUTORS · 219

    INDEX · 221

foreword

WIM VAN DAELE

Ahead of you lies *Eating beside Ourselves*, a selection of research essays and intercalary conversations that pursue the relations, thresholds, and boundaries of food and eating. Relations abound in food studies, yet they are all too often taken for granted as a savoir faire in studying food *in relation to* other social domains, whether the body, commensality, ritual, political economy, migration, or the structures of the mind—but what of relations themselves? To query the natures and specifications of food's relations with more-than-human life, I organized the symposium "Food's Entanglements with Life," from which this volume took root. The symposium took place in Oslo, Norway, in September 2016; it was generously supported by the European Research Council and the Wenner-Gren Foundation for Anthropological Research, and it became just one event in a larger process, preceded by intense preparations and discussions among panelists and followed by the further concoction of this volume, edited by Heather Paxson.

The symposium began from the premise that *entanglement* offers a more relationally and materially grounded approach to the study of food than does the well-known credo that food is "good to think." Recognizing that food is not merely a passive mirror in which to study society, and inspired by the insights of such scholars as Karen Barad, Annemarie Mol, and Manuel DeLanda, my aim with the symposium was to highlight the ways food both is enacted by and takes part in shaping society through its entanglements with life. Food thus emerges as a key agent with which to work anthropologically in studying life, social and biological, as reflected in the symposium's full title, "Food's Entanglements with Life: How Is It Good to Work With?" The symposium was organized around three panel workshops that examined related themes: (1) the fragility and precariousness of food's entanglements in health and well-being, chaired by philosopher Lisa Heldke; (2) the tensions between sensorial intimacies and scaled abstractions in food as it entangles with different social contexts, chaired by anthropologist David Sutton;

and (3) the entanglements forged by food between humans and nonhumans, chaired by anthropologist Heather Paxson. That third workshop is the basis of the present volume.

Eating beside Ourselves takes food studies beyond food to detail relations of eating. The very distinction between food and eating is actually peculiar as each is implied in the other. We need only look at the Dutch word—*eten*—which merges the substantive of food and the verb of eating: food/eating, as it were. This volume's focus on eating, *and* on the multiplicities it entails, is a fresh elaboration of food/eating; drawing on rich and vivid empirical research, it offers a much-needed contribution to food studies. Moreover, the chapters encompass eaters besides human beings (as multiple as "we" are), discussing nonhuman and other-than-human agents as varied as cows, cats, reindeer, sugarcane, ventilators, stars, and the placenta. Throughout, the chapters are themselves connected by intercalary pieces in which the contributors collegially converse with one another to move forward together, yet in a nonunitary way. *Eating beside Ourselves* is a singular plural.

Relations may be everywhere, but they acquire a special qualification in the intimacy of both eating and in-*corpo*-ration. Relating joins food/eating in being plural, heterogeneous, and ambivalent. As Marilyn Strathern has taught us, relations do more work than just relating. These chapters expand the field of relations to query *thresholds* in a double sense: as relational boundaries and as tipping points catalyzing transformation. In the first sense, we can think of relations as carrying boundaries within them while boundaries also connect the two aspects they separate, as in a door that both separates and connects two rooms. The notion of the threshold in the second sense, as a tipping point, complexifies the opposition between relation and boundary, and between stability and transformation, as it involves multiple intensities and degrees of each. Suffused with relations in the forms of thresholds and transformations, *Eating beside Ourselves* demonstrates these to be generative apparatuses indeed with which to work.

acknowledgments

This book began as a workshop, "Human/Non-human Boundary Work," conceived and convened as part of the symposium "Food's Entanglements with Life: How Is It Good to Work With?" organized by Wim van Daele in collaboration with Thomas Hylland Eriksen, Marianne Elisabeth Lien, and Harry West. Held in Oslo, Norway, in September 2016, the three-day symposium was generously funded by a research grant from the European Research Council on Overheating (no. 295843, grantee Thomas Hylland Eriksen). After a sudden drop in global oil prices months before the event depreciated the Norwegian kronor and the symposium's budget, in relation to the US dollar, by 30 percent, Wim van Daele submitted a secondary grant and won additional support from the Wenner-Gren Foundation for Anthropological Research (CONF-722). We express our warm gratitude to Wim for his creative vision and steadfast leadership in convening the symposium, and to Thomas Hylland Eriksen and the Department of Social Anthropology at the University of Oslo for the gracious hosting. Our lively and inspiring discussions with other participants at the symposium—David Sutton, Lisa Heldke, Cristina Grasseni, Julie Guthman, Abby Wilkerson, and many others—galvanized us to pursue this book project.

The following year, 2017, nearly all of this volume's contributors reconvened for a roundtable discussion, "Eating beside the Human: Intercalary Exchanges on Food's Thresholds," at the meeting of the Society for Social Studies of Science, held in Boston, Massachusetts. Here we worked out a plan for the short intercalary exchanges that, as thresholds, both border and connect the traditional research chapters that otherwise constitute this volume.

We are indebted to Ken Wissoker and Joshua Tranen at Duke University Press for supporting this project and patiently waiting for it all finally to come together, and to Lisl Hampton for ushering it through the production process.

We are grateful to the entire production team, with special thanks to Aimee Harrison for her brilliant cover design. The comments and suggestions from two anonymous reviewers pushed us in good ways. Alex Rewegan provided valuable end-stage assistance, and Matthew John Phillips did an expert job with the index.

We give thanks to our families, friends, and messmates, and for renewed opportunities for commensality.

Introduction

....

EATING BESIDE OURSELVES

HEATHER PAXSON

> Eating is a liminal activity, occurring at the threshold between "inside" and "outside" the body.... As such it represents both opportunity and danger, and so it stands to reason that it would be freighted with significance that bears upon values and the relative worth of different ways of life.
>
> —CAROLYN KORSMEYER, "INTRODUCTION: PERSPECTIVES ON TASTE," *THE TASTE CULTURE READER*

TRANSFORMATIVE ACTS AND PROCESSES OF EATING—TASTING, ingesting, digesting, metabolizing—serve to nourish bodies, but they accomplish much else besides. They nourish relations and in this way share features with acts of care (Abbots, Lavis, and Attala 2015). They materialize social differences and in this way participate in gendered (and sexist), racializing (and racist), and classed (and classist) body politics (e.g., Bourdieu 1984; Counihan 1999; Witt 1999; Williams-Forson 2006; Bobrow-Strain 2012; Tompkins 2012; Garth and Reese 2020). They take forms understood to be "normal" or "abnormal" and in this way contribute to the stigmatization of conditions that interfere with "ordinary" living, whether these conditions stem from disability (Lance 2007; Taylor 2017), chronic illness (Solomon 2016; Moran-Thomas 2019), or acute poverty (Fitchen 1997; Mansfield and Guthman 2015; Bowen, Brenton, and Elliott 2019). Building on and expanding the work of food studies, this volume approaches eating and feeding as sites of transformation across a variety of bodies and selves, not only among but also beside ourselves, as humans.

Eating, after all, is not strictly a human activity. *Eating beside Ourselves* asks what can be learned by recognizing that what makes food *food*, in both substance and significance, concerns its relation to a myriad of eaters—not only human eaters but others besides. In turning organic substances into food, acts of eating create webs of relations, interconnected food chains organized by relative conditions of edibility, through which eaters may in turn become eaten. "As a mode of doing," note Sebastian Abrahamsson, Filippo Bertoni, Annemarie Mol, and Rebeca Ibáñez Martín (2015, 15), "eating crucially includes transforming: food into eater and eater into a well-fed rather than an undernourished creature. But, as it is through eating and feeding that diverse beings or substances fuse, in the end you never quite know who or what has done it." Hannah Landecker (2015, 257) writes similarly, "'You' and 'what you eat' are difficult to define, if you contain both generations and multitudes, and what you eat turns out... to itself contain worlds of industry and production." As both myriad and cumulative, the eating self recalls the digital self described by Brian Rotman in *Becoming beside Ourselves*. In the digital age, he writes, "Self-other boundaries thought previously to be uncrossable" are increasingly breaking down; the "I" of the digital self "is *porous*, spilling out of itself, traversed by other 'I's networked to it, permeated by the collectives of other selves." Plural and distributed, the "I" is "becoming beside itself" (2008, 8). For Rotman, becoming "beside oneself" is "a form of temporal change, becoming party to a condition other than one's own" (103). The digital self is a condition of living at the threshold of self and other(s), present and future. The condition of eating, we propose, is similar.

Eating beside Ourselves explores how acts and processes of eating partake in the ongoing making and unmaking of ontologies (the body, the self), taxonomies (food/not-food, raw/fermented), and judgments (inedible, delicious, disgusting). To bring to the center of our analyses the various forms of ingestion enacted by other-than-human animals, plants, and microbes—as well as by a diversity of humans—we must expand our view of "eating." Eating, in this volume, may not always enlist mouth or tongue. Eating, for example, may in placental mammalians take place within a pregnant body, across the threshold of the placenta (Yates-Doerr, chapter 6), or it may transpire across the fungal matrix providing the rootstock of grapevines access to minerals in surrounding soil (Heath, chapter 7). Eating may extend, too, to unexpected and even counterintuitive processes, describing, for instance, how trauma or COVID-19 patients may be "fed" oxygen through a ventilator (Solomon, chapter 5).

Contributors to this volume build on their own previous work on the sciences of food and nutrition to think through questions of difference-making and boundary-crossing. Amy Moran-Thomas, Harris Solomon, and Emily Yates-Doerr have all studied manifestations of the global diabetes epidemic as a metabolic condition, without presuming the matter to be a problem of overconsumption or "poor dietary choices." Hannah Landecker, Alex Blanchette, Marianne Elisabeth Lien, Deborah Heath, and I have written variously about agriculture's or aquaculture's manifold, multispecies ecologies of food production, including its "nested metabolisms" (Landecker 2011, 187). As part of the 2016 Oslo symposium "Food's Entanglements with Life," the idea behind the workshop "Human/Non-human Boundary Work," from which this volume emerged, was to bring together insights about the transformative agency of metabolism with the holistic perspective exemplified by multispecies ethnographies of agricultural relations. What resulted from that workshop, as our ongoing discussions have made clear, is a keen sense that eating is not a singular thing. Our contribution to food studies goes beyond bringing to it a multispecies approach inflected by science and technology studies (STS). Our intervention, instead, is to call attention to the many kinds of ingestions and transcorporealities that are often overlooked when we think of eating as thoughtfully deliberate, a fundamentally *cultural* matter of intention and meaning.

Consider the notion, by now a commonplace, that eating is an act of incorporation, of taking into the body elements of the surrounding world. As Anna Meigs observed in her 1987 article "Food as a Cultural Construction," anthropologists have often presumed that what *food* is, culturally speaking—what makes substances edible and palatable to some but not to other groups of people—has largely to do with cultural perceptions of those intrinsic qualities, material and symbolic, that are understood to be incorporated through eating into bodies and selves (e.g., Fischler 1988). Human commensality, the collective experience of "eating at the same table," has thereby been taken to suggest that such incorporation is at once individual and corporate: "If eating a food makes one become more like that food, then those sharing the same food become more like each other" (Fischler 2011, 533).[1] But if, "for us humans," culture means that "eating is never a 'purely biological' activity" (Mintz 1996, 7), eating is never a "purely cultural" activity either. If the human body of anthropology in the latter half of the twentieth century was "a recipient body that can be acted upon, rather than a dynamic site of interspecies mutuality and evolutionary change" (Lien, Swanson, and Ween 2018, 12), today's anthropologists increasingly perceive "a fluidity between bodies and worlds that foregrounds relations instead of entities" (Ford 2019); on this view, "humans are inseparable from surrounding environments and also function as environments themselves" (Ford 2019). Questions of eating, then, expand further to probe the uneven metabolic and epigenetic inheritances from generations of industrial farming and food production; the gut microbiome's connections to infrastructures of hygiene, sanitary water, and pharmaceutical care as well as to the predigestive role of fermentation; and bodily embeddedness in chemical ecologies that contribute to health risks and life chances.

Inside the body, too, as Annemarie Mol (2008, 30) observes, "the absorption of particles into its bloodstream is selective" but not as a matter of custom, volition, or personal taste: "I will never master which of [an apple's] sugars, minerals, vitamins, fibres are absorbed; and which others I discard," she writes. Biting, chewing, and swallowing may bring food substance into the (human) body via the threshold of the mouth, but further, involuntary activity by stomach acids and gut bacteria is required to break down that substance into small-enough bits to pass across the lining of the bowel and to complete the excorporation that is required for proper digestion and absorption. The digestive tract is, perhaps surprisingly, the largest endocrine organ in the human body, lined with cells bearing "taste" receptors that sense what is ingested, triggering manifold digestive responses and shaping appetite, nausea, and satiation, all well beyond conscious perception (Sternini, Anselmi, and Rozengurt 2008). This amazing gut lining, assisted by its more-than-human microbiome, is a body threshold, serving as much as a selectively protective skin against internalized elements from the outside as it is a site and means of absorption of welcome nutrients. The multifarious digestive tract is also asked to do *cultural* work. Pointing to a shift in "culinary imperialism" from advancing the cultural distinction of taste (Heldke 2012) to the privileged imperative of health, Hiʻilei Julia Hobart and Stephanie Maroney (2019) analyze, for example, how Indigenous "cures"—from Hawaiian Taroena marketed as an easily "assimilable" superfood to the promotion of "ancestral" fecal microbiota transplants derived from the excrement of Hadza people "hunting and gathering" in East Africa (see also Rest 2021)—draw on primitivist ideologies in promising to soothe dyspeptic or revive dysbiotic "white digestive systems" degraded by a "modern" diet of highly processed foods.

At the same time, Donna Haraway's (2008, 301) recognition that those with whom we humans "share a table" include other, more or less companionate species leads us to a revised notion of commensality. Commensality, we note, is an ecological concept as well as a gastronomic one. In biology a commensal relation obtains between individuals of two species in which one derives food or other necessities from the other without either harming or benefiting the latter directly; commensal relations are neither parasitic nor mutualist but something in between. Whether species interactions among messmates are best characterized as commensal, parasitic, or mutualist is not always easy to determine (Lorimer 2018). Human "messmates," as Haraway names them, include the bacteria that cause fermentation and enable digestion; the pets, vermin, and livestock that consume the scraps of human eating and industry; the mycorrhizal association between fungi and plant roots crucial to plants' ability to draw nourishment from soils; and the animals, wild and domesticated, that end up on some people's plates. Subject to changing conditions and pressures, relations among messmates are continuously being worked out.

To get at these relations, we aim to link materialist analyses of food's composition, availability, and accessibility to ethnographic perspectives on how particular foods and other nutritive substances may be understood to nourish or deplete, to comfort or repulse particular eaters—human as well as other-than-human. Our contention is that, by doing so, we can gain greater political purchase on the complex, planetary politics of contemporary food systems, in which living things are variously, sometimes confusingly, implicated as eaters and feeders and as food.

At the Threshold of Eating...

Our key analytic is the *threshold*. One meaning of *threshold*, the line crossed in entering a space, signals a border crossing. Eating, in this sense, is readily viewed as a thresholding project: "The act of choosing what to put into our mouths is a kind of 'boundary-work' in which"—by differentiating "food" from "not-food"—"we sort out the line between what is us and what is other" (DuPuis, Garcia, and Mitchell 2017, 1; see also Lien, chapter 4). A second meaning of *threshold* marks a baseline or an upper limit beyond which a particular phenomenon will occur or "characteristic behaviors [will] deviate from known patterns or trends" (Petryna 2018, 571). Concerned more with volumes and intensities than with lines, thresholds of this sort test known limits or capacities—for example, a human body's limited capacity to "tolerate" an allergen, toxic exposure, or high blood sugar—and they challenge established standards (tolerance levels, baselines) and protocols for standardization (Star and Lampland 2009). Our focus on the threshold is indebted to Amy Moran-Thomas, whose *Traveling with Sugar* (2019) chronicles diabetes in southern Belize, documenting how patients are able to manage (for a time) to live with off-the-charts blood sugar levels that challenge biomedical thresholds of survivability—a threshold put at stake by other thresholding projects, such as shopping for often unaffordable seafood and vegetables in a so-called tropical country whose local fisheries and agricultural economy have been compromised by ecological degradation and conditioned by a colonialist, export-oriented turn toward the Global North.

Far from being marginal to daily social life, critical thresholds are sites of intensification rather than attenuation, as Arnold van Gennep ([1909] 1960) and Victor Turner (1967) taught us of the limen. They may mark the beginning of transformative change, as in crossing from a state of health to a state of illness, or vice versa. Or they may affirm the limits of transformative potential, the point beyond which accommodation or adjustment is no longer possible, as when falling below a minimum threshold of nourishment to sustain life itself (Gremillion 2003; Solomon, chapter 5)—or to sustain "a particular kind of living," adequate "for the social, cultural, and personal dimensions of a good life," as Hanna Garth powerfully demonstrates in her *Food in Cuba* (2020, 5), or as Juliet Schor (2010) theorizes in terms of "plentitude," emphasizing environmental as well as social sustainability. Food sovereignty movements set as a threshold a group's ability to control the means and mechanisms of their own food's production and distribution (Mares 2019; Mihesuah and Hoover 2019).

Edibility nicely illustrates the analytic of the threshold. Consider how both forms that thresholds take—as line crossed and as capacity limit—participate in the making and unmaking of edibility, determining the status of a given substance as food with respect to the identity and condition of a particular eater. The successful passage of a foodstuff *across* the bodily threshold of an eater, affirming edibility, depends on that eating body's *capacity* to receive and incorporate it. A substance's status as edible food and an organism's status as an eater are thus mutually realized. Eating's inherent liminality as a process by which edibility is rehearsed, or refuted, through ritual enactment has been much remarked on, as by Carolyn Korsmeyer in this chapter's epigraph. "During the liminal period," Victor Turner tells us, "neophytes"—or, here, eaters—"are alternately forced and encouraged to think about their society, their cosmos, and the powers that generate and sustain them" (1967, 105). In discerning edibility, palatability, food safety, sufficiency, and the like, potential eaters participate in a variety of gastro-political contests, on materially uneven grounds.

In exploring through the lens of the threshold "food's power to entangle biological bodies within wider political and cultural structures" (Abbots 2017, 11), our focus is less on bodily incorporation than on mutual transformation, less on the agency of "eating bodies" (Mol 2008) or the philosophical question of what it means to "be human" (Mol 2021) than on processes of world-making (Landecker, chapter 2; Van Daele 2013, 2018; Yates-Doerr 2015)—evoking the worlds of industry and global trade but also the unmaking and remaking of the everyday cultural and ecological worlds of myriad inhabitants (Bertoni 2013). The notion of the threshold, serving alternately as portal and as barrier, reminds us that if food brings entities together—makes commensal—it also delineates, holds apart (see Yates-Doerr, chapter 6). The threshold gives force to the partiality of food's capacity to make and to relate, and to the messy unevenness of commensality (Abrahamsson and Bertoni 2014).

… Food Is a Medium of Contact

To get at eating's threshold dynamics, we extend Arjun Appadurai's notion of *gastro-politics*, by which he called attention to the ways foods serve as "important media of contact between human beings" (1981, 495), while offering an account of how such contact is socially regulated, policed, and exploited in domestic settings. Our interest is complementary, focusing on how foods serve as "media of contact" at other thresholds besides human social interactions. In particular, we regard food as a medium of multispecies relations, and we consider how food's porosity connects organisms to their manifold environments.

The gastro-political thresholds in which we are interested are mediated by social rules but also by (micro)biopolitics, capitalism, and technoscience. The glucometer; the knife; the ventilator; the wood-fired grill; the scientifically formulated feed fed to the hogs destined to be reconstituted as pork chops, pet food, and a thousand other commercial products—such thresholding objects, featured in the chapters that follow, are densely embedded in relations of inequality and constrained choice. The "techno-intimacies" they mediate are not always chosen, or even wanted (Weston 2017). Such mediating devices reveal how eating, at the thresholds of the natural and the artificial, the human and the other-than-human, the individual and its milieu, often occurs beside ourselves, as culture-bearing humans with tastes and appetites, as we become party to the conditions of *other* transformations, standards, appetites, and forces.

By bringing into focus the fundamental porosity of bodies—be they organisms, social groups, or nations—the analytic of the threshold calls attention to the role of *regulatory* functions—metabolic, gastro-political, and state enacted—in reinscribing, redrawing, or rending constructions of bodily integrity (Jusionyte 2018). Consider, for example, what food-safety scandals, as evidence of a lack of oversight, or *mis*regulation, reveal about postsocialist states. Elizabeth Dunn (2008) has interpreted botulism-prone home canning practices in postsocialist Georgia as emblematic of the decaying post-Soviet state, arguing that the Soviet decline of centralized, industrial food production left Georgians with a taste for canned foods but not the practical knowledge of how to safely re-create those tastes (and that storage capacity) in domestic spaces. In postsocialist Bulgaria, Yuson Jung (2009, 2016) observed that food shoppers faced with unaccustomed consumer choice approached goods with suspicion, ever on the lookout for "fake" (*mente*) products, be they cheap knockoffs of name brands, physically adulterated items, or otherwise falsely advertised goods. Such skepticism about the "realness" of their food, in Jung's analysis, reflects a postsocialist self-perception of marginalization, a feeling of being not fully included in the so-called global economy, and reveals the significance of food as a "medium for social trust and global belonging" (2016).

Recognizing that eating transpires across many forms of ingestion, not all of which entail choosing which foods to put into "our" mouths, this volume focuses on the ways eating and feeding mediate potential crossings and overtoppings at thresholds among (1) different conditions or states of being, (2) organisms of different species, and (3) living beings and their surrounding environment, or milieu (Canguilhem 2001).

BETWEEN CONDITIONS OR STATES OF BEING

Acts and processes of eating and feeding mediate thresholds between different conditions or states of being both for food substances (edible/inedible, safe/toxic) and for eaters (parasitic/commensal, autonomous/pregnant, healthy/ill, living/dying). Addressing how eating is understood to mediate *conditions of health and illness* in the human body could fill a volume of its own. By way of illustration, suffice it to point out the flaws of nutrition science's dominant paradigm, the "energy balance theory," in which "healthy" eating rests on a quantitative equilibrium of calories taken in through eating, and calories expended through physical activity (Mudry 2009; Gálvez 2018). From research into digestion and metabolism, it is becoming clear that a calorie from fat and a calorie from carbohydrate (sugar) do not move through the threshold that is metabolism in the same way; a calorie is *not* a calorie. Fantasies of universal exchange are increasingly challenged by the specificity of biochemical action: for example, carbohydrate cooked at high temperatures under dry conditions might ricochet off DNA in a damaging fashion, while fat may feed or suppress inflammatory signals depending on its kind, the relative ratio to other fats in the diet, or the emulsifiers it travels with in any given foodstuff (Furman et al. 2019).

Both nutritional paradigms—weighing all food calories as equivalent sources of potential energy and excess, and distinguishing between the metabolic effects of fats and carbohydrates when ingested by the body—are based on ideal-typic notions of foods. Standard dietary advice consistently "overlooks the chemical composition of processed foods and beverages and the effects of consuming those chemicals" (Gálvez 2018, 111). If a fat-free fruit popsicle with added sugars is no better an alternative for weight loss than a creamy ice cream bar, a lime-green popsicle might well be a better choice than a cherry pop with Red Dye 40—at least for young eaters with attention-deficit/hyperactivity disorder (ADHD). Nutritionism has yet to catch up with the fact that so much of our food today inescapably contains *nonfood* in the form of added flavorings and colorings, nutritional fortifications, preservatives, and fillers (González Turmo 2007, 45), if not also harmful contaminants, such as pesticide residues or adulterants introduced to processed foods to reduce costs (Yan 2012).

A forceful example of this is given by Emily Yates-Doerr (2012) in tracking what happens when the "nutritional black-boxing" that informs public health campaigns developed in the United States crosses national, economic, and cultural thresholds to reach Guatemala. Nutritionists working in Guatemala present what they imagine to be straightforward lessons in how to identify nutritionally "good" and "bad" foods—green vegetables, since they have vitamins, are good and should be eaten; sugar, because it is sweet, is also bad and should be avoided—and so they are flummoxed when the classificatory reductions (calories, vitamins) of "nutritionism" (Scrinis 2008) fail to take hold. Yates-Doerr not only explains how reductive thinking about food remains disconnected from people's everyday social and sensory experiences of cooking and eating but also demonstrates how, in Elizabeth Dunn's (2009, 119) words, a "standard without an appropriate infrastructure cannot be put into force without major upheavals in the physical environment and the social organization of production." The government of Guatemala requires sugar fortification as a means of preventing nutritional deficiencies; the box of sugar found on the kitchen table of most households is thus labeled "Sugar with Iron." Consequently, Yates-Doerr (2012, 297) watched women spoon sugar into their drinks, explaining it was "for the vitamins."

In *Traveling with Sugar*, Amy Moran-Thomas (2019, 89) reflects on the ironies attached to "normal sugar" levels for diabetic patients in Belize, who often live with levels of blood sugar and pressure "beyond the ranges programmed into devices like glucometers and digital home blood pressure cuffs." "What does 'normal' sugar even mean here?" she asks (90, see also chapter 1), reminding us again that standards without an infrastructure to uphold them lose their significance (Dunn 2009). Jessica Hardin (2021) relatedly analyzes "the problem of vegetables" in Samoa. Grown in household gardens for cash trade and nutritionally promoted as "good" vitamin-rich foods, vegetables register the subjunctive quality of both health and wealth by promising the possibility of health *as if* they were affordable to eat. "Health," Hardin (2021, 435) writes, "is impossible to achieve because of the doubling of ever-receding thresholds whereby vegetables index both the promise of wealth (despite the presence of poverty) and the promise of health (despite the presence sickness).... As these thresholds shift, their definitions change, making them all the more impossible to achieve."

Picking up on the involuntary dimensions of ingestion, Harris Solomon (2016, 5), in his study of diabetes and "metabolic living" in India, forwards an analytic of *absorption*, by which he means "the possibility for bodies, substances, and environments to mingle, draw attention to each other, and even shift definitional parameters in the process." He writes, "A study of metabolic illness grounded in absorption, in contrast to one that assumes overconsumption as its starting point ... can open up key questions in the context of chronic diseases connected to food: Who and what become the eater and the eaten? What is nutrition and what is poison? Who and what set the boundaries of inside and outside, delineating organism and environment?" (5). Such questions take us beyond ourselves, as humans, to consider species and other boundaries.

AMONG SPECIES

Theories of domestication have long grappled with the role of food as a medium of contact among species (Lien 2015; Swanson, Lien, and Ween 2018). Domestication is not taming, nor is it making placid. Domestication is about (unequal) cohabitation within a given environment, including modifications made to the conditions of eating, resulting in the coevolution of species and concomitant transformations of lands and watersheds (Noske 1989; Tsing 2012). Such changes entail not only "biological processes of alteration to organisms" but also "social and cultural changes in both humans and animals" (Russell 2007, 30; see also Leach 2003; Anderson 2004)—including changes in eating and in producing bodily and other wastes. A multispecies relation, domestication may be simultaneously beneficial and deleterious to inhabitants, for commensal organisms that share environments may have different needs and conditions of flourishing. At the same time, "many of the effects associated with human domestication practices," including metabolic effects, "are unintended" and may go unrecognized (Lien, Swanson, and Ween 2018, 17).

We often imagine food as a medium of transmission conveying sustaining matter and energy into eating bodies from the surrounding environment, including the organisms of other species. Yet the scientific term for the assimilation and generation of nutrients, *metabolism*, is capacious and includes the processing of toxicants and oxygen within and between cells, bodies, and species. These relations are both spatial and temporal; metabolism reformats the matter of living beings in ways that are understood further to impact not-yet-living beings, through epigenetic processes (Valdez 2018). Metabolically speaking, plants and other animals are just as much "eaters" as are people and are equally reliant on the metabolic activity of microbes. What can we understand better about eating "by allowing metabolic relations writ large to decenter human food as the object of inquiry?" (Landecker, chapter 2). One thing we can see is that food chains unfold not only laterally across species but also generationally, mutually transforming bodies and environments over time (Moran-Thomas, chapter 1; Yates-Doerr, chapter 6; Heath, chapter 7). At the level of everyday practice, too, eating and its effects—providing nourishment, producing interconnectedness as well as difference—are similarly species interdependent.

Consider fermented foods. Biological anthropologists and nutrition scientists view fermentation as a form of predigestion, meaning that eaters of fermented foods benefit from the added bioavailability of minerals and vitamins made possible by the prior microbial metabolism (Amato et al. 2021). As Megan Tracy writes, "Fermentation, then, is not simply about converting matter but is also about the transformations it effects on its 'eaters' and 'eatens'" (2021, s277; see also Yamin-Pasternak et al. 2014). Harnessing the transformative agencies of bacteria, yeasts, and fungi, agriculturalists and pastoralists, no less than scientists working in industrial food labs, endeavor to manipulate metabolic processes toward better (human) living through systematically designed and integrated feeding practices for livestock, plants, and microbes (Heath, chapter 7; Lee 2015; Raffaetà 2021). What makes for "better" living through fermentation is, of course, a (microbio-)*political* question, as Daniel Münster (2021) tellingly demonstrates in his study of how an agricultural ferment (see also chapter 7) popular in South India—concocted from the microbially rich dung of native cows, nourished with "cow urine, ground pulses, sugar, soil, and water"—is employed by farmers both to revitalize depleted agricultural soils and to make exclusionary, "bionativist" claims in support of Hindu nationalism.

Cheese making is an ancient fermentation-based biotechnology for food preservation. "Whereas industrial cheese makers seal off their productive process from the surrounding environment," writes Harry West (2013, 322) "artisan producers seek to engage actively with their environment" (see also Paxson 2013). They do so "in the vat" by adjusting their recipe, tweaking temperature, technique, and the timing of various steps to work *with* rather than *against* "natural" variability in both their milk and their ambient environments, conditioned by seasonal, weather-dependent, and climatological factors as well as by the effects of human activity.[2] In aging facilities, too, artisans manage the microbial environment through control of humidity, air circulation, and temperature to cultivate conditions in which wheels of cheese may grow so-called natural rinds. Created by successive waves of bacteria and fungi colonizing the surface of a cheese, a cheese rind or crust is what microbiologists call a *biofilm*, or microbial mat (Wolfe et al. 2014). But not all microbes are welcome. Just as organic farmers cultivate the habitats of owls and hawks so that *they* might take care of rodent pest control in the field, artisan cheese makers cultivate the "good" microbes that might outcompete "bad" ones (not only pathogens but also bacteria judged to produce malodorous decomposition) for nutrients in a cheese, resulting in competitive exclusion. As one cheese maker explained to me, evoking a microcosmic farm, "We want to cultivate the right soil, if you will, for the right things to grow." I have described this approach to cheese making as "post-Pasteurian" (2008, 2013) to highlight how it takes *after* and, indeed, carries on the Pasteurian ethos of hygiene by dutifully enacting proper sanitation, while also moving *beyond* an antiseptic food-safety orthodoxy informed by industrial scales and methods of manufacturing to embrace the aid of ambient fermentative and flavor-generating microbes, including uncharacterized or "wild" ones. Post-Pasteurian cheese making is an exercise in microbial domestication. Harry West (2013) calls it learning to "think like a cheese."

Dairy milk, in turn, is the outcome of domesticated cows, goats, or sheep feeding on dry and fermented hay and pasture grasses containing cellulose, which ruminants (unlike other mammals) are able to digest owing to the metabolic assistance of microbes residing in their four-chambered guts. Thanks to further activity by microbes, the fodder that healthy dairy animals eat and digest—hay and fresh grasses, pulses, wild onions or flowers, fermented corn silage, or total mixed rations—directly influences the nutritional composition and taste of their milk and the subsequent flavor profile of a raw-milk cheese (or the meat of a suckling lamb or calf, known as *veal*). Ruminating and lactating cows, sheep, and goats are, with microbes and people, symbiotically essential to cheese "ecologies of production," assemblages of multispecies, metabolic, social-economic, and political forces that are enlisted into agricultural value-making projects (Paxson 2013, 31). Writing of raw-milk cheese making in the Italian Alps, Roberta Raffaetà details "how fermentation participates in the composition of different human, more-than-human, and microbial spacetimes" (2021, s323)—what she calls *utopias, heterotopias,* and *atopias*—through which cheese's ecologies of production are variously fetishized, valorized, or transcended in the service of distinct ideological visions and economic endeavors.

Beyond what dairy animals eat, the habituated, species-specific *manner* in which they graze and selectively take in food further contributes to the quality characteristics of their milk (Paxson 2013, 45–46). Goats, I was told by their keepers, are nervous animals; fearful of lacking enough to eat, they wind up eating everything in sight. If the flavor of goats' milk is of concern, goats' eating should be monitored. Sheep, in contrast, nibble delicately at the tops of pasture grasses; as a sheep dairy farmer explained, cheese made from their milk thus tends to be uniformly flavored and relatively mild.

Cows dig into it when out on pasture, taking into their mouths hunks of sod with bits of soil still clinging to the root structures of grasses. When cows chew their cud, what they are chewing is previously swallowed food that has been microbially fermented (predigested) in the reticulum, the second of a cow's four stomach compartments, and then regurgitated (burped up) for further mechanical processing. All that chewing further breaks down the cellulose in hay and grasses, enabling further digestion as well as releasing additional flavor compounds. For this reason some scientists point to the particular potential of cheese made from cow's milk to express pronounced flavors of pasturage—one element of what the French call the *terroir* of a cheese. Along with grinding teeth, antacid saliva, and a muscular tongue for pushing around cud, the chambers of a cow's stomach, including their varied microbiomes, are all agents of cow "eating." In turn, the composite agency of cow eating, in addition to the material composition of cow feed, influences the flavor of cheese made from cow's milk, particularly when spared the heat treatment of pasteurization.

At the same time, "cow taste," that is, bovine taste for cow feed, is itself influenced by the human manipulations of domesticated husbandry. Describing the sensory work employed by dairy farmers in selecting optimal feed, Katy Overstreet (2018a, 2018b) introduces us to a Wisconsin farmer who pokes at bales of hay at auction, searching for the right mix of grasses and legumes, in optimally dry condition, to promote his cows' digestive health without compromising the high-volume milk production that the industry has come to expect. On most dairy farms today, feed optimization is accomplished in the form of total mixed rations (TMR), industrially manufactured, standardized feed composed of vitamins, minerals, nutritional components, and possibly medicines and growth promoters, bulked up with the by-products of industrial agriculture and manufacturing (see Landecker, chapter 2). Although "TMR diets are designed to deliver an optimally balanced nutritional package in every bite," Overstreet observed that cows often thwarted this design by eating on their own terms—"cows often push the feed around with their noses and tongues in order to eat the pieces that they prefer"—or by refusing to eat the rations altogether (2018b, 72). Chopping TMR into smaller bits might undercut choosy cow eating, but by reducing roughage it would also cause them digestive problems. Instead, she explains, Wisconsin dairy farmers attempt to mask the bitter taste of medicated feed rations by applying a "dressing" of synthetic flavor enhancers (see Blanchette, chapter 3). Overstreet interprets Wisconsin farmers' tendency to apply feed dressings with commercial names like "Caramel Delight" as a projection of their own Midwestern taste for sweetness—a regional proclivity that Overstreet (2018a, 64–65) registered ethnographically as a culinary outsider from California. In the end, she proposes to regard cow "taste" as "transcorporeal," something that "moves through and across bodies," human and bovine (2018a, 54). Similarly, the tastes and appetites of animals not only contribute to the flavor of flesh eaten by humans (Weiss 2016) but may also, for example, lead "farmers to send their sheep up hills where herbs are growing" and "butchers to buy lambs from farmers with hillside land" (Yates-Doerr and Mol 2012, 53)—or such proclivities may participate in the mobility of migrating herds, as with reindeer, whose taste for mushrooms facilitates their herding by humans (Lien, chapter 4). This book explores the significance of transcorporeal taste not only for eaters thus connected but also for the wider political, economic, and environmental worlds in which they dwell.

BETWEEN ORGANISM AND ENVIRONMENT

Cheese, I have suggested, may be regarded as the living manifestation of ruminant and microbial bodies incorporating and transforming bits of their environment: eating, digesting, metabolizing. This may be cause for celebration, as in claims to terroir foods and wine, valued for expressing distinctive characteristics "typical" of their place and customary method of production (Paxson 2013, 282–83; see also Barham 2003; Trubek 2008; Demossier 2011). It can also be cause for alarm. Some years ago, the safety of buffalo-milk mozzarella made in its home region of Campania was called into doubt when the Italian Ministry of Health announced that buffalo-milk mozzarella from twenty-five facilities tested positive for dioxins, chemical compounds known as persistent environmental pollutants, noting "the strong likelihood that the dioxin contamination was due to local forage and feed" (Biasetti 2008, 2). Fingers were pointed at years of profitable and largely illegal trade in toxic waste dominated by another local product of Campania: the Camorra (Italian mafia); surely, illegal landfills were the cause of dioxins seeping into the groundwater that fed water buffalo via "forage and feed."

A focus on the threshold helps make clear that while eating and feeding can be intentional (if contingent) acts of crossing borders, of actively bringing into the body elements of the surrounding world, they nonetheless share features with the more passive process of environmental or toxic *exposure* (Landecker 2011, 173; Agard-Jones 2014; Shapiro 2015; Murphy 2017; Liboiron, Tironi, and Calvillo 2018; Creager and Gaudillière 2021; Moran-Thomas, chapter 1). Toxins, absorbed into living organisms, are often eaten. The nonfood substances that many foods today contain, "which they used not to contain" (González Turmo 2007, 45), include added fillers and nutritional supplements but also uninvited contaminants, antibiotics, and pesticides. Becky Mansfield (2011) notes that decades of industrial waste runoff into waterways has meant that heavy metals such as mercury have become an essential part of the nutritional composition of top-predator fish, such as tuna and swordfish. Such toxicants not only cross thresholds but can reorder or disrupt them, affecting biological and cultural foodways alike (Hoover 2017). Describing a marine ecology of production, Elspeth Probyn (2016, 15–16) writes, "There is no privileging the inside or outside of any individual body. If one eats bluefin tuna, one eats at the top of the trophic system, ingesting the heavy metals the tuna has eaten across this history. Human eaters get a taste of what we have wreaked. We eat oil slicks, and the chemicals used to disperse them eat into our flesh. Fish eat the microplastics used in daily skin care; humans eat the fish and the microplastics; and fish and human bodies intermingle. And of course that 'we' gets eaten up too, differentiated, fragmented, and fractured." Precisely because "bodies and environments are porous to each other" (Solomon 2015, 178), the health of organisms and of species is fully enmeshed with the health of marine, land, and atmospheric environments. Consequently, "laboratory and policy concern for 'eating well' increasingly entails consideration for how foods are cultivated, transported, packaged and processed by a range of human and non-human bodies" (Sanabria and Yates-Doerr 2015, 119).

Moreover, the indeterminacy of the threshold reminds us to regard ingestion as a site of not only incorporation, willful or otherwise, but also its antitheses: rejection, indigestion, revulsion. Food allergies and autoimmune diseases alike are understood to occur when a body's immune system has trouble distinguishing among "self," "food" ("food" being that which can safely become incorporated into "self"), and "nonfood" (that which is toxic or pathogenic to self). "Food allergic living," as Danya Glabau (2019) observes, is often oriented around keeping "nonfood" out of the allergic body by keeping it out of the allergenic home, maintaining a domestic threshold of bodily safety through persistent hygiene. An alternative strategy is to "teach" the immune system to tolerate potentially dangerous substances through repeated low-dose exposure. As Richard Cone and Emily Martin write, the gut's immune system "learns to recognize and accept ('tolerate') food, allowing it to be absorbed into the blood and lymph. It also learns to recognize dangerous pathogens and toxins ingested along with food and helps prevent them from being absorbed" (2003, 239)—that is, by causing people to be sick. That ingesting small amounts of a "foreign" substance can "train" the immune system to tolerate it is the reasoning behind ingesting local honey (full of environmental pollen) to reduce suffering associated with hay fever.

In a fascinating twist on the idea of oral tolerance, Elizabeth Roberts's study of toxicity and persistence in an impoverished neighborhood in Mexico City demonstrates that selective "permeation" of bodies by toxic substances (sugary soda, drugs) can contribute to a "protective porosity, which sustains life at collective levels" (2017, 613). Sending a child to school with a water bottle filled with contraband soda may lead to a prediabetic state of health, but first—and foremost—it fills the child with the sustenance of a mother's love (see also Fitchen 1997). In Roberts's reading, the soda conveys material comfort as it is "let in" both bottle and body, while it also mediates the child's persistence by throwing up a social-emotional protective barrier against an environment neglected by state care—an environment that, like the running water provided by a state government that is trusted by no one in the neighborhood, may indeed cause sickness and other harm. As such, the study demonstrates how toxic harm not only "disrupts order and existing relations" but sometimes "also *maintains* systems, including those that produce inequity and sacrifice" (Liboiron, Tironi, and Calvillo 2018, 333).

Whereas Roberts argues that potential benefits can be gained by developing a tolerance for nutritionally "bad" foods, Annemarie Mol (2009) extends the notion of oral tolerance in a different direction, to entertain the possibility of "teaching" a body to accept, even to appreciate, food that is not only "good" for a healthy body but also "good" in an ethical sense, providing tangible benefits to communities of producers or to the environment. I have witnessed this notion play out in recreational taste education in which connoisseurship, the cultivation of a knowing palate, is retrained to include (selective) knowledge about the means and methods of food production. At the 2009 California Artisan Cheese Festival, for example (see Paxson 2016), Cowgirl Creamery's founding cheese makers, Sue Conley and Peggy Smith, introduced a tasting session by explaining that they would "talk about cheeses in terms of the place they're made in, and how place contributes to the cheese." Their rhetoric points to how ethically, socially *good food* and food that *tastes good* are brought together through a taste education that promotes artisan practices no less than artisanal products (see also Weiss 2016). The Cowgirls' cheese flight featured a simple, fresh cheese selected "to showcase [the] hard work" of the organic dairy farmer who provided the milk and "how he's taken care of the land and his animals." As tasters, we were invited to draw a causal connection between the "good, clean" milk flavor of the cheese and the farmer's "good, clean," environmentally conscious dairying practice. His pastures, we learned, are free of herbicides and chemical fertilizers; the cows are never treated with hormones or antibiotics to boost production volume. Conley and Smith went on to describe in some detail a newly installed methane digester, apparently without worry that our senses would suddenly register suggestive hints of manure in the odor and taste of the cheese. Instead, we were meant to taste the goodness of greenhouse gas mitigation! Including methane digesters in the "taste of place" (Trubek 2008) is a mode of "making taste public" (Counihan and Højlund 2018).

Here, in much the way Mol (2009) envisions cultivating the good taste of a consumer-citizen, eaters with "good taste" are enjoined to taste "good" qualities that materialize *beside* the food itself—and even to imagine, through the fantasy of tastes yet to come, the realization of more just and sustainable futures. But for whom? Cows, sheep, goats, bacteria, and fungi actively participate, through eating, in cheese making but not under conditions of their own choosing (Paxson 2013, 40). Among humans, eating continues to be enlisted in the social reproduction of class, caste, and gender and remains "a site of racial anxiety" (Tompkins 2012, 2). Exploring not only the plurality but also the diversity of eating's agencies and actions requires constant attention to the uneven, world-making power dynamics in which they are enlisted. For this reason this book is as much about ingestion, digestion, indigestion, and incorporation—about bodies and the relations they enter into and contain—as it is about food and eating.

Thresholding Projects

The chapters that follow take up and address eating and feeding as *thresholding projects*, processes and activities that mediate or regulate border crossings, that test the limits and capacities of various sorts and scales of boundaries, and that may reveal hidden or overlooked borders or regulating mechanisms. These may be intentional or unintended, successful or failed. With the potential either to reinforce or to transgress, thresholding projects push up against and may expand established ways of doing, being, feeling, relating: "Boundaries can also be that place where new ways of being get worked out and incorporated into a new whole" (DuPuis, Garcia, and Mitchell 2017, 1). Nodding to Elizabeth Roberts's (2017, 615) call to take "into account not only the (often quantitative) practices that make boundaries but also what those boundaries have to offer," thresholding projects also include efforts at boundary maintenance amid ongoing crossings and overflows.

Throughout the ethnographic cases presented here, we also see people confront *ethical thresholds* as they are pressed into moral trade-offs, or acquiesce to making moral accommodations, because that is what it takes to remain above or below a certain threshold to get by, to persist. People's decisions over eating and feeding are often decisions about who we are and would like to be as family members, caregivers, people of faith, professionals, communities, societies. Awareness of the persisting paradox of abundance and hunger that characterizes the contemporary global food system could drive any of us beside ourselves with worry over what and how to eat and to feed others (Poppendieck 1998; Levenstein 2003; Patel 2007).

The volume begins with Amy Moran-Thomas's composite reflections on the shape-shifting, world-making carbohydrate substance of sugar. Inspired by visiting the warehouses and factories of London's "sugar mile," Moran-Thomas follows how sweetness's power spills far beyond the commodity chains described by Sidney Mintz (1985) to trace the mediations of sugar's life-sustaining and life-taking power in Belize from the afterlives of plantation labor to diabetic limb loss today. In her sweeping account of sugar's metabolic transformations—as something eaten and as itself all-consuming—bodies, chemistries, technologies, and environments are all shown to be entangled in the ecological webs of global, racial capitalism. Her exploration of imbricating thresholds serves as a sort of parallel introduction to the volume's broader themes.

Drilling down into technoscience histories, chapters by Hannah Landecker and Alex Blanchette update readings of animal domestication and commensality for an era of industrially processed foods and feed, as the feeding of one organism or species can now be formatted as the by-product of providing sustenance to another. They demonstrate edibility and palatability to be an effect and, indeed, legitimation of scaling up other forms of alimentary production. By detailing the biochemical, economic, and technoscientific mediations that have come to constitute "the food of our food" (at least for the carnivores among us), Landecker excavates the "the industrialization of metabolism" itself to suggest how the rise of medicated livestock feed has reformatted the "biochemical milieu" of modern life. Blanchette shows not only that house cats express taste preferences, signaling that felines enjoy some understanding of yumminess, but also that cats' preferences have, for the food industry, come to mean an expanded economic ability to exploit the industrial hog, which in turn means cheaper cuts of pork for wider human consumption. Cat eating and human eating are thus mutually informed in ways that are mediated by endlessly partible pigs.

Drawing on three decades of fieldwork conducted in North Norway, Marianne Elisabeth Lien's chapter explores food's involvement in ongoing practices that enact, stabilize, and negotiate boundaries and thereby take part in the *making and unmaking* of insides and outsides, of people and things, of food and not-food. (Such an approach contrasts with one that would regard food as *transcending* boundaries, as if the insides and outsides of such bounded entities as bodies, species, or social groups had an independent existence from one another.) Lien shows boundary-crossing processes—of slaughtering, cooking, sharing, tasting, ingesting—to be full of ambiguity and often experienced with ambivalence. Such vital uncertainties are revealed by fieldwork that is "less about collecting facts than about paying attention to the moments when the facts falter," as Lisa Stevenson (2014, 2) describes in her wondrous ethnography of "life beside itself" in the Canadian Arctic.

In this vein, too, Harris Solomon's chapter on critical care in an overcrowded trauma ward in Mumbai, India, stages commensality beside the hospital bed to analyze the ventilator-assisted "feeding" of oxygen. When ventilators, a mediating technology for respiration, must be rationed, who has the right to adjudicate the threshold between life and death—or between allowing to stay living and giving over to dying? How do families and healthcare providers make sense of this moral ecology of feeding breath? Tragically, Solomon's analysis of a singular trauma ward came to have global relevance as the coronavirus pandemic took hold in early 2020, with a second wave overwhelming India in early 2021.

Continuing to think, through feeding, about biomedical understandings of and efforts at a more fundamental means of life support, Emily Yates-Doerr draws attention to the "miraculous conduit" of the human placenta, a threshold organ that materializes metabolic contradictions by being, at once, "harmful and healthy, wanted and repellent, life-giving and deadly, self and other." How, and with what repercussions for personhood, are women held responsible—and how do they hold themselves responsible—for the avolitional act of "feeding" a fetus growing in the womb? (see also Markens, Browner, and Press 1997). By exploring through personal experience how exceeding acceptable sugar levels can transform a woman's pregnancy from a relation of idealized commensality to a more threatening parasitism requiring biomedical management, Yates-Doerr experiments with ethnographic narration to make evident incongruities among body, experience, and subjecthood.

If insides and outsides fold in on one another in many of these chapters, scalar distance between the organismic and the planetary, and even the cosmic, also collapses—an insight that the biodynamic winegrowers about whom Deborah Heath writes in her chapter not only perceive but work to operationalize. Bringing a "gentle empiricism" to a viticultural ecology of production, biodynamic growers follow celestial cues in creating compost and other "preps" (preparations) to feed vineyard soils—or, more directly, to nourish the mycorrhizal interface, a fungal threshold that mediates between soils and plant roots, and beyond. As one biodynamic vintner tells Heath, "Preps aren't about agency. They're like catalysts to communication between soil and the cosmos." We are returned to magical gardens, introduced in the epigraph to this book—although not as Bronislaw Malinowski (1935) viewed those of the Trobriand Islanders. Today, as Heath traces, a growing reckoning with the colonial and racial-capitalist origins of this planet's contemporary environmental crises is inviting dialogue and collaboration between ecological sciences and Indigenous food and soil sovereignty activism, edging a path toward multispecies justice (Celermajer et al. 2021).

A final note. In the spirit of our discussions beginning in Oslo, and in a desire to play in this volume with the forms that thresholds might take, the chapters that follow are connected and augmented by short intercalary exchanges between authors. We approached these lively, dialogical pieces as conversational passes, as in a relay, allowing authors to pull out and reflect further on phenomena, ambivalences, and conceptual tensions that weave throughout the chapters, especially those having to do with *processing, (in)edibility, giving, transgression,* and *nourishment*. Their explicitly collaborative method means further to acknowledge—and to celebrate—the reality that no one writes alone. Numerous influences permeate and reformat our thoughts, arguments, and phrasings as scholars; indeed, this introduction has been significantly strengthened by the incorporation of insights and suggested wording from my collaborators.

By offering broader reflections on the contemporary study of food and eating, and on social theory more generally, the connective intercalary passes invite readers to grasp the baton and to pursue new thresholds in food studies.

ACKNOWLEDGMENTS

This introduction has undergone numerous revisions in close dialogue with Alex Blanchette, Deborah Heath, Hannah Landecker, Marianne Elisabeth Lien, Amy Moran-Thomas, Harris Solomon, and Emily Yates-Doerr: I learned a lot from, and greatly enjoyed, our collective effort that unfolded over several years. This chapter has further benefited from constructive feedback from Elizabeth Ferry, Stefan Helmreich, Wim van Daele, and the anonymous reviewers for Duke University Press. A late draft was enriched by bringing this project into dialogue with another: the Wenner-Gren Foundation Symposium "Cultures of Fermentation," organized by Jessica Hendy, Matthäus Rest, Mark Aldenderfer, and Christina Warinner, held in October 2019 in Sintra, Portugal; see the supplemental issue of *Current Anthropology* 62, no. S24 (2021). My appreciation goes to MIT Libraries for providing a subvention for an open-access version of this chapter and others.

NOTES

1. By the same token, eating the foods of "exotic others" is often scripted into what Lisa Heldke (2012) names "culinary imperialism," revealing how "adventurous," recreational eating motivated by gustatory pleasure and status enhancement also participates in the conflation of racial and ethnic differences, reproduces colonialist relations of resource extraction, and depoliticizes the material conditions under which so-called ethnic foods developed historically and are cooked and served today.

2. For more detailed and nuanced discussions of how cheese makers negotiate and manipulate numerous material-organic variables in raw-milk cheese manufacture, particularly under conditions of "paucimicrobial" milk, see Rest (2021); and Demeulenaere and Lagrola (2021).

REFERENCES

Abbots, Emma-Jayne. 2017. *The Agency of Eating: Mediation, Food and the Body.* London: Bloomsbury.

Abbots, Emma-Jayne, and Anna Lavis, eds. 2013. *Why We Eat, How We Eat: Contemporary Encounters between Foods and Bodies.* London: Routledge.

Abbots, Emma-Jayne, Anna Lavis, and Luci Attala, eds. 1995. *Careful Eating: Bodies, Food and Care.* Farnham, UK: Ashgate.

Abrahamsson, Sebastian, and Filippo Bertoni. 2014. "Compost Politics: Experimenting with Togetherness in Vermicomposting." *Environmental Humanities* 4 (1): 125–48.

Abrahamsson, Sebastian, Filippo Bertoni, Annemarie Mol, and Rebeca Ibáñez Martín. 2015. "Living with Omega-3: New Materialism and Enduring Concerns." *Environment and Planning D: Society and Space* 33 (1): 4–19.

Agard-Jones, Vanessa. 2014. "Spray." *Somatosphere*, May 27, 2014.

Amato, Katherine R., Elizabeth K. Mallott, Paula D'Almeida Maia, and Maria Luisa Savo Sardaro. 2021. "Predigestion as an Evolutionary Impetus for Human Use of Fermented Food." *Current Anthropology* 62 (S24): S207–19.

Anderson, Virginia DeJohn. 2004. *Creatures of Empire: How Domestic Animals Transformed Early America.* Oxford: Oxford University Press.

Appadurai, Arjun. 1981. "Gastro-Politics in Hindu South Asia." *American Ethnologist* 8 (3): 494–511.

Barham, Elizabeth. 2003. "Translating Terroir: The Global Challenge of French AOC Labeling." *Journal of Rural Studies* 19 (1): 127–38.

Bertoni, Filippo. 2013. "Soil and Worm: On Eating as Relating." *Science as Culture* 22 (1): 61–85.

Biasetti, Dana. 2008. *Italy: Agricultural Situation: Dioxin in Italian Buffalo Mozzarella Cheese.* Global Agriculture Information Network Report, no. IT8006. USDA Foreign Agricultural Service, April 1, 2008. http://apps.fas.usda.gov/gainfiles/200804/146294161.pdf.

Bobrow-Strain, Aaron. 2012. *White Bread: A Social History of the Store-Bought Loaf.* Boston: Beacon.

Bourdieu, Pierre. 1984. *Distinction: A Social Critique of the Judgment of Taste.* Translated by Richard Nice. New York: Routledge.

Bowen, Sarah, Joslyn Brenton, and Sinikka Elliott. 2019. *Pressure Cooker: Why Home Cooking Won't Solve Our Problems and What We Can Do about It.* New York: Oxford University Press.

Canguilhem, Georges. 2001. "The Living and Its Milieu." *Grey Room*, no. 3, 7–31.

Celermajer, Danielle, David Schlosberg, Lauren Rickards, Makere Stewart-Harawira, Mathias Thaler, Petra Tschakert, Blanche Verlie, and Christine Winter. 2021. "Multispecies Justice: Theories, Challenges, and a Research Agenda for Environmental Politics." *Environmental Politics* 30 (1–2): 119–40.

Cone, Richard, and Emily Martin. 2003. "Corporeal Flows: The Immune System, Global Economies of Food, and New Implications for Health." In *Social and Cultural Lives of Immune Systems*, edited by James M. Wilce Jr., 232–66. London: Routledge.

Counihan, Carole. 1999. *The Anthropology of Food and the Body: Gender, Meaning, and Power*. New York: Routledge.
Counihan, Carole, and Susanne Højlund, eds. 2018. *Making Taste Public: Ethnographies of Food and the Senses*. London: Bloomsbury.
Creager, Angela N. H., and Jean-Paul Gaudillière, eds. 2021. *Risk on the Table: Food Production, Health, and the Environment*. New York: Berghahn.
Demeulenaere, Élise, and Mathilde Lagrola. 2021. "Des indicateurs pour accompagner 'les éleveurs de microbes.'" *Revue d'Anthropologie de Connaissance* 15 (3). http://journals.openedition.org/rac/24953.
Demossier, Marion. 2011. "Beyond *Terroir*: Territorial Construction, Hegemonic Discourses, and French Wine Culture." *Journal of the Royal Anthropological Institute*, n.s., 17 (4): 685–705.
Dunn, Elizabeth. 2008. "Postsocialist Spores: Disease, Bodies, and the State in the Republic of Georgia." *American Ethnologist* 35 (2): 243–58.
Dunn, Elizabeth. 2009. "Standards without Infrastructure." In *Standards and Their Stories: How Quantifying, Classifying, and Formalizing Practices Shape Everyday Life*, edited by Martha Lampland and Susan Leigh Star, 118–21. Ithaca, NY: Cornell University Press.
DuPuis, E. Melanie, Matt Garcia, and Don Mitchell. 2017. "Food across Borders: An Introduction." In *Food across Borders*, edited by Matt Garcia, E. Melanie DuPuis, and Don Mitchell, 1–23. New Brunswick, NJ: Rutgers University Press.
Fischler, Claude. 1988. "Food, Self and Identity." *Social Science Information* 27 (2): 275–92.
Fischler, Claude. 2011. "Commensality, Society and Culture." *Social Science Information* 50 (3–4): 528–48.
Fitchen, Janet. 1997. "Hunger, Malnutrition, and Poverty in the Contemporary United States: Some Observations on Their Social and Cultural Context." In *Food and Culture: A Reader*, edited by Carole Counihan and Penny Van Esterik, 384–401. New York: Routledge.
Ford, Andrea. 2019. "Introduction: Embodied Ecologies." *Fieldsights*, Society for Cultural Anthropology, April 25, 2019. https://culanth.org/fieldsights/introduction-embodied-ecologies.
Furman, David, Judith Campisi, Eric Verdin, Pedro Carrera-Bastos, Sasha Targ, Claudio Franceschi, Luigi Ferrucci, et al. 2019. "Chronic Inflammation in the Etiology of Disease across the Life Span." *Nature Medicine* 25 (12): 1822–32.
Gálvez, Alyshia. 2018. *Eating NAFTA: Trade, Food Policies, and the Destruction of Mexico*. Oakland: University of California Press.
Garth, Hanna. 2020. *Food in Cuba: The Pursuit of a Decent Meal*. Stanford, CA: Stanford University Press.
Garth, Hanna, and Ashanté M. Reese, eds. 2020. *Black Food Matters: Racial Justice in the Wake of Food Justice*. Minneapolis: University of Minnesota Press.
Gennep, Arnold van. (1909) 1960. *The Rites of Passage*. Translated by Monika B. Vizedom and Gabrielle L. Caffee. Chicago: University of Chicago Press.

Glabau, Danya. 2019. "Food Allergies and the Hygienic Sublime." *Catalyst: Feminism, Theory, Technoscience* 5 (2): 1–26.

González Turmo, Isabel. 2007. "The Concepts of Food and Non-food: Perspectives from Spain." In *Consuming the Inedible: Neglected Dimensions of Food Choice*, edited by Jeremy MacClancy, Jeya Henry, and Helen Macbeth, 43–52. New York: Berghahn Books.

Gremillion, Helen. 2003. *Feeding Anorexia: Gender and Power at a Treatment Center*. Durham, NC: Duke University Press.

Haraway, Donna J. 2008. *When Species Meet*. Minneapolis: University of Minnesota Press.

Hardin, Jessica. 2021. "Life before Vegetables: Nutrition, Cash, and Subjunctive Health in Samoa." *Cultural Anthropology* 36 (3): 428–57.

Heldke, Lisa. 2012. "Let's Cook Thai: Recipes for Colonialism." In *Food and Culture: A Reader*, edited by Carole Counihan and Penny Van Esterik, 394–408. 3rd ed. New York: Routledge.

Hobart, Hiʻilei Julia, and Stephanie Maroney. 2019. "On Racial Constitutions and Digestive Therapeutics." *Food, Culture and Society* 22 (5): 576–94.

Hoover, Elizabeth. 2017. *The River Is in Us: Fighting Toxics in a Mohawk Community*. Minneapolis: University of Minnesota Press.

Jung, Yuson. 2009. "From Canned Food to Canny Consumers: Cultural Competence in the Age of Mechanical Production." In *Food and Everyday Life in Postsocialist Europe*, edited by Melissa L. Caldwell, 29–56. Bloomington: Indiana University Press.

Jung, Yuson. 2016. "Food Provisioning and Foodways in Postsocialist Societies: Food as Medium for Social Trust and Global Belonging." In *Handbook in Food and Anthropology*, edited by James L. Watson and Jakob A. Klein, 289–307. London: Bloomsbury.

Jusionyte, Ieva. 2018. *Threshold: Emergency Responders on the US-Mexico Border*. Oakland: University of California Press.

Korsmeyer, Carolyn. 2005. "Introduction: Perspectives on Taste." In *The Taste Culture Reader: Experiencing Food and Drink*, edited by Carolyn Korsmeyer, 1–9. Oxford: Berg.

Lance, G. Denise. 2007. "Do the Hands That Feed Us Hold Us Back? Implications of Assisted Eating." *Disability Studies Quarterly* 27 (3). https://doi.org/10.18061/dsq.v27i3.23.

Landecker, Hannah. 2011. "Food as Exposure: Nutritional Epigenetics and the New Metabolism." *BioSocieties* 6 (2): 167–94.

Landecker, Hannah. 2015. "Being and Eating: Losing Grip on the Equation." *BioSocieties* 10 (2): 253–358.

Leach, Helen M. 2003. "Human Domestication Reconsidered." *Current Anthropology* 44 (3): 349–68.

Lee, Victoria. 2015. "Mold Cultures: Traditional Industry and Microbial Studies in Early Twentieth-Century Japan." In *New Perspectives on the History of Life Sciences and Agriculture*, edited by Denise Phillips and Sharon Kingsland, 231–52. Heidelberg: Springer Cham.

Levenstein, Harvey. 2003. *Paradoxes of Plenty: A Social History of Eating in Modern America*. Berkeley: University of California Press.
Liboiron, Max, Manuel Tironi, and Nerea Calvillo. 2018. "Toxic Politics: Acting in a Permanently Polluted World." *Social Studies of Science* 48 (3): 331–49.
Lien, Marianne Elisabeth. 2015. *Becoming Salmon: Aquaculture and the Domestication of a Fish*. Oakland: University of California Press.
Lien, Marianne Elisabeth, Heather Anne Swanson, and Gro B. Ween. 2018. "Introduction: Naming the Beast—Exploring the Otherwise." In *Domestication Gone Wild: Politics and Practices of Multispecies Belonging*, edited by Heather Anne Swanson, Marianne Elisabeth Lien, and Gro B. Ween, 1–32. Durham, NC: Duke University Press.
Lorimer, Jamie. 2018. "Hookworms Make Us Human: The Microbiome, Ecoimmunology, and a Probiotic Turn in Western Health Care." *Medical Anthropology Quarterly* 33 (1): 60–79.
Malinowski, Bronislaw. (1935) 1965. *Coral Gardens and Their Magic*. Vol. 1, *Soil-Tilling and Agricultural Rites in the Trobriand Islands*. Bloomington: Indiana University Press.
Mansfield, Becky. 2011. "Is Fish Health Food or Poison? Farmed Fish and the Material Production of Un/Healthy Nature." *Antipode* 43 (2): 413–34.
Mansfield, Becky, and Julie Guthman. 2015. "Epigenetic Life: Biological Plasticity, Abnormality, and New Configurations of Race and Reproduction." *Cultural Geographies* 22 (1): 3–20.
Mares, Teresa. 2019. *Life on the Other Border: Farmworkers and Food Justice in Vermont*. Oakland: University of California Press.
Markens, Susan, C. H. Browner, and Nancy Press. 1997. "Feeding the Fetus: On Interrogating the Notion of Maternal-Fetal Conflict." *Feminist Studies* 23 (2): 351–72.
Meigs, Anna. 1987. "Food as a Cultural Construction." *Food and Foodways* 2 (1): 341–57.
Mihesuah, Devon A., and Elizabeth Hoover, eds. 2019. *Indigenous Food Sovereignty in the United States: Restoring Cultural Knowledge, Protecting Environments, and Regaining Health*. Norman: University of Oklahoma Press.
Mintz, Sidney. 1985. *Sweetness and Power: The Place of Sugar in Modern History*. New York: Penguin.
Mintz, Sidney. 1996. *Tasting Food, Tasting Freedom: Excursions into Eating, Culture, and the Past*. Boston: Beacon.
Mol, Annemarie. 2008. "I Eat an Apple: On Theorizing Subjectivities." *Subjectivity* 22 (1): 28–37.
Mol, Annemarie. 2009. "Good Taste: The Embodied Normativity of the Consumer-Citizen." *Journal of Cultural Economy* 2 (3): 269–83.
Mol, Annemarie. 2021. *Eating in Theory*. Durham, NC: Duke University Press.
Moran-Thomas, Amy. 2019. *Traveling with Sugar: Chronicles of a Global Epidemic*. Oakland: University of California Press.
Mudry, Jessica. 2009. *Measured Meals: Nutrition in America*. Albany: State University of New York Press.

Münster, Daniel. 2021. "The Nectar of Life: Fermentation, Soil Health, and Bionativism in Indian Natural Farming." *Current Anthropology* 62 (s24): s311–22.

Murphy, Michelle. 2017. "Alterlife and Decolonial Chemical Relations." *Cultural Anthropology* 32 (4): 494–503.

Noske, Barbara. 1989. *Humans and Other Animals: Beyond the Boundaries of Anthropology*. London: Pluto.

Overstreet, Katy. 2018a. "How to Taste like a Cow: Cultivating Shared Sense in Wisconsin Dairy Worlds." In *Making Taste Public: Ethnographies of Food and the Senses*, edited by Carole Counihan and Susanne Højlund, 53–67. London: Bloomsbury.

Overstreet, Katy. 2018b. "'A Well-Cared for Cow Produces More Milk': The Biotechnics of (Dis)Assembling Cow Bodies in Wisconsin Dairy Worlds." PhD diss., Aarhus University.

Patel, Raj. 2007. *Stuffed and Starved: From Farm to Fork, the Hidden Battle for the World Food System*. New York: Melville House.

Paxson, Heather. 2008. "Post-Pasteurian Cultures: The Microbiopolitics of Raw-Milk Cheese in the United States." *Cultural Anthropology* 23 (1): 15–47.

Paxson, Heather. 2013. *The Life of Cheese: Crafting Food and Value in America*. Berkeley: University of California Press.

Paxson, Heather. 2016. "Rethinking Food and Its Eaters: Opening the Black Boxes of Safety and Nutrition." In *The Handbook of Food and Anthropology*, edited by Jakob A. Klein and James L. Watson, 268–88. London: Bloomsbury.

Petryna, Adriana. 2018. "Wildfires at the Edges of Science: Horizoning Work amid Runaway Change." *Cultural Anthropology* 33 (4): 570–95.

Poppendieck, Janet. 1998. "Want amid Plenty: From Hunger to Inequality." *Monthly Review* 50 (3): 125–37.

Probyn, Elspeth. 2016. *Eating the Ocean*. Durham, NC: Duke University Press.

Raffaetà, Roberta. 2021. "Microbial Antagonism in the Trentino Alps: Negotiating Spacetimes and Ownership through the Production of Raw Milk Cheese in Alpine High Mountain Summer Pastures." *Current Anthropology* 62 (s24): s323–33.

Rest, Matthäus. 2021. "Preserving the Microbial Commons: Intersections of Ancient DNA, Cheese Making, and Bioprospecting." *Current Anthropology* 62 (s24): s349–60.

Roberts, Elizabeth. 2017. "What Gets Inside: Violent Entanglements and Toxic Boundaries in Mexico City." *Cultural Anthropology* 32 (4): 592–619.

Rotman, Brian. 2008. *Becoming beside Ourselves: The Alphabet, Ghosts, and Distributed Human Being*. Durham, NC: Duke University Press.

Russell, Nerissa. 2007. "The Domestication of Anthropology." In *Where the Wild Things Are Now: Domestication Reconsidered*, edited by Rebecca Cassidy and Molly Mullin, 27–48. Oxford: Berg.

Sanabria, Emilia, and Emily Yates-Doerr. 2015. "Alimentary Uncertainties: From Contested Evidence to Policy." *BioSocieties* 10 (2): 117–24.

Schor, Juliet. 2010. *Plentitude: The New Economics of True Wealth*. New York: Penguin.

Scrinis, Gyorgy. 2008. "On the Ideology of Nutritionism." *Gastronomica* 8 (1): 39–48.

Shapiro, Nicholas. 2015. "Attuning to the Chemosphere: Domestic Formaldehyde, Bodily Reasoning, and the Chemical Sublime." *Cultural Anthropology* 30 (3): 368–93.

Solomon, Harris. 2015. "Unreliable Eating: Patterns of Food Adulteration in Urban India." *BioSocieties* 19 (2): 177–93.

Solomon, Harris. 2016. *Metabolic Living: Food, Fat, and the Absorption of Illness in India*. Durham, NC: Duke University Press.

Star, Susan Leigh, and Martha Lampland. 2009. "Reckoning with Standards." In *Standards and Their Stories: How Quantifying, Classifying, and Formalizing Practices Shape Everyday Life*, edited by Martha Lampland and Susan Leigh Star, 3–34. Ithaca, NY: Cornell University Press.

Sternini, Catia, Laura Anselmi, and Enrique Rozengurt. 2008. "Enteroendocrine Cells: A Site of 'Taste' in Gastrointestinal Chemosensing." *Current Opinion in Endocrinology, Diabetes, and Obesity* 15 (1): 73–78.

Stevenson, Lisa. 2014. *Life beside Itself: Imagining Care in the Canadian Artic*. Oakland: University of California Press.

Swanson, Heather Anne, Marianne Elisabeth Lien, and Gro B. Ween, eds. 2018. *Domestication Gone Wild: Politics and Practices of Multispecies Relations*. Durham, NC: Duke University Press.

Taylor, Sunaura. 2017. *Beasts of Burden: Animal and Disability Liberation*. New York: New Press.

Tompkins, Kyla Wazana. 2012. *Racial Indigestion: Eating Bodies in the 19th Century*. New York: New York University Press.

Tracy, Megan. 2021. "Missing Microbes and Other Gendered Microbiopolitics in Bovine Fermentation." *Current Anthropology* 62 (s24): s276–86.

Trubek, Amy. 2008. *The Taste of Place: A Cultural Journey into Terroir*. Berkeley: University of California Press.

Tsing, Anna. 2012. "Unruly Edges: Mushrooms as Companion Species." *Environmental Humanities* 1 (1): 141–54.

Turner, Victor. 1967. *The Forest of Symbols: Aspects of Ndembu Ritual*. Ithaca, NY: Cornell University Press.

Valdez, Natalie. 2018. "The Redistribution of Reproductive Responsibility: On the Epigenetics of 'Environment' in Prenatal Interventions." *Medical Anthropology Quarterly* 32 (3): 425–42.

van Daele, Wim. 2013. "Igniting Food Assemblages in Sri Lanka: Ritual Cooking to Regenerate the World and Interrelations." *Contributions to Indian Sociology* 47 (1): 33–60.

van Daele, Wim. 2018. "Food as the Holographic Condensation of Life in Sri Lankan Rituals." *Ethnos* 83 (4): 645–64.

Weiss, Brad. 2016. *Real Pigs: Shifting Values in the Field of Local Pork*. Durham, NC: Duke University Press.

West, Harry. 2013. "Thinking like a Cheese: Towards an Ecological Understanding of the Reproduction of Knowledge in Contemporary Artisan Cheese Making." In *Understanding Cultural Transmission in Anthropology: A Critical Synthesis*, edited by Roy Ellen, Stephen J. Lycett, and Sarah E. Johns, 320–44. Oxford: Berghahn.

Weston, Kath. 2017. *Animate Planet: Making Visceral Sense of Living in a High-Tech Ecologically Damaged World*. Durham, NC: Duke University Press.

Williams-Forson, Psyche A. 2006. *Building Houses out of Chicken Legs: Black Women, Food, and Power*. Chapel Hill: University of North Carolina Press.

Witt, Dorris. 1999. *Black Hunger: Soul Food and America*. Oxford: Oxford University Press.

Wolfe, Benjamin E., Julie E. Button, Marcela Santarelli, and Rachel J. Dutton. 2014. "Cheese Rind Communities Provide Tractable Systems for In Situ and In Vitro Studies of Microbial Diversity." *Cell* 158 (2): 422–33.

Yamin-Pasternak, Sveta, Andrew Kliskey, Lilian Alessa, Igor Pasternak, and Peter Schweitzer. 2014. "The Rotten Renaissance in the Bering Strait: Loving, Loathing, and Washing the Smell of Foods with a (Re)acquired Taste." *Current Anthropology* 55 (5): 619–45.

Yan, Yunxiang. 2012. "Food Safety and Social Risk in Contemporary China." *Journal of Asian Studies* 71 (3): 705–29.

Yates-Doerr, Emily. 2012. "The Opacity of Reduction: Nutritional Black-Boxing and the Meanings of Nourishment." *Food, Culture and Society* 15 (2): 293–313.

Yates-Doerr, Emily. 2015. "The World in a Box? Food Security, Edible Insects, and 'One World, One Health' Collaboration." *Social Science and Medicine* 129: 106–12.

Yates-Doerr, Emily, and Annemarie Mol. 2012. "Cuts of Meat: Disentangling Western Natures-Cultures." *Cambridge Journal of Anthropology* 30 (2): 48–64.

chapter one

Sweetness across Thresholds at the Edge of the Sea

AMY MORAN-THOMAS

> The machinery of the sugar mill, once installed and set in motion, soon becomes almost indestructible, since even when it is partially dismantled, its transformative impact will survive it for many years. Its track will be inscribed within Nature itself, in the climate, in the demographic, political, social, economic, and cultural structures of the society to which it once was joined.
>
> —ANTONIO BENÍTEZ-ROJO, THE REPEATING ISLAND

THE AIR TASTED AND SMELLED LIKE BURNT SUGAR THE MORNING I WALKED past the stretch of factories outside London. When Sidney Mintz evoked industrial contexts like this iconic "sugar mile" in *Sweetness and Power* (1985), he described the changing tastes that accompanied factory routines and lifestyles, showing how the lives of working people who once populated these factories were materially connected to the lives and dispossessions across sugar plantations on the other side of the Atlantic. I walked through the parking lot of one of the abandoned nineteenth-century jam factories Mintz had written about. Its gate was covered in ivy; an antique surveillance camera was dissolving into rust. Nearby walls were marked with graffiti from long-lost union strikes against bankrupt or offshored companies. Someone had left a single men's dress shoe in the watchman's booth. Today nearly all the other factories in the Silvertown area outside London have been abandoned, but not the sugar refinery. "KEEPING SWEET," its large, bright signs read. "TASTE THE SUNSHINE."

By 2018, long gone were the days when business was so good that the Tate and Lyle could market a line of sugar cubes exclusively for circus bears. Most working-class jobs have long since been taken over by machines; someone I met said the few remaining human positions in the factory mainly belonged to engineer types with PhDs who monitored chemistry or programmed computers. But there is still a building called the Royal Sugar Shed to house the queen's personal supply (today owned by a US conglomerate), with piles of white sugar as high as sand dunes (see figure 1.1).

As with Mintz's questions, the interconnections around sugar that I was trying to understand began on the other side of the ocean that fed this waterway outside London. Along the Caribbean coast of the small Central American country of Belize, a decade ago people had told me endless stories about the chronic conditions they more often called "sugar." The rising blood sugar levels and severe complications described by patients in Belize seemed to far exceed the focus on personal responsibility through which rising rates of diabetes are more often cast in public health rubrics. Over the fifteen years since those ethnographic relationships began, I have been working to place the stories of sugar that people wanted to share into a sketch of the

FIGURE 1.1 Piles of unrefined sugar in a warehouse outside London, near the dock that receives shipments of cane from Belize. Chris Ratcliffe/ Bloomberg/ Getty Images.

larger historical and material contexts that have also played a role in shaping such disproportionate "body burdens" (Agard-Jones 2015). And so, like many scholars trying to examine blood sugar in relation to sugar's much longer histories (Reese 2021; Hatch 2016; Klingle 2015; Doucet-Battle 2021), I found myself returning time and again to Mintz's emblematic work on sugar—with a growing appreciation for its capacity to move between a global account of racial capitalism and individual life histories (Mintz 1974), including its insistence on interconnected histories that also uneasily position European-descended researchers in any account of Caribbean plantations' legacies.[1]

And yet—watching a boat arriving at the outer London factory's shores that morning and wondering if it was one of the shipments of sugarcane that still arrive here regularly from Belize—I paused, wondering how this scene fit into an understanding of commodity chains today. After all, the questions about blood sugar at the center of my ethnographic project were something much more diffuse than the products of these massive piles of sugarcane and whatever they were turned into. The people I spoke with on both sides of the Atlantic were not so easy to label as either producers or consumers, or even some rearrangement of those earlier terms. And while certain scenes from a sugar factory might crystallize one aspect of what contributes to the unequal global reach of diabetes today—cheap processed foods are often marketed disproportionately in nonwhite places—the commodity chains that blood sugar highlighted made it impossible to consider food and medicine in different frames from each other or from the porous ecologies that their infrastructures impinged on.[2] Sugar's deliberately crafted markets were already unwieldy to follow, but accidental aftereffects and by-products of commodities also played a key role in the stories about sugar that people I had met in Belize were calling to public attention. Accumulating over time, these material afterlives and accretions can have deep and quite often harmful implications for the health of atmospheres, microbes, plants, and animals alongside humans. Following the messiness of sugar's sequelae resulted in something less like a canonical project on eating or farming practices. It was more like piecing together a composite picture of commodity chains that have been cracking and breaking apart for centuries, leaking across food webs and histories that can live on and build up within bodies of all kinds.

I did not yet know how to read those signs when I first walked Belize's southern coast, observing what washed up along the tideline. But like my interviews about the health of people and places, the tide arriving from the deep ocean presented a knot of entwined lives I did not know how to untangle: the last nylon strings of "ghost nets" that now make up half of the ocean's plastic debris, long abandoned by people fishing but still catching life until they unravel; curds of broken Styrofoam in clotted algae; hunks of dying coral from the heat-bleached reef; thin, gleaming strips of brown seaweed that looked as if they'd been unspooled from the reels of an old cassette tape. Odds were that most of the bright microplastic shards had once been food containers, perhaps ejected from passing cruise ships decades ago in order to be worn down to such confetti-sized slivers. I watched as local women deftly swept the day's debris from their stretch of beach, treating the sand underfoot like the floor of a well-tended kitchen.

Media headlines about diabetes always seem to show bodies getting bigger, but the stories I heard in this stretch of Caribbean Central America more often focused on fears of getting smaller. The wear of high blood glucose levels within veins and arteries frequently accumulated into nerve damage and limb amputations, so common that such injuries appear in the Belizean Kriol dictionary simply as *sweet foot* (Crosbie et al. 2005). If you sat and talked with people, missing body parts were often central to how they told stories and measured time. Some felt phantom pains or dreamed at night about running. Others watched with dread as it happened in their families. Nurses said that feet bitten by venomous snakes were easier to heal than the injured limbs that people described simply as "sugar."

In Belize the common name for diabetes traveled across languages: *súgara* in Garifuna, *shuga* in Belizean Kriol, *azúcar* in Spanish, *kiha kiik* in Kekchi Maya, or *ch'uhuk k'iik* (sweet blood) in Mopan and Yucatec Maya. More than one out of every four people (and one in three women) had type 2 diabetes in the southern district of Stann Creek, and diabetes had become the leading cause of death countrywide (Gough et al. 2008). For a time, I used to think "sugar" was a popular synonym that meant diabetes. I came to realize over time, though, that these labels often slipped into each other but were not really the same. The effects of sugar routinely exceeded common understandings of diabetes problems. Sugar was alive in the landscape. It named something that escaped from the many containers—biomedical, industrial, technoscientific—of expert accounting. I began to think that any stable account of sugar's contradictory meanings would miss the very thing that people named as the chronic conditions they were trying to live with.

Life rearranged by past plantation sciences of sugar remained subtly legible across the landscape, biologies touched by historical events and still present far beyond genetic and epigenetic lenses alone: in rearranged plants and seeds and food systems, access to synthetic and herbal medicines, changing weather patterns, dispossessed lands, lost limbs and family members. These disquieting absences and unwanted changes at times factored palpably in the travails of bodies and families trying to heal against histories of violence and their legacies today.

Colonial sugar economies across the Caribbean were driven by "unequal ecological exchange," Jason Moore (2000, 426) noted, not only by human labor extraction. Sometimes I tried to picture what the old forest in Stann Creek District looked like before it was logged and burned to clear fields for plantations. Inhabiting a hobbled landscape, some interviewees told me they wanted to grow vegetables, but now the soil along the highway was too poor to grow anything but oranges and bananas. Had it always been that way? This legacy was not only about land in law but also about its biology. Once sugarcane grows in certain ground, it depletes nutrients from the soil. This paves the way for further industrial monocropping, since it often leaves behind exhausted land that requires heavy doses of petrochemical pesticides and fertilizers in order for food plants to grow.

"In 2002–2007, the sugar industry alone produced 5,074,261 to 5,950,123 gallons of liquid waste per year," the Belize Ministry of Health noted in 2014. Recent orange and banana blights had further driven the use of pesticides, the report added: "Wash waters and irrigation run-offs contaminate the watershed in the two southernmost districts—Stann Creek and Toledo . . . where runoff and chemical pollution affect adjacent water bodies" (32). Pesticides found in a Stann Creek water sample included cadusafos, ethoprop, acetochlor, fenamiphos, oxamyl, carbofuran, chlorpyrifos, dimethyl tetrachloroterephthalate, chlorothalonil, trifluralin, malathion, lead, and mercury; levels peaked where the Stann Creek river meets the sea (Alegria, Carvalho-Knighton, and Alegria 2009).

I didn't then know the names of the chemicals they put on sugarcane in Belize, but I tasted them once, biting to peel a cane stalk straight from the fields with my teeth. The white powder flaked dry on my tongue and dissolved without flavor. Later, a friend and I stood staring at the names of the agricultural chemicals made from petrochemicals advertised on a sign in town: Actara, Amistar, Cruiser, Curyam, Flex, Gesaprim, Gramoxone, Karate, Ridomil Gold, Syngenta. Somehow, the advertised list felt taboo to discuss: the shopkeeper did not want to talk about which ones he sold for sugar and which ones he sold for other monocrops, like oranges and bananas. The term *pesticide drift* that I read about sounded like a sinister enigma. But lab tests in Belize measure it: glyphosate, better known by the brand name Roundup, was found in six out of six test sites in Stann Creek (Kaiser 2011).

FIGURE 1.2 A nineteenth-century sugar machine, left behind by Confederate settlers in Belize, rusting into the landscape. Photo by Amy Moran-Thomas.

An abundance of population studies elsewhere suggests that the growth in both type 1 and type 2 diabetes is exacerbated by exposure to pesticide runoff from agricultural and other synthetic chemicals and pollution in food, air, and waterways. The haze of what Vanessa Agard-Jones (2013; 2015) calls "accreted violence" from agricultural pesticides remains a legacy throughout the Caribbean and Latin America. In this context of limited foods and abundant chemicals, one woman's name for her glucose meter, "sugar machine," struck me as an apt frame for the way this region—if not much of the agro-industrial world system—is fast becoming a sugar machine.[3]

A number of older people with diabetes I met in Belize diagnosed or monitored their glucose by smelling and tasting sweetness in their urine. Others first realized they had diabetes by noting insects gathering in the places they urinated, drawn to consume the sugar. For them, "sugar" was not an abstract unit mediated by technologies or paperwork—bodily sugar had a sensibility and flavor, a literal taste. And, of course, blood sugar reflects much more than the sweets someone has eaten. Since all carbohydrates turn into glucose in the body, foods like flour tortillas and white rice can cause high sugar levels in bodily fluids too. The ants can't tell whether a glucose molecule was broken down from cane or white flour, was once sucrose or fructose. By then it is just sugar, and they are there to eat it next.

Sugar not only reveals scales but also *produces* them, like the genes described by Ian Whitmarsh (2013) elsewhere in the Caribbean. When a diabetic ulcer refuses to heal, some hospitals actually apply a topical poultice of sugar, which for unknown reasons has at times more medical efficacy than many antibiotics (Biswas et al. 2010). Certain foods may be disproportionately eaten due to a history of exploitation, but people have also learned ways to make "dietary disaster" (Beckles 2014) delicious, and often there is "clearly life surging around the sugary rite," as Michael Taussig (1989, 14) once wrote in critique of Mintz. Sugar holds contradictory meanings: eating and getting eaten; histories of hardship and labor but also of love, pleasure, and luxury; both wealth and poverty; security and danger; terror and intimacy; violence and comfort; age-old and growing new; hunger and indulgence; invigorated and devastated agriculture; ancient human staple and disobedient Frankenfood; chronic injuries and proximity to normalized death—but also sweet gestures of tenderness and care marshaled for survivance.

Unacknowledged scars of sugar could be read as one of many distillations in the "climate" in which premature "Black deaths are produced as normative," as Christina Sharpe (2016, 7) describes—or, for others, as part of "the labor of living in the face of an expectant and a foretold cultural and political death," as described by Audra Simpson: "With settler colonialism came... a radical shift in Indigenous diets and their bodies. As a result their blood is excessively 'sweet' and has a high prevalence of diabetes—a bodily indicator of these spatial and dietary transitions" (2014, 6). Yet as scholars from Sylvia Wynter (1971) to Malcom Ferdinand (2022) have observed, these legacies hold profound impacts not only for people but also for the earth itself. History's dramatic transplantations of people, plants, and land tenure also made such ecological legacies part of the intergenerational texture of *simultaneous time*, "where the future, past, and present are mutually constitutive" (Thomas 2016, 183). In this view, the sequelae of plantations spilled out materially as well as psychically: in agricultural chemicals leaking from monocropped fields into waterways, in the carbon emissions of industrial agricultural and food transport, in the racial orders that continue to expose people unequally to these material effects. In this way, diabetes again disturbingly echoes earlier logics of sugar, as Saidiya Hartman (2007, 31) writes of such afterlives: "Death wasn't a goal of its own but just a by-product of commerce, which has had the lasting effect of making negligible all the millions of lives lost."

In Belize, sugar's machinery had come and gone from the southern region, leaving only rubble on the edges of a global system where the outpost of British Honduras was a fringe node at best. The Confederate families flying flags of Dixie are long gone. But sugar remains iconic of the larger shifts that such colonial forms have unleashed on a global scale: motors of industrial agriculture and ecological extractions; chemicals used to grow crops on spent soils; plantations that led to corporations (Manjapra 2018); machines rusted in place in fields yet still in motion across landscapes and inside the cells of human bodies, even when left behind by all accounts (see figure 1.2).

The old pipe jutting over the river at the abandoned cane fields of Libertad looked like an oil pipeline, but it was built for molasses. For a brief time after 1989, a Jamaican company called PetroJam leased the old sugar estate and refined its molasses into ethanol for US markets. But by the time I visited, only sugarcane was being loaded into the tugboats I watched preparing for export. Staring into the water that some call "the river of strange faces," I thought of Kara Walker's art installation in the old Domino Sugar factory in Brooklyn (see Walker 2014), where pools of dissolved sugar water reflected each visitor back at themselves. Now that sweet crude oil has been drilled in Belize, there are jokes that even the land has gotten sweet blood.

Coral Gardens and Their Metabolism

Colonial anthropologists left a deeply uncomfortable legacy around metabolism, such as in Bronislaw Malinowski's *Coral Gardens and Their Magic* ([1935] 1965; see epigraph, this volume). Malinowski's stubborn view that metabolism referred only to a single human body, processing intentionally eaten food, became part of his broader misrecognition and ethnographic dismissal of the practices of feeding the land and feeding the ancestors that he notoriously observed in the Trobriand Islands.

Many public health pamphlets around the world today, still framing metabolism and nutrition reductively, are unable to account for "nutrition" in ways that allow for interrelated bodies across generations or scales. Yet in Belize, when hospitals were at times unable to help patients manage their diabetes, many people I met asked me to include in this storytelling their work reaching out to the ancestors through meals and other forms of attention to probe other existential thresholds of healing.[4] C., a Garifuna woman I had first met in the hospital, invited me to accompany her to one such meal, a practice offered to restore relations with the land and with the dead. The sand and waves that day were filled with tiny bits of plastics, blended with the offerings being buried in the beach and submerged into the sea to feed the ancestors. It takes decades for food containers to photo-degrade into the tiny bright slivers found on the beach and in the waves. Little pieces of garbage get eaten by fish, moving up the food chain. The ancestral offerings represented a restorative force, a means of summoning spirits to rebuild (Valentine 2002), but the plastic remainders inside animals and in the land and water where the food was buried were a more enigmatic kind of "co-presence" (Beliso-De Jesús 2014, 503). I wondered, Was this also feeding the land and the dead? What about the living?

In this view, not only do human bodies metabolize their ecologies, but our environments in turn metabolize both humans and the long-lasting traces of people's activities. Hannah Landecker traces the intellectual history of metabolism, noting that for such scientists as Hans Jones, "*metabolism made it possible in the first place for there to be an inside and an outside*" (2013, 196)—part of demarcating where a given boundary of "the environment" or "the body" was taken to begin or end. Such a focus on bodily "absorption," Harris Solomon (2016, 5) writes in *Metabolic Living*, "can open up key questions in the context of chronic diseases related to food: Who and what become the eater and the eaten? What is nutrition and what is poison? Who and what set the boundaries of inside and outside, delineating organism and environment?"

By the time I spent a year in Belize in 2010, more and more hunks of coral were washing up on the beaches undigested by parrotfish. About half the reef had died, and the coral skeletons that I saw took many forms: white spine-shaped columns, airy hunks of calcified sponge, and brittle broken fans. According to scientists, the Mesoamerican Reef—like most coral today—is also showing signs of metabolic disorders. It has trouble with its own food supply: the algae-like zooxanthellae that coral polyps harvest for carbohydrates, "much as farmers harvest corn" (Kolbert 2014, 142), struggle to survive in warming oceans. High temperatures "cause the metabolism of the algae—which give coral reefs their brilliant colors and energy—to speed out of control, and they start creating toxins. The polyps recoil.... When heat stress continues, they starve to death" (Innis 2016, 1; see also Harvell 2019; Young 2008; Braverman 2018).

This loss of sustenance is the primary cause of coral bleaching, reef death, and the displacement of resident fish and other aquatic species. Other processes further compound the impacts of climate change on sea life: sea levels are rising, the oceans are becoming more acidic, and unchecked mining and foreign building projects are accelerating coastal erosion in parts of Belize. Some residents describe these shoreline erosions in terms of consumption too: "The sea is eating the shore."

Diabetes was one of the key examples that physician-philosopher Georges Canguilhem wrote about in *The Normal and the Pathological*. He was fascinated by the many microevents that preceded the first time sugar could be found "pouring over a threshold" in the kidneys, the moment when detectable glucose (always present in human blood) suddenly leaked into urine and became legible as a disorder. He argued that "the pathological cannot be linearly deduced from the normal," the way graphs tend to depict it. Instead, health was "a margin of tolerance," Canguilhem wrote, "for the inconsistencies of the environment" (1991, 190, 197). How does this notion of a "margin of tolerance" resonate with the blood sugar readings—ranging from 62 to 718 mg/dL—facing the patients I met in one morning in a Belize City clinic? The majority of the measurements I was invited to record that day clustered in patterns that would be considered astronomically high elsewhere. Only two of sixteen patients registered in the range (80–120 mg/dL) defined in medical textbooks at the time as "normal." What does "normal" sugar even mean, when a great majority of people living with diabetes are labeled "outliers"? If applying the narrower range of "normal" blood sugar levels (80–110) that later came to be promoted by many pharmaceutical companies, only one of the sixteen patients who asked me to record their readings that day would qualify—a reminder of how moving a threshold's definition changes the biology being treated and produced in practice. The majority of those sixteen people tested that morning registered blood sugars over 300 mg/dL—such a high level that, if chronically sustained, severe complications are almost certain. But that was the low end of the range in which C. spoke of feeling normal. When C. was given insulin to bring her glucose down from what the hospital considered dangerous and back to "normal," she began to throw up.

Today "inconsistencies of the environment" are so pervasive that Canguilhem's ideas about the "ex post facto normal" have become important for approaching ecological losses as well as the erosion of human health, as David Bond (2013) argues: disasters often produce what later comes to be imagined as the lost baselines of "normal" environs. The Belizean coral reef that C. lived alongside had itself undergone disease and bleaching events in 1995, 1998, 2005, 2010, 2015, and 2016. Surviving patches have already lived beyond what scientists once estimated as the reef's "thresholds of temperature tolerance" (Richardson 2009, 33), its survivability tested in ways that often remind me of "normal" blood sugar appearing in diabetes clinics along that same stretch of coast. Yet when "changes in degree become changes in kind," Donna Haraway (2015, 159) observes, "all the stories are too big and too small." There are "waxing and waning thresholds of life" (Singh 2015, 402) being demarcated all around: "epidemic thresholds," like the one the World Health Organization declared that diabetes has crossed; "pain thresholds," debated around when and how diabetic nerve damage should be medicated; "thresholds of exposure," which define permissible levels of toxic chemicals (see also Langston 2011; Hecht 2019; Mitman, Murphy, and Sellers 2004). Adriana Petryna (2018, 573) calls drawing such lines for tractable action "horizoning work": "perceiving critical thresholds, determining baselines, and carving out footholds" as part of a "fine-tuned awareness of jeopardy amid incomplete knowledge, and for labors of continuous recalibration amid physical worlds on edge."

A little at a time, capacities might gradually change beyond what once seemed like hard limits (see figure 1.3). "Life tries to win against death in all senses of the verb.... Life gambles against growing entropy," Canguilhem (1991, 236) wrote. Exceeding experts' predictions, at times the intensities of death in life could create powerful modes of alter-survival (Murphy 2017). When diabetic deaths and injuries were statistically "normal," stabilizing outliers became something besides pathological—opening instead toward the possibility of transcendence. Some people in Belize explained to me how they lived with their symptoms as miracles.

When a woman named Bea, for example, noticed the two perfect pink circles that opened spontaneously on each foot, she recognized the symmetrical marks. She took fastidious care of the wounds in collaboration with her doctor. But Bea could discern nothing that she had done to "deserve" her diabetic injuries, as she explained, and their strong resemblance to Catholic stigmata helped her to bear the fact that they would not heal. She said that she knew others in town with similar marks. "Many are chosen."

How is expertise constructed in different ways around death and survival? Diabetes caregivers often presented threshold definitions as "natural" facts, using them as tools to navigate uncertain biology. The specific ways that blood sugar's thresholds were defined and reworked often took on a meaningful life of their own, sustaining the possibilities of "wellness despite sickness" (Hardin 2016; see also Hardin 2019) along the unstable edges between religion and medicine.

Thresholds around us were also changing, most visibly at "the edge of the sea" (Carson [1955] 1998). Some old myths used to say the bubbled seaweed that people call sargasso never died, but most locals recall that occasional tangles of it had always washed up along the coast in Belize at certain times

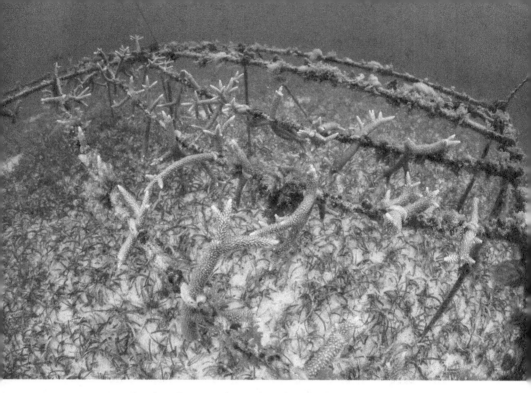

FIGURE 1.3 Coral reef repair projects have become popular in Belize, part of ongoing local attempts to sustain fish and sea life. Ethan Daniels/Stocktrek/Getty Images.

of year. But after 2010, thick, pungent tides of dead sargasso carried by the Gulf Stream began washing up along Belizean shorelines. While raking the decaying yellow and brown weeds, people I knew debated whether the die-off possibly had something to do with the BP oil spill. Or maybe the carcinogenic plasticizers used to hide the oil. Or the underwater heat waves killing off life of all kinds. Over time, though, the toxic superblooms in Belize keep getting worse. By 2019 anthropologist Siobhan McCollum would describe how miles of sargasso washed up on the beach in a matter of hours with an overpowering stench. Some in Belize attributed part of the issue to industrial fertilizer runoff from agricultural plantations as far away as Brazil.

Phosphorus and nitrogen have historically been reaped from poor regions and brought to wealthy empires to replenish agricultural fields and plantations with depleted soil. By the mid-1800s, England and the United States, in particular, were vying for control of guano islands in South America (especially Peru), across the Caribbean, and around the world. Influenced by the sciences of metabolism of his era, Karl Marx wrote that this movement of life-supporting soil nutrients from poor places to wealthy ones—what he called metabolic "rift"—interacted with human politics and the ecological displacements of capitalism, as it "disturbs the metabolic interaction between man and the earth" (quoted in Foster 2000, 155–56).

Although phosphorus and nitrogen are now industrially produced and chemically manipulated as well as mined raw, the afterlives of their nutrient cycles have cascading implications for metabolism across scales. The putrid-smelling algae blooms they fuel often kill off other sea life, including overstressed coral, which in turn fossilizes some of the excess phosphorus in the calcifications of its polyps. Dead coral is thus sometimes also mined for industrial phosphorus, which in turn gets sold as fertilizer to add nutrients to keep plantation soil viable.

Belize is relatively unpolluted compared to most places on the earth today. The country has one of the smallest carbon footprints in the world. To me, this beauty made observing its harmed ecologies all the more unsettling: even there, it was also happening. In a place that evoked the imagery of tropical paradise that postcards try to capture, traces of mutation felt both invisible and hyperreal. Certain lagoons still harbored moon jellyfish and algae that glowed blue when disturbed, but the gnarled roots of many mangrove trees caged disturbing quantities of plastic debris. The distant sea looked a pristine azure blue on clear days, and manatees with brown noses sometimes swam up to the docks. Other times what I mistook for a first sign of a sea animal on the horizon ended up being garbage. The most visually prominent items in this tidal trash were plastic bags, floating in the waves like listless jellyfish, and Styrofoam, known in Belizean Kriol as *sea bread*—as if even the earth were being fed a sick diet.

According to the US Environmental Protection Agency (2008), each "floating city" of approximately three thousand cruise ship passengers discharges an average of 210,000 gallons of sewage and one million gallons of gray water into the oceans each week. This includes toxins and oil, discarded and expired chemicals, batteries, fluorescent lights, explosives, paint thinners, and solid waste such as plastic bottles and food containers. Toxicologists note that plastic leaks bisphenol A and other endocrine-disrupting chemicals into the environment. What Sarah Vogel (2009) has called the "politics of plastics" is part of how people and chemical environs become literal parts of each other's biologies, disturbingly embroiled in human capacities for plasticity and change.

Seeing dead fish floating in the water, I wondered, What counted as an environmental "sentinel"—as such figures are often cast in ecological writing—in the past, or now? In 2010 a sea turtle washed up in southern Belize with crude petroleum in its mouth. One nurse told me that when she was growing up, some days they used to hear the sounds of dynamite in the distance, as foreign entrepreneurs hunted for oil underwater along the Belizean reef. In the aftermath of the explosions, a tide with dead tropical fish and paralyzed stingrays would be swept onto the sand. Belize has worked to curb the worst of these practices, but ambient exposures from other times and places linger.

An older man named Edwin once showed me his favorite trees nearby. He talked about global warming a lot but mostly about the little ways he saw climate change making its way into daily life. It was ruining the best mangoes, the rare blue kind that grew behind his sister's house. And the price of fish was rising steeply, almost doubled in recent memory. It made him worry about the ocean. Edwin was born in a fishing village during the "times of abundance," back "in Lucy days," when a trawler named *Lucy* used to ply the Belizean coast buying up whatever fish were caught. But now that fish and shellfish were starting to become scarce, he had more trouble buying what used to be an everyday food. This impacted the kinds of protein people could afford to eat, especially people with less money. Some thought the fish scarcity had to do with the rise of shrimp farms and their antibiotic-laden wastewater that was killing local sea life, while shrimp are primarily exported to enrich diets abroad. Edwin hoped the shortage could be attributed instead to climate change's contribution to new patterns of weather: his fishing friends noted an increase in winds from the southeast that drove the fish into deeper ocean or to coasts elsewhere. That was the most optimistic scenario. Competing theories held that they had simply died.

Even for an outsider like me, it was disturbing to observe grilled fish becoming scarcer on kitchen tables and in local shops because of rising prices. In some places it was easier to find the "fish" sold in spray bottles—FISH being the common generic name in Belize for chemicals that kill biting insects by design but can also kill aquatic life as a side effect. Seeing them lined up on supermarket shelves made me picture a dystopian future zoo of aerosol animals, with a room of cans holding samples of whatever toxic mix helped to kill off the creature on its label. Whenever we went grocery shopping together, one friend and I made jokes that took on hints of compulsive ritual, as if to remind each other of the species going missing. We were probably projecting deeper anxieties onto those fairly trivial canisters, supercharged by the fact that most of the chemicals on the loose around us were not labeled at all. But everyone was still breathing, drinking, and eating them. One local study about the effects of DDT compared thinning eggshells and the reproductive implications of the chemical for various groups of crocodiles in Belize. But the research team could not find a control group of unexposed animals for comparison; many of the contaminated crocodiles were sex shifting from males into anatomical females, likely owing to the organic pesticides in their waterways (Pepper et al. 2004). The same hormonal pathways that trigger such changes in aquatic animals have been linked to diabetes as well as to breast and prostate cancer in humans (Hayes and Raz 2016), but the effects on people were not being measured in this context. Likewise, the study mentioned earlier about pervasive contamination from the diabetogenic chemical Roundup in Stann Creek (Kaiser 2011) was conducted out of concern for jaguars. Many biologists and researchers from wealthy institutions abroad came to study wildlife ecologies in Belize, but very few scrutinized what the ambient chemicals harming crocodiles and jaguars might also mean for the health of human residents.

Issues like this are part of the reason some observers today argue that diabetes should be considered an issue of not only "global health" but also "planetary health" (Horton, Beaglehole, and Bonita 2014). For some, the language of "planetary" is uneasy too—the optics through which we know this scale were largely born of the visual technologies of nuclear war, Joseph Masco (2010) observes, and the rallying call toward shared causes and effects can gloss over how unevenly collective risks are distributed. Yet the debate does prompt reflection on how *global* is also a paradoxical word. It is supposed to mean a thing in its entirety—yet a globe is modeled as hollow inside, a static shell. In contrast, *planet* models something animate, in the sense Kath Weston (2017) describes—emphasizing the earth as a living character, not an inert stage for human politics. Though "planetary" is a label weighted with baggage of its own, such reframings also represent an attempt within health policy to acknowledge more complicated relational thresholds around what Kim TallBear (2011) calls "the life/not life binary."[5]

These are key dimensions of health that certain earlier generations of social thinkers were not often forced to reckon with. "Well, if there has been so much change, it is not the climate that has changed," Michel Foucault (2007, 22) once wrote, commenting on a description of weather in Virgil, "the political and economic interventions of government have altered the course of things." In this framing, nature was assumed to be a receiving template for governance. But the realities that this overlooked even in Virgil's time (and certainly in Foucault's) are becoming more difficult to bracket. A living piece of earth is many things besides an inert territory; unruly oceans and atmospheres may not respond at all to the strategic designs of local sovereigns within the state in question or on a human timescale.

Yet even human timescales are a kind of threshold making, one people like C. were working to reach beyond in search of healing. When I watched the canoes full of sweet desserts and abundant food being paddled out to sea to feed the ancestors that dwelled there, I thought of all that had happened in the space of the deep ocean that I could not begin to comprehend. The thresholds such rituals aimed to rearrange were transformative and restorative to collective connections, allowing C. to survive long past the point when available science had run out. Sometimes when C. was found in a state of collapse, the local Kriol nurse could not tell whether she was experiencing a diabetic coma or spirit possession. C. explained that she was learning how aspects of high sugar might be harnessed as transcendence. She continued having intimate encounters with the dead there, including many who had already died of diabetes. When spirits were offered the rich foods they loved most, sometimes they revealed to her what to do next.

Carbohydrates and Hydrocarbons

Sugar was first explained to me as the experience of watching a loved one slowly disappear from a family album. I recalled the matter-of-factness of one man's voice as he recounted what had happened to his wife, turning each page of his album and repeating the word *sugar*. He paged through a family album on the kitchen table in his home on Belize's south coast, showing me pictures of their family. He smiled back at the old photos of her as a Garifuna teacher standing firm beside a rural schoolhouse. We watched as on the pages she became a mother, then a grandmother. The next time Mrs. P. appeared in the album, she was suddenly on crutches. "Sugar," Mr. P. said simply as he paged forward in time, the photographs sharpening in color and filling with grandchildren. In a family Christmas picture, his wife's entire right foot was missing. At one wedding, both of Mrs. P.'s legs were gone below the knee. We watched her disappear a piece at a time from the pictures, until she was absent altogether.

Later, that scene kept looping in my memory: Mr. P. turning the album's pages carefully so as not to crinkle its plastic sleeves, the photographic record of loss a surreal counterpoint to the stories he told about raising a family and caring for the generations to come. About the harrowing parts, he only ever repeated, "Sugar." Back then, I didn't know about the dozens of different cellular pathways and blood capillary injuries by which you can lose a limb to diabetic sugar's wears. But I could never forget how he narrated a series of slow losses that somehow had come to feel inevitable. When people like C., whom I had met in my short year there, began to go missing from pictures too, I thought of how many different versions of tenderness and disappearance are playing out in family albums across Belize and around the world, part of some much larger story of sugar.

In London I had traveled up to the highest point in the city, the Coca-Cola London Eye. From inside its wheeling glass pods, I looked out from this latest sugar machine toward the museum exhibit on sugar and slavery that I had visited inside an old Docklands sugarhouse. Its narratives recounted how ships from the Caribbean routinely arrived there to be unloaded in Blood Alley—thus named not because those same holds carried humans during another leg of those vessels' triangle trade routes, but because the cones of crystallized sugar had sharp edges that cut the British laborers carrying them. More severe injuries elsewhere were present mostly in cryptic traces: the museum displayed a drinking ladle from the renowned slain Garifuna leader Satuye, which had been mounted like a trophy and traded to England by former French allies once Garinagu ancestral lands, on what later became the island of St. Vincent, were turned into colonial sugar plantations.

Staring through the corporate soda logos emblazoned on the glass pods' windows, I could see Buckingham Palace and the Parliament buildings where historian Hilary Beckles and other leaders from CARICOM countries like Belize recently gathered to present their policy proposal (see figure 1.4), including health-care investments for diabetes as a form of repair and apology for colonial injustices (see Beckles 2013, 2014).[6] I had told myself that a UK trip made sense, in part, to better reckon with my own position in sugar's connected histories. Perhaps that had been another displacement, I realized, looking out onto London's skyline through a US corporate emblem.

The time-lapse quality of disappearances from photo albums is now evident not only with people but also with shorelines and other places gradually disappearing piece by piece. Such scales of chronic global consumption—of carbohydrates and hydrocarbons, the fuel of people and machines—have been materially linked for centuries. "Oil and sugar would seem to have little in common," Vincent Brown reflects on evolving forms of hydrocarbons, yet "we are reminded of how the consumption of fossil fuel has been closely associated with the machinery of death" (2008, 124). Such stories are there in the coal- and oil-powered factories once populated by the British laborers consuming sugar, and in the ways Caribbean sugar refining requires coal and other fossil fuels for heat (Mitchell 2011, 16–17). They are there in the petrochemicals contributing to diabetes and entering bodies, and in the calories of fuel spent on transporting calories of food (Wilk 2007) as overheating climates remake

FIGURE 1.4 View over Buckingham Palace, where a request for diabetes infrastructures to address colonial legacies of sugar was presented by Caribbean reparation advocates, as seen from the Coca-Cola London Eye in 2018. Photo by Amy Moran-Thomas.

center and peripheries. Like wild cane growing ragged along roads in Belize, the English sugar refineries puffing on without working-class labor appeared both evacuated and alive, continuing to unleash forces in the world.

Scientific models of the coming century suggest grim forecasts about these material afterlives: that sugar will do harm in an increasing number of bodies, and that carbon's atmospheric effects will harm many living things' chances to survive. One could imagine, from London, a future where the fixes of "halfway technologies" like geo-engineering are enough for a while: carbon-capture technologies filtering the atmosphere something like the washings of dialysis machines; solar engineering projects injecting particles into the stratosphere as routinely as people inject insulin. One could imagine that these stories about struggles for access to technologies in the face of chronic wear may grow to an atmospheric scale (Moran-Thomas 2019; Mizelle 2020)—that unequal infrastructures for repair work could produce unevenly normalized death for planetary bodies, in addition to human ones.

But amid those ominous thoughts in Silvertown, I also heard about an improvised museum of sugar factory artifacts inside the old Tate Social Institute, assembled by its migrant squatters who recycle and repair computers. I was glad to find that tiny crack of ethnographic surprise to interrupt my thoughts of bleak models. It reminded me of the hope and chances I had seen people like C. create for each other, in ancestral feedings and so many forms of care work. The cracks in such models are filled with people, and people are doing things that posit a future.

Maybe I traveled to London searching for some kind of acknowledged interrelation, a mutual awareness of all that was still happening across the world around sugar's thresholds. But the closest thing I found was the warped slogan "Out of the Strong Came Forth Sweetness," flaking off the derelict Lyle sugar factory's giant golden molasses tin, dominating the landscape with its eerie image of bees emerging from a dead lion—among the oldest corporate logos in the world. Not the parable I was looking for, just another unresolvable riddle. I was trying to locate some sign of responsibility for linked histories but found only empty houses all around the sugar factory, some bearing little notes on their doors: "POSTMAN—NOBODY LIVES HERE."

I stood at the water's edge and looked through the fog at the abandoned industrial mills and distant cranes putting up glass-fronted condos, rumored to be owned mostly by investors from Dubai and China. Locals said that the digging releases smells from the earth of whichever factory used to sit above: creosote, telegraph rubber, perfume chemicals. "In understanding the relationship between commodity and person, we unearth anew the history of ourselves," Mintz (1985, 214) wrote as his book's last line. But if I was honest while watching the cranes dig into the ground below the "sugar mile," I still wasn't sure what was being unearthed in this history of ourselves, except how unevenly commodities' potent afterlives lingered in relations and bodies of all kinds.

ACKNOWLEDGMENT

This essay is adapted from several chapters of *Traveling with Sugar: Chronicles of a Global Epidemic*. I am deeply grateful to all of those who contributed to this project.

NOTES

1. Mintz credited his grasp of these relations to the foundational work of Eric Williams in *Capitalism and Slavery* ([1944] 2005), on which Cedric Robinson (1983), in developing the term *racial capitalism*, would also build to extend

Williams's arguments about how enslavement and settler colonialism had made free-trade capitalism possible.

2. These reflections unfold in dialogue with the key insights of scholars who have deeply examined this issue across segregated "food geographies" both across the United States (Reese 2019; Garth and Reese 2020; Hoover 2017; Hassberg 2020; Jernigan 2018; Hatch 2016; Penniman 2018) and elsewhere in the world (Gálvez 2018; Roberts 2017; Garth 2013, 2020; Llewellyn 2013; Vaughan, Adjaye-Gbewonyo, and Mika 2021; Solomon 2016; Yates-Doerr 2015; Carruth and Mendenhall 2019; Wilk 2006, 2007; Gálvez, Carney, and Yates-Doerr 2020). They have also been informed by many studies on how diabetes and related chronic conditions are shaped by diagnostic technologies and the illnesses they define and make biomedically legible (Liggins 2020; Whitmarsh 2011; Tuchman 2020; see also Landecker 2015), continuously inflecting how they are lived in turn (Biehl and Petryna 2013; Mol 2008; Livingston 2005; Benton 2015).

3. Much of the region's sugar, once refined (often elsewhere), will return again to Caribbean and Latin American markets as sweet packaged food products—part of the global circuits of production and consumption that Frantz Fanon long ago foresaw as the next stage of exploitation: "The colonies have become a market. The colonial population is a customer who is ready to buy goods," which Fanon viewed as part and parcel of "that violence which is just under the skin" (1963, 38). Historian Sir Hilary Beckles (2014) notes that the disembodiments related to diabetes therefore have especially discomforting resonance in Caribbean and Latin American regions today, writing from Barbados that these trademark injuries of sugar are resurrecting its reputation as "the amputation capital of the world. It is here that the stress profile of slavery and racial apartheid; dietary disaster and psychological trauma; and addiction to the consumption of sugar and salt, have reached their highest peak. The country is now host to the world's most virulent diabetes and hypertension epidemic. [The British] Parliament owes the people of Barbados an education and health initiative." For much more on the meanings of sugarcane and its entwined psychic and infrastructural legacies, see Reese (2021); Brown (2018); Mizelle (2021); Hatch (2016); Toomer ([1923] 2019); James ([1938] 1989); Doucet-Battle (2021); Las Casas (1906); and Stoler (2013). For more on the converging Caribbean histories and silences briefly referenced here, see Trouillot ([1995] 2015); Palacio (1982, 2005); Scott (2018); Reid et al. (2018); Taylor (2016); Beckles (2013); and Wynter (1971).

4. These reflections are also shaped by ongoing conversations in anthropology about the political and existential meaning of various converging "thresholds" (see Jusionyte 2018). Memorably, in the longer history of anthropology, Victor Turner's theories described the betwixt-and-between threshold states that he called "liminality," building on the work of Arnold van Gennep. Turner wrote, "The attributes of liminality or of liminal personae ('threshold people') are necessarily ambiguous, since this condition and these persons elude or slip through the network of classifications that normally locate states and positions in cultural space" (1967, 359). Many anthropologists have since reflected on these ideas of

liminality and thresholds—spaces of transformation, open on both ends. For Turner, the way out of the liminal state was through ritual practice. But in situations of chronic conditions, it was not always possible to find a ritual that worked. Getting caught in its betwixt-and-between, neither-nor state can recall what it is like for patients to live with chronic diagnoses, Jean Jackson argues, classified by biomedicine as "ambiguous beings" (2005, 332). Yet a "liminal figure—one that haunts the very field of power that excludes her"—at times also sheds light on those fields' definitions, Angela Garcia (2010, 149) offers. "Such a liminal position can animate a critically different reflection on medicine and society, a reflection that need not accept things as they are," Arthur Kleinman (1997, 3–4) notes.

5. These reflections also unfold in relation to much larger conversations in anthropology about interspecies writing (e.g., Todd 2017; Paxson and Helmreich 2014; Besky and Blanchette 2019; Livingston and Puar 2011).

6. The regional alliance of CARICOM (the Caribbean Community and Common Market) includes not only island nations but also mainland countries such as Belize, Guyana, and Suriname. See CARICOM Reparations Commission (2013).

REFERENCES

Agard-Jones, Vanessa. 2013. "Bodies in the System." *Small Axe* 17 (3): 182–92.

Agard-Jones, Vanessa. 2015. "Chlordécone." Paper presented at the Manufacturing of Rights, Beirut, May 14, 2015. YouTube video, 14:49. https://www.youtube.com/watch?v=yvqVkR4Iuqs.

Alegria, Henry, Kathy Carvalho-Knighton, and Victor Alegria. 2009. *Assessing Land-Based Sources of Pollutants to Coastal Waters of Southern Belize*. Final report, project NA07NOS4630029. National Oceanic Atmospheric Administration (NOAA). https://repository.library.noaa.gov/view/noaa/590.

Beckles, Hilary. 2013. *Britain's Black Debt: Reparations for Caribbean Slavery and Native Genocide*. Kingston, Jamaica: University of West Indies Press.

Beckles, Hilary. 2014. "Address to the British Parliament on Reparations," July 16, 2014. Reprinted in *Wadadli Pen*, November 21, 2014. https:/wadadlipen.wordpress.com/2014/11/21/fyi-sir-hilary-beckles-addresses-the-british-parliament-on-reparations/.

Beliso-De Jesús, Aisha. 2014. "Santería Copresence and the Making of African Diaspora Bodies." *Cultural Anthropology* 29 (3): 503–26.

Belize Ministry of Health. 2014. *Belize Health Sector Strategic Plan, 2012–2024*. Pan American Health Organization. https://extranet.who.int/nutrition/gina/en/node/39409.

Benítez-Rojo, Antonio. 2001. *The Repeating Island: The Caribbean and the Postmodern Perspective*. Durham, NC: Duke University Press.

Benton, Adia. 2015. *HIV Exceptionalism: Development through Disease in Sierra Leone*. Minneapolis: University of Minnesota Press.

Besky, Sarah, and Alex Blanchette, eds. 2019. *How Nature Works: Rethinking Labor on a Troubled Planet*. Albuquerque: University of New Mexico Press.

Biehl, João, and Adriana Petryna, eds. 2013. *When People Come First: Critical Studies in Global Health*. Princeton, NJ: Princeton University Press.

Biswas, Atanu, Manish Bharara, Craig Hurst, Rainer Gruessner, David Armstrong, and Horacio Rilo. 2010. "Use of Sugar on the Healing of Diabetic Ulcers: A Review." *Journal of Diabetes Science and Technology* 4 (5): 1139–45.

Bond, David. 2013. "Governing Disaster: The Political Life of the Environment during the BP Oil Spill." *Cultural Anthropology* 28 (4): 694–715.

Braverman, Irus. 2018. *Coral Whisperers: Scientists on the Brink*. Oakland: University of California Press.

Brown, Vincent. 2008. "Eating the Dead: Consumption and Regeneration in the History of Sugar." *Food and Foodways* 16 (2): 117–26.

Canguilhem, Georges. 1991. *The Normal and the Pathological*. Translated by Carolyn R. Fawcett. New York: Zone Books.

CARICOM Reparations Commission. 2013. "10-Point Reparation Plan." http://caricomreparations.org.

Carruth, Lauren, and Emily Mendenhall. 2019. "'Wasting Away': Diabetes, Food Insecurity, and Medical Insecurity in the Somali Region of Ethiopia." *Social Science and Medicine* 228:155–63.

Carson, Rachel. (1955) 1998. *The Edge of the Sea*. New York: Houghton Mifflin.

Crosbie, Paul, Yvette Herrera, Myrna Manzanares, Silvana Woods, Cynthia Crosbie, and Ken Decker, eds. 2005. *Kriol-Inglish Dikshineri*. Belmopan, Belize: Belize Kriol Project.

Doucet-Battle, James. 2021. *Sweetness in the Blood: Race, Risk, and Type 2 Diabetes*. Minneapolis: University of Minnesota Press.

Fanon, Frantz. 1963. *The Wretched of the Earth*. Translated by Constance Farrington. New York: Grove.

Ferdinand, Malcom. 2022. *Decolonial Ecology: Thinking from the Caribbean World*. Cambridge: Polity.

Foster, John Bellamy. 2000. *Marx's Ecology: Materialism and Nature*. New York: Monthly Review Press.

Foucault, Michel. 2007. *Security, Territory, Population: Lectures at the Collège de France, 1977–78*. Edited by Michel Senellart. Translated by Graham Burchell. New York: Palgrave Macmillan.

Gálvez, Alyshia. 2018. *Eating NAFTA: Trade, Food Policies, and the Destruction of Mexico*. Oakland: University of California Press.

Gálvez, Alyshia, Megan Carney, and Emily Yates-Doerr. 2020. "Chronic Disaster: Reimagining Noncommunicable Chronic Disease." *American Anthropologist* 122 (3): 639–40.

Garcia, Angela. 2010. *The Pastoral Clinic: Addiction and Dispossession along the Rio Grande*. Berkeley: University of California Press.

Garth, Hanna, ed. 2013. *Food and Identity in the Caribbean*. London: Bloomsbury.

Garth, Hanna. 2020. *Food in Cuba: The Pursuit of a Decent Meal*. Stanford, CA: Stanford University Press.

Garth, Hanna, and Ashanté M. Reese, eds. 2020. *Black Food Matters: Racial Justice in the Wake of Food Justice*. Minneapolis: University of Minnesota Press.

Gough, Ethan, Englebert Emmanuel, Valerie Jenkins, Lorraine Thompson, Enrique Perez, Alberto Barcelo, Robert Gerzoff, and Edward Gregg. 2008. *Survey of Diabetes, Hypertension and Chronic Disease Risk Factors*. Belize City: Pan American Health Organization and Belize Ministry of Health.

Haraway, Donna J. 2015. "Anthropocene, Capitalocene, Plantationocene, Chthulucene: Making Kin." *Environmental Humanities* 6 (1): 159–65.

Hardin, Jessica. 2016. "'Healing Is a Done Deal': Temporality and Metabolic Healing among Evangelical Christians in Samoa." *Medical Anthropology* 35 (2): 105–18.

Hardin, Jessica. 2019. *Faith and the Pursuit of Health: Cardiometabolic Disorders in Samoa*. New Brunswick, NJ: Rutgers University Press.

Hartman, Saidiya. 2007. *Lose Your Mother: A Journey along the Atlantic Slave Route*. New York: Farrar, Straus, and Giroux.

Harvell, Drew. 2019. *Ocean Outbreak: Confronting the Rising Tide of Marine Disease*. Oakland: University of California Press.

Hassberg, Analena Hope. 2020. "Nurturing the Revolution: The Black Panther Party and the Early Seeds of the Food Justice Movement." In *Black Food Matters: Racial Justice in the Wake of Food Justice*, edited by Hanna Garth and Ashanté M. Reese, 82–106. Minneapolis: University of Minnesota Press.

Hatch, Anthony Ryan. 2016. *Blood Sugar: Racial Pharmacology and Food Justice in Black America*. Minneapolis: University of Minnesota Press.

Hayes, Tyrone, and Guy Raz. 2016. "How Do Common Chemicals Affect Frogs, Rats—and Maybe Us?" NPR, October 21, 2016. https://www.npr.org/templates/transcript/transcript.php?storyId=497844694.

Hecht, Gabrielle. 2019. "Air in the Time of Oil." *Los Angeles Review of Books*, January 21, 2019. https://blog.lareviewofbooks.org/provocations/air-time-oil/.

Hoover, Elizabeth. 2017. *The River Is in Us: Fighting Toxics in a Mohawk Community*. Minneapolis: University of Minnesota Press.

Horton, Richard, Robert Beaglehole, and Ruth Bonita. 2014. "From Public to Planetary Health: A Manifesto." *Lancet* 383 (9920): 847.

Innis, Michelle. 2016. "Climate-Related Death of Coral around World Alarms Scientists." *New York Times*, April 9, 2016.

Jackson, Jean. 2005. "Stigma, Liminality, and Chronic Pain: Mind-Body Borderlands." *American Ethnologist* 32 (3): 332–53.

James, C. L. R. (1938) 1989. *The Black Jacobins*. New York: Vintage.

Jernigan, Kasey. 2018. "Embodied Heritage: Obesity, Cultural Identity, and Food Distribution Programs in the Choctaw Nation of Oklahoma." PhD diss., University of Massachusetts, Amherst.

Jusionyte, Ieva. 2018. *Threshold: Emergency Responders on the US-Mexico Border*. Oakland: University of California Press.

Kaiser, Kristine. 2011. "Preliminary Study of Pesticide Drift into the Maya Mountain Protected Areas of Belize." *Bulletin of Environmental Contamination and Toxicology* 86 (1): 56–59.

Kleinman, Arthur. 1997. *Writing at the Margin: Discourse between Anthropology and Medicine*. Berkeley: University of California Press.

Klingle, Matthew. 2015. "Inescapable Paradoxes: Diabetes, Progress, and Ecologies of Inequality." *Environmental History* 20 (4): 736–50.

Kolbert, Elizabeth. 2014. *The Sixth Extinction: An Unnatural History*. New York: Henry Holt.

Landecker, Hannah. 2013. "Metabolism, Reproduction, and the Aftermath of Categories." *S&F Online* 11 (3). https://sfonline.barnard.edu/life-un-ltd-feminism-bioscience-race/metabolism-reproduction-and-the-aftermath-of-categories/.

Landecker, Hannah. 2015. "Antibiotic Resistance and the Biology of History." *Body and Society* 22 (4): 19–52.

Langston, Nancy. 2011. *Toxic Bodies: Hormone Disruptors and the Legacy of DES*. New Haven, CT: Yale University Press.

Las Casas, Bartolomé de. 1906. "Narrative of the Third Voyage of Columbus as Contained in Casas's History." In *The Northmen, Columbus and Cabot*, edited by Julius Olson and Edward Bourne, 317–66. New York: Charles Scribner's and Sons.

Liggins, Arlena S. 2020. *Making Diabetes: The Politics of Diabetes Diagnostics in Uganda*. New York: Columbia University Press.

Livingston, Julie. 2005. *Debility and the Moral Imagination in Botswana*. Bloomington: Indiana University Press.

Livingston, Julie, and Jasbir K. Puar. 2011. "Interspecies." *Social Text* 29 (1): 3–14.

Llewellyn, Robin. 2013. "Rediscovering the Half-Forgotten Farms of the Garifuna." *Los Angeles Review of Books*, January 13, 2013.

Malinowski, Bronislaw. (1935) 1965. *Coral Gardens and Their Magic*. Vol. 1, *Soil-Tilling and Agricultural Rites in the Trobriand Islands*. Bloomington: Indiana University Press.

Manjapra, Kris. 2018. "Plantation Dispossessions: The Global Travel of Agricultural Racial Capitalism." In *American Capitalism: New Histories*, edited by Sven Beckert and Christine Desan, 361–88. New York: Columbia University Press.

Masco, Joseph. 2010. "Bad Weather: On Planetary Crisis." *Social Studies of Science* 40 (1): 7–40.

McCollum, Siobhan. 2019. "The Cultural Impacts of Sargassum Invasion." Belize NICH/Institute for Social and Cultural Research Symposia, April 4, 2019.

Mintz, Sidney. 1974. *Worker in the Cane: A Puerto Rican Life History*. New York: W. W. Norton.

Mintz, Sidney. 1985. *Sweetness and Power: The Place of Sugar in Modern History*. New York: Penguin.

Mitchell, Timothy. 2011. *Carbon Democracy: Political Power in the Age of Oil*. New York: Verso.

Mitman, Gregg, Michelle Murphy, and Christopher Sellers, eds. 2004. *Landscapes of Exposure: Knowledge and Illness in Modern Environments. Osiris* 19. Chicago: University of Chicago Press.

Mizelle, Richard M., Jr. 2020. "Hurricane Katrina, Diabetes, and the Meaning of Resiliency." *Isis* 111 (1): 120–28.

Mizelle, Richard M., Jr. 2021. "Diabetes, Race, and Amputations." *Lancet* 397 (10281): 1256–57.

Mol, Annemarie. 2008. "I Eat an Apple: On Theorizing Subjectivities." *Subjectivity* 22 (1): 28–37.

Moore, Jason W. 2000. "Sugar and the Expansion of the Early Modern World Economy." *Fernand Braudel Center Review* 23 (3): 409–33.

Moran-Thomas, Amy. 2019. *Traveling with Sugar: Chronicles of a Global Epidemic*. Oakland: University of California Press.

Murphy, Michelle. 2017. "Alterlife and Decolonial Chemical Relations." *Cultural Anthropology* 32 (4): 494–503.

Palacio, Joseph. 1982. "Food and Social Relations in a Garifuna Village." PhD diss., University of California, Berkeley.

Palacio, Joseph, ed. 2005. *The Garifuna: A Nation across Borders—Essays in Social Anthropology*. Benque Viejo del Carmen, Belize: Cubola Books.

Paxson, Heather, and Stefan Helmreich. 2014. "The Perils and Promises of Microbial Abundance: Novel Natures and Model Ecosystems, from Artisanal Cheese to Alien Seas." *Social Studies of Science* 44 (2): 165–93.

Penniman, Leah. 2018. *Farming While Black: Soul Fire Farm's Practical Guide to Liberation on the Land*. London: Chelsea Green.

Pepper, Christopher B., Thomas R. Rainwater, Steven G. Platt, Jennifer A. Dever, and Todd A. Anderson. 2004. "Organochlorine Pesticides in Chorioallantoic Membranes of Morelet's Crocodile Eggs from Belize." *Journal of Wildlife Diseases* 40 (3): 493–500.

Petryna, Adriana. 2018. "Wildfires at the Edges of Science: Horizoning Work amid Runaway Change." *Cultural Anthropology* 33 (4): 570–95.

Reese, Ashanté M. 2019. *Black Food Geographies: Race, Self-Reliance, and Food Access*. Chapel Hill: University of North Carolina Press.

Reese, Ashanté M. 2021. "Tarry with Me: Reclaiming Sweetness in an Anti-Black World." *Oxford American*, no. 112. https://www.oxfordamerican.org/magazine/issue-112-spring-2021/tarry-with-me.

Reid, Basil A., Peter E. Siegel, Nicholas P. Dunning, Corinne L. Hofman, Stéphen Rostain, Victor D. Thompson, and Scott M. Fitzpatrick. 2018. "Caribbean and Circum-Caribbean Farmers: An Introduction." In *The Archaeology of Caribbean and Circum-Caribbean Farmers 6000 BC–AD 1500*, edited by Basil A. Reid, 1–32. New York: Routledge.

Richardson, Robert. 2009. "Belize and Climate Change: The Costs of Inaction." Belmopan, Belize: UN Development Program.

Roberts, Elizabeth. 2017. "What Gets Inside: Violent Entanglements and Toxic Boundaries in Mexico City." *Cultural Anthropology* 32 (4): 592–619.

Robinson, Cedric. 1983. *Black Marxism: The Making of the Black Racial Tradition*. Chapel Hill: University of North Carolina Press.

Scott, Julius S. 2018. *The Common Wind: Afro-American Currents in the Age of the Haitian Revolution*. New York: Verso.

Sharpe, Christina. 2016. *In the Wake: On Blackness and Being*. Durham, NC: Duke University Press.

Simpson, Audra. 2014. *Mohawk Interruptus: Political Life across the Borders of Settler States*. Durham, NC: Duke University Press.

Singh, Bhrigupati. 2015. *Poverty and the Quest for Life*. Chicago: University of Chicago Press.

Solomon, Harris. 2016. *Metabolic Living: Food, Fat, and the Absorption of Illness in India*. Durham, NC: Duke University Press.

Stoler, Ann Laura, ed. 2013. *Imperial Debris: On Ruins and Ruination*. Durham, NC: Duke University Press.

TallBear, Kim. 2011. "Why Interspecies Thinking Needs Indigenous Standpoints." *Fieldsights*, Society for Cultural Anthropology, November 18, 2011. https://culanth.org/fieldsights/why-interspecies-thinking-needs-indigenous-standpoints.

Taussig, Michael. 1989. "History as Commodity." *Critique of Anthropology* 9 (1): 7–23.

Taylor, Christopher. 2016. *The Black Carib Wars: Freedom, Survival, and the Making of the Garifuna*. Jackson: University of Mississippi Press.

Thomas, Deborah A. 2016. "Time and the Otherwise: Plantations, Garrisons and Being Human in the Caribbean." *Anthropological Theory* 16 (2–3): 177–200.

Todd, Zoe. 2017. "Fish, Kin and Hope: Tending to Water Violations in *amiskwaciwâskahikan* and Treaty Six Territory." *Afterall* 43:102–7.

Toomer, Jean. (1923) 2019. *Cane*. New York: Penguin Classics.

Trouillot, Michel-Rolph. (1995) 2015. *Silencing the Past: Power and the Production of History*. Boston: Beacon.

Tuchman, Arleen. 2020. *Diabetes: A History of Race and Disease*. New Haven, CT: Yale University Press.

Turner, Victor. 1967. *The Forest of Symbols: Aspects of Ndembu Ritual*. Ithaca, NY: Cornell University Press.

US Environmental Protection Agency. 2008. *Cruise Ship Discharge Assessment Report*. EPA Report # 842-R-07-005. Washington, DC: Oceans and Coastal Protection Division, Office of Water. https://nepis.epa.gov/Exe/ZyPDF.cgi/P1002SVS.PDF?Dockey=P1002SVS.PDF.

Valentine, Jerris J. 2002. *Garifuna Understanding of Death*. Belmopan, Belize: National Garifuna Council of Belize.

Vaughan, Megan, Kafui Adjaye-Gbewonyo, and Marissa Mika, eds. 2021. *Epidemiological Change and Chronic Diseases in Sub-Saharan Africa: Social and Historical Perspectives*. London: UCL Press.

Vogel, Sarah A. 2009. "The Politics of Plastics: The Making and Unmaking of Bisphenol A 'Safety.'" *American Journal of Public Health* 99 (s3): s559–66.

Walker, Kara. 2014. "A Subtlety, or the Marvelous Sugar Baby." Art 21, May 23, 2014. Video, 9:37. https://art21.org/watch/extended-play/kara-walker-a-subtlety-or-the-marvelous-sugar-baby-short/.

Weston, Kath. 2017. *Animate Planet: Making Visceral Sense of Living in a High-Tech Ecologically Damaged World*. Durham, NC: Duke University Press.

Whitmarsh, Ian. 2011. "American Genomics in Barbados: Race, Illness, and Pleasure in the Science of Personalized Medicine." *Body and Society* 17 (2–3): 159–81.

Whitmarsh, Ian. 2013. "Troubling 'Environments': Postgenomics, Bajan Wheezing, and Lévi-Strauss." *Medical Anthropology Quarterly* 27 (4): 489–509.

Wilk, Richard. 2006. *Home Cooking in the Global Village: Caribbean Food from Buccaneers to Ecotourists*. Oxford: Berg.

Wilk, Richard. 2007. "The Extractive Economy: An Early Phase of the Globalization of Diet, and Its Environmental Consequences." In *Rethinking Environmental History: World-System History and Global Environmental Change*, edited by Alf Hornborg, J. R. McNeill, and Joan Martinez-Alier, 179–98. Lanham, MD: AltaMira.

Williams, Eric. (1944) 2005. *Capitalism and Slavery*. Chapel Hill: University of North Carolina Press.

Wynter, Sylvia. 1971. "Novel and History, Plot and Plantation." *Savacou* 5:95–102.

Yates-Doerr, Emily. 2015. *The Weight of Obesity: Hunger and Global Health in Postwar Guatemala*. Oakland: University of California Press.

Young, Colin. 2008. "Belize's Ecosystems: Threats and Challenges to Conservation in Belize." *Tropical Conservation Science* 1 (1): 18–33.

chapter two

The Food of Our Food

MEDICATED FEED AND
THE INDUSTRIALIZATION
OF METABOLISM

HANNAH LANDECKER

WHAT DO FOOD ANIMALS EAT? MOST ATTENTION TO THIS QUESTION tends to focus on contaminants that might reach humans (McEvoy 2016). Yet the biomass of domesticated animals far outstrips that of humans on earth, and thus the materials that flow into and out of them do so at a scale that is environmentally and historically consequential well beyond any individual eaters (Bar-On, Phillips, and Milo 2018). Bucolic images of chickens in barnyards or cows in grassy fields aside, the majority of food animals raised in the United States eat complex mixtures of macronutrients, drugs, and supplements variably called *condimental feed, formulated feed, manufactured feed*, or *medicated feed*. The term *medicated feed* emerged late in the nineteenth century and was adapted in the twentieth to mean small amounts of supplement added to a bulk amount of fodder, whether that be vitamins, minerals, enzymes, amino acids, medicines, growth promoters, or a smell or flavor enhancer—or more likely a complex combination of these. Medicated feed now shapes the nutrition, growth, and health of most food animals in the United States for their entire lives.

This chapter focuses on the quotidian but profound remaking of the materiality of eating in the science and industry of animal feeding in the United States. I sketch a big picture: the wholesale remaking of streams of matter and energy among microorganisms, plants, animals, and humans in the twentieth century. In the development of the medicated feed industry, existing metabolic relationships within and among animals, plants, and microbes were sundered, selectively augmented, and reconnected anew. My focus is not on any single case of industrialization within this picture—beef or milk or hormones or chickens—but on the industrialization of metabolism itself (Marcus 1993; DuPuis 2002; Boyd 2001; Schrepfer and Scranton 2004).

The systematic remaking, rescaling, and reordering of matter's movement through bacteria, plants, and animals is what makes the history of medicated feed significant. It constitutes a wholesale rearrangement of relations constituting the metabolic web in which human eating is hung. *Metabolism* describes the biochemical processes by which organisms use food and oxygen and process drugs and toxins. It is an organized set of biochemical reactions: enzymes catalyze the conversion of substances into different forms and use or produce energy for the cell or body. Metabolic relations also link individuals and species to one another, as the metabolic output of one organism may furnish materials necessary to another's life. To industrialize means to introduce industry at a large scale, to reorganize an economy for the purpose of manufacturing. It might seem counterintuitive that this should occur in the microscopic realm of the biochemistry of the agricultural cell, but this is what I mean in using the phrase *industrialization of metabolism* literally: metabolic processes such as fat synthesis were targeted for augmentation or acceleration relative to others, and key enzymes were employed to scale up particular chemical conversions in and between organisms. Scientists and industrial feed manufacturers moved from questions of *nutritional insufficiencies* to problems of *metabolic efficiencies*, retooling and accelerating systems of chemical conversions.

In the context of this volume, metabolism is both an important empirical site for understanding food production and a heuristic: Can we understand eating better by allowing metabolic relations writ large to decenter human food as the object of inquiry? By focusing on metabolism, not food, this study contributes to a growing social science literature at several levels. First, the cultural, medical, and political prominence of metabolic disorders such as diabetes has brought scholarly attention to what is done in the name of metabolic health at the level of societies and individuals (Yates-Doerr 2015; Solomon 2016; Guthman 2011; Roberts 2017; Moran-Thomas 2019). Examining medical and social efforts to manage metabolic disorder, this work asks: (1) How do people organize action around metabolism? (2) What kind of concept is it? I extend these questions by focusing on metabolism as the technical object of intervention in animal feed science. As such, metabolism is a set of biochemical relations that both formats and is formatted by economic and social life.

Simultaneously but quite separately, twentieth-century theoretical uses of metabolism as a framework for measuring ecosystem dynamics are making a return in systems analysis approaches, tracking the fate of energy and matter across ecological or social units from ponds to cities (Mitman 1992). This approach is quantitative, for example, in Vaclav Smil's (2013) astonishing estimates of the relative biomass of plants, wild animals, domesticated animals, and humans after sustained "harvesting [of] the biosphere"; and qualitative, as in the revival of Karl Marx's critiques of agriculture under capitalism in light of ecological crisis, which John Bellamy Foster (2000) terms a theory of "metabolic rift." Marx decried the rupture in cycles of growth and decay caused by taking nitrogenous waste such as bird guano from its origin (Peru) and shipping it to Europe to increase agricultural production in nitrogen-depleted soils.[1] Jason Moore (2015) argues that the world has seen a historical "metabolic shift" in which humans do not so much cause a rift in nature, damaging an ecology that is outside of themselves, as remake the material natural world (of which they are a part) through unrelenting capital accumulation. Capitalism, he argues, does not have an ecology, it *is* an ecology, one brought to the breaking point as low-cost extraction becomes more difficult. Jonathan Wells offers a related framework in *The Metabolic Ghetto* (2016), arguing that food is power and that systemic inequalities in social power under capitalism manifest as systemic inequalities in metabolic health; Wells also sees capitalism as a root cause and explanatory ground for the contemporary human condition.

This account of animal feed treads a middle ground between ethnographic study of any one instance of metabolism in medicine or culture and the world-historical macroscale of capitalism as an explanation. Here I follow historian Tiago Saraiva, who in his work on animal and plant science in fascist Europe has argued convincingly for a refusal to accept that all forms of control of life are the same. Rather than seeing fascist pig breeding as yet another form of biopolitics and therefore capable of being equated to capitalist pig breeding as two variations of a general process of modernization, Saraiva asks how "the increasing ability to tinker with plant and animal life ... enabled the materialization of different political projects, alternative modernities, good and bad" (2016, 12). The question is not how fascism was a pregiven "context" that shaped the pig or the potato but the reverse: how these technical practices and new organismal forms themselves constituted, informed, or enabled fascist regimes and particular social collectives. Technoscientific organisms, he argues, are a form of world-making.

What kind of modernity is made by feeding practices? While it is clear that medicated feed designed to make more animal products in less time with less input is an instance of increasing capital accumulation, herein lies the beginning of inquiry rather than its conclusion: What worlds are made in and through the industrialization of metabolism? Quite literally, what is constituted, what gets suppressed, and what is transformed? How exactly is cheap food made possible, and with what specific effects on the material conditions of contemporary life? Indeed, for those who care less about social theory and who want to know what this history means for human health, concrete details of medicated feed's components and the industrialization of metabolism provide insight into the nature of human diets today, raising new questions about the systemic rather than the overtly toxic impacts of these hidden practices.

The history of animal feeding over the twentieth century is a complicated story, even if limited to the United States. Accordingly, while recounting events chronologically, I have focused the narrative to reflect three facets of the industrialization of metabolism: conversion, scale, and acceleration. The first analyzes the animal as a machine converter of matter and energy between 1880 and 1920, the period in which "scientific feeding" was established. The second section turns to more profound metabolic rearrangements that came with a shift from obsessions with protein to single molecules, particularly vitamins and amino acids. Microbial fermentation and synthetic chemistry were used to mass-produce key nutrients, lowering costs. The joining of microbial metabolism, chemical synthesis, and animal metabolism into new chains of consumption and conversion between 1920 and 1960 meant new kinds of relations but also new scales and proportions for the organic molecules moving along these conduits.

The third aspect of industrializing metabolism is temporal: getting animals to maturity and market faster. Acceleration is already implicit in the conversion and rescaling of nutrient flows, but postwar growth promoters further foreshortened animal life. This section discusses growth promoters, from substances that encouraged growth to full potential (such as vitamins) to substances that changed the ratio of food to growth (such as antibiotics). I conclude by discussing the historical centrality of growth in nutrition science and animal husbandry, and its occlusion of alternative questions that should be asked concerning the food of our food.

Animals as Chemical Converters: Protein Obsessions in the Early Twentieth Century

Organisms have been seen in terms of machines (and machines in terms of organisms) in many ways over the course of history (Canguilhem 2000). Animal metabolism as a chemical "converter of matter and energy" is a peculiar species of this analogy (Armsby and Moulton 1925). This language of chemical conversion and an obsession with protein originates with agricultural science in nineteenth-century Europe but takes a specifically American form in the twentieth century at the nexus of farming and manufacturing. I begin with the logic and thereby arrive at the practice of the animal as chemical converter.

The animal converter is different from the "human motor" focus of nutrition science in this period (Aronson 1982; Rabinbach 1992; Carpenter 1994; Cullather 2007; Mudry 2009; Neswald 2013). The human motor needed calories—fuel for socially and economically important activities of working and fighting, or perhaps, for elites, thinking or athleticism. Protein was often subsumed into the calorie question in research on human nutrition (Treitel 2008). By contrast, the job of animals was tied to matter that farmers could sell and consumers could eat. Energy was important in its conservation: manuals of animal feeding included advice on "Principles That Relate to Restfulness" to ensure costly feed was not wasted as movement and heat (Shaw 1907, 96–109). But animal nutrition was focused on protein matter first, with energy a distant second; meat was sold by the pound, milk by the gallon, wool by the bale.

This framework is best understood via Henry Prentiss Armsby (1853–1921), founding director of the Institute for Animal Nutrition at Pennsylvania State University, president of the Society for Agricultural Science, translator of German manuals of feeding standards, founder of the American Society of Animal Nutrition, and ardent investigator of the chemical and physical "laws" of animal nutrition.[2] He saw the animal body as the obligatory passage point between the inedible and the edible: "Only the smaller portion of the solar energy or the proteins which are stored up in the farmer's crops is directly available for man's use.... [T]he essential function of the animal in a permanent system of agriculture is the conversion of as large a proportion as possible of these inedible products into forms whose matter and energy can be utilized by the human body" (1917, xv). Unlike animal labor power, substitutable by "inanimate motors," animal metabolism was the sole way to access most of the energy and protein in plants: for conversion of "the by-products of the farm and factory into human food, there is as yet no suggestion of an agency which can take the place of the animal body" (xv).

Armsby's writings usefully represent the agricultural science of his time. The purpose of elucidating laws of nutrition was to make the most profitable use of the world's matter. The purpose of instruments such as respiration calorimeters was to "gain as intimate a knowledge as possible of the fundamental laws governing the nutrition of farm animals, so that the transformation may be effected with the least possible waste, and, on the other hand, the ability so to apply these laws as to secure the greatest economic return, since *it must never be forgotten that the criterion of success in agriculture is not a maximum production but a maximum profit*" (xv–xvi, emphasis added). Armsby's generation strove to import German agricultural science into American farming practices, which involved a "glorification of albuminous substances"—those containing nitrogen (Mendel 1923, 12). The question of how the nitrogen in soil was turned into plants, and how those plants were turned into animal matter, was the central preoccupation of the day (McCay 1973). Because the animal body could build up a "a great variety of specific proteins which are peculiar to itself and which differ in properties and chemical structure from the proteins... of the vegetable kingdom," protein metabolism was the specific site of profit maximization (Armsby 1917, 161).

Energetics were important, but Armsby highlighted that the enzymes and hormones running metabolism were themselves proteins, each a combination of different amino acids. Thus, the "machinery" of metabolism had to be provisioned precisely: "No amount of coal under the boiler will enable an electric plant to furnish a normal amount of current if the insulation of the generator is defective. For example, if tryptophan is necessary for the formation of some essential internal secretion, a diet lacking that substance, however much energy it might furnish, would fail to support the organism permanently" (184). In other words, animal metabolisms were converters made of protein components; animal nutrition science was charged with knowing just what was needed when to construct and run those converters most efficiently.

Here at the nexus of protein, efficiency, and profit, a growing manufacturing sector became sutured to academic biochemistry and the physiology of animal growth. High-protein feed could produce more weight but not necessarily more profit, depending on its cost. The ideal was a low-cost, high-protein feed. If we think of the emergence of the manufactured feed industry as a set of pushes and pulls from different sectors, a protein-dominated outlook led to a pull by science-advised farmers, just as the manufacturing sector was providing a push. A history of the international chemical industry between 1900 and 1930 drily observes of fertilizer production that the "American attitude to the size of chemical works... was, in short, to build a large plant and then find a market for the products" (Haber 1971, 176). Therefore, one does not have to presume that the pull preceded the push, which in this case stemmed from problematic processing wastes in other industries.

Fish entrails from canning plants on the West Coast and carcass trimmings in the Midwest and South constituted intrusive, rotting urban hazards, alongside "tankage" from animal rendering (Kiechle 2017). Growing markets for plant oils generated voluminous mash wastes. While it was a long-standing practice to feed leftover mash from brewing beer to animals, this was a local phenomenon, with cattle yards beside breweries turning brewing waste into milk for city dwellers (DuPuis 2002).[3] Processing technologies of homogenizing, drying, and pelleting developed for storing and transporting foods over time and distance changed these local waste economies. Tankage became "crackling" and was pelletized; dried distiller's grains began to move along the same rail corridors that alcohol and meat did. The use of dairy in feeds increased substantially around 1910 when it could be easily transported and evenly mixed into other fodder materials in dried form. Farmers had often used homegrown milk as a feed supplement on their own farms; now it became a farm input.

The result was a boom after 1900 in small feed-manufacturing companies and the transformation of existing ones. Cereal and oil producers diversified, entering the feed industry as they commercialized processing by-products. Promotion of "scientific feeding" was of mutual interest for government, companies, and agricultural science institutions. Efficiency did not merely mean a ration that would produce the maximum liveweight, nor was it purely a matter of feed cost: it could be the most expensive per bag or ton—but it should be the cheapest per dozen eggs, per gallon milk, or per pound of meat produced (Haecker 1903). The economic stakes were high: the population of the country expanded by almost 30 million people between 1900 and 1920, a 40 percent gain in a mere twenty years; manufacturing industries were rapidly expanding; and transport and infrastructure projects were connecting geographically disparate areas—moving agricultural products along new railways and roads (Hobbs and Stoops 2002; Cronon 2009).

Feeds of the 1910s–1920s increased protein content by adding buttermilk, fish meal, or bonemeal to a bulk grain material. Ful-O-Pep Growing Mash, introduced in 1917 by Quaker Oats (see figure 2.1), was marketed with a typical mix of economic and nutritional logic: "At every bite the chicks get just the things they should have. Your profit doesn't depend on what the feed costs; it depends on what it costs to raise your birds." Titled "It's the EARLY BIRD that gets the PROFIT," the advertisement makes clear that the farmer buying this

FIGURE 2.1 Advertisement for Ful-O-Pep Growing Mash, *Poultry Science* 6 (1927).

"balanced" ration will get to market first with bigger birds and earlier eggs. "Just the things they should have" ties wasteful feeding practices explicitly to the question of profit.

Teaching farmers "scientific feeding" was a key outcome of the early manufactured feed industry, a legacy that lasted long past the particular constituents of any one feedstuff. Purina Mills, established in 1894, sent out a female "crew of experts... all over the country to teach those desiring to know how to obtain greater results from poultry and cattle through scientific and balance feeding" (*Atlanta Constitution* 1923, 15). Instruction was free; feed was not. Learning to farm by accounting—calculating the net of inputs and outputs—was integral to agricultural modernization (Fitzgerald 2003). By 1920 fortified feeds and "premix" combinations became the norm. In 1929 the market of prepared feeds consisted of more than 750 manufacturers and was valued at $400 million, outpacing the total value of agricultural machinery and parts manufactured in 1929, at $278 million (Olmstead and Rhode 2008, 276).[4]

According to *The Golden Anniversary of Scientific Feeding*, published in 1947 to celebrate fifty years of the animal feed industry, the production of more meat, milk, and eggs was a fortunate side effect of the main event: the "development of a great industry... the feed processing and manufacturing industry... which today represents a volume of more than two billion dollars a year" (Wherry 1947, 1). It became possible to see the purpose of animals anew: as participants in consumption. The growth potential of animals was the basis of the new industry. Animal growth was thereby industrial growth. From this point of view, animals existed to grow the manufactured feed industry.

A "Practical Chemical Economy": Vitamins, Amino Acids, and the Articulation of Microbial and Animal Metabolism, 1920–1960

A practical chemical economy in the future depends quite as much upon our exploration of the fundamentals of microbial metabolism as upon the exploration of petroleum chemistry.

—R. E. BUCHANAN, "MICROBIAL METABOLISM AND AGRICULTURE"

The story recounted thus far fits well with accounts of American foodways during the late nineteenth and early twentieth centuries, from the vertical integration of food-processing industries (Chandler 1977) to technical innovations in baking chemistry, meat eating, and milk drinking (Horowitz 2006). As E. Melanie DuPuis (2002) points out in her excellent history of fresh milk in America, such changes were never just about the milk or the cow but involved a thoroughgoing transformation of landscape and labor, from alfalfa fields to transport networks to experts and salesmen. The next stage in the development of medicated feed could be told in this vein of social history of consumption and health: the rise of vitamins and the concept of deficiency diseases, the moral nature of dietary advice, the advent of the medicated feed salesmen, the equation of meat with virility, the impact of war (Bentley 1998; Biltekoff 2013; Collingham 2013). Or, equally, one could follow the masterful lead of social historians of the corporation and show the annexation of plant and animal functions to twentieth-century corporate bodies (Roy 1999; Boyd and Watts 2013).

Yet I have insisted on highlighting the industrialization of metabolism rather than that of food, animals, or agriculture per se. Such a perspective provides a different analytic path, focusing on metabolic processes in and between organisms as technological work objects in the hunt for efficiency. How does this framing change what we see? Significantly, the pig or the cow as a discrete entity recedes as the biochemical interrelationship between organisms is foregrounded for enhanced mechanization and production. Such foregrounding was done by the historical actors themselves. The realization that humans, animals, plants, and microbes were enmeshed in universal shared metabolic processes was transformative for scientific and philosophical concepts of life as well as for the eminently practical matter of feeding an increasing number of agricultural animals. Discovery and manufacture of vitamins drove a view of "man and animals as parasites of bacteria," dependent on microbes, which in turn drove practices of mass-culturing bacteria and fungi to produce essential nutrients at scale (Rahn 1945, 227).

This section concerns the yoking of animal to microbial metabolism. Whereas in the protein years the main players in the animal feed industry were grain producers or food manufacturers channeling extracts from whole animals and plants into animal protein production, fine chemical companies increasingly pushed upstream, combining vitamin preparations and other single-molecule feed supplements into specifically formulated premixes of raw concentrates sold onward to feed distributors, who then combined them with bulk feedstuffs. At the same time—in the same feed bags—medicinal substances increased in importance, as agriculture intensified and animals were kept in closer quarters and in larger numbers, such that "the feed mixer has had to assume the role of pharmacist and then incidentally, ventured into what was presumed to be the field of veterinary medicine" (Lubbehusen 1956, 9). I will discuss growth promoters shortly; first I focus on the rescaling and rearrangement of metabolic relations between organisms by tracing the emergence of vitamin logics and the corresponding industrial microbiology that reshaped animal life between 1920 and 1960.

VITAMINS AND MICROBES

To illustrate how microbial and animal metabolisms move into new scales of distribution and modes of connection in the twentieth century, I trace two streams of activity: vitamin research and industrial microbiology. These initially separate endeavors were merged in technologies of microbial fermentation in the 1920s, by the 1950s becoming a scene in which vitamins, enzymes, and amino acids were produced at the scale of tons and were ubiquitously constitutive of animal feeds.

Vitamins emerged as discrete conceptual and technical objects in the early twentieth century from medical research in humans, bacterial nutrition studies, and agricultural science. The word *vitamine* was coined in 1911, and the corresponding concept of the "deficiency disease" was proposed for conditions such as beriberi or scurvy caused by nutritional lack rather than infection (Funk 1912). As "efficient agents" capable of cures, vitamins were likened to hormones. Both appeared to investigators as "drug-like and communicative substances," biological chemicals with potency to regulate bodies (Schwerin, Stoff, and Wahrig 2013, 13).

Vitamins emerged from and profoundly changed attitudes toward the workings of intermediary metabolism, as entirely different metabolic objects from the intensively researched proteins, fats, and carbohydrates. The concept of the "biochemical lesion" of vitamin deficiency illustrates how vitamins appeared to researchers as akin to watch jewels, crucial to the larger mechanism (Lipmann 1969). In pigeons used to model beriberi, debilitating muscle spasms arose after dietary transition to polished rice, as thiamin (vitamin B_1) was lost with the brown rice husk. Deficiency manifested as opisthotonos—muscle spasms bending the bird's neck and head completely backward against the body. This condition could be dramatically reversed in half an hour by an injection of thiamin. British biochemist Rudolph Peters showed in the 1930s that pyruvate—a metabolic intermediary normally converted to acetate and carbon dioxide—built up in the brain tissues of these birds (Meiklejohn, Passmore, and Peters 1932). This blockage could be "cured" in pigeon brain slices by adding thiamin, one of the "early indications that vitamins had a metabolic function" (Lipmann 1969, 3). The speed and totality of the cure indicated "it must be a biochemical change rather than one which has gone as far as structural alterations," and Peters argued it was time for "medicine to transfer attention in pathology to the initial biochemical changes rather than to the final microscopic picture" (1952, 143, 144). Disease shifted from visible lesions to invisible but biochemically measurable and chemically malleable changes.

The effects of thiamin deficiency manifested throughout the body. "In vain have we endeavored to find *the* specific effect of a deficiency of the substance and yet it is credited with almost panacean properties. The reason is, we believe, that carbohydrate metabolism cannot go forward in any living cell without thiamin" (Williams 1938, 563). Despite being present in tissues in amounts below one part per million, vitamins were systemically essential. In other words, it was not just that vitamins regulated "the body" in some hand-waving manner observed in animal feeding trials. Rather, vitamins were necessary passage points for crucial segments of metabolic sequences in every cell in every body. As such, they were fine tools of biochemical dissection of the intricacies of intermediary metabolism. The rapidity and specificity of fixing a biochemical lesion showed the vitamin to be a powerful lever for reaching into metabolism and tuning it.

Vitamin function across human, animal, plant, and microbial cells was universal enough that one could observe common deficiency defects across a huge diversity of life-forms: microbes, rats, pigeons, sick people. Investigators of intermediary metabolism increasingly turned to microbes in the 1920s in research on vitamins. Bacteria could be cultured in controlled media and responded unequivocally when specific metabolic pathway elements were added or subtracted—by growing or not. Investigators realized that microbes, particularly pathogens, and animal cells often share nutritional requirements. Sensitivity to the presence of particular substrates was used to find new vitamins or to quantify the presence of known ones, such as bacterial assays for riboflavin (Snell and Strong 1939).

At the same time, microbes were shown to be incredible chemical producers in their own right. The attempt to dissect intermediary metabolism *interior* to cells and organisms led to a realization of profound metabolic interdependencies *between* microbes and animals (Kluyver 1959). A bacterial culture in its growth phase generates many elements of cellular life, such as nucleic acids and lipids, and by-products of energy metabolism, such as ethanol, acetone, citric acid, and lysine—or vitamins, thereby providing essential nutrients for animals. Microbes could be used to dissect metabolism's inner workings and, once the necessary substances were thereby identified, to *produce* metabolic entities vital to humans and animals.

INDUSTRIAL MICROBIOLOGY: SCALING UP

Vitamin production became a matter of scale via industrial microbiology. Initially, microbes were seen as "work-machines" analogous to the animal converter, also turning cheap materials into valuable substances such as acetone or alcohol (Bud 1994). However, elaboration of the interdependencies of intermediary metabolism soon moved them into series, rather than parallel, with one process feeding into another. At the same time, the isolation, structural analysis, and chemical synthesis of vitamins proceeded apace. Sometimes part of the production sequence was microbial and the rest synthetic, as with manufacturing of vitamin C. Beginning in the 1920s, chemical, alcohol, and pharmaceutical manufacturers came onto the scene where food and oil processors had dominated.

The story of the Commercial Solvents Corporation (CSC) is representative of the course charted by others. Founded in 1917 by the Allied War Board for microbial production of acetone to serve in explosives manufacture, the company's initial task was to industrialize the fermentation process discovered by Chaim Weizmann for the war effort. Taken over by private owners after 1919, the CSC's plants in Terre Haute, Indiana, and Peoria, Illinois, converted Midwest grain supplies into a wide range of fermentation products, including alcohol. A popular history of the CSC published in 1936, aptly named *One Thing*

Leads to Another, recounts stepwise moves from explosives manufacture to animal nutrition, including the acquisition of molasses distributors and the spin-off of a subsidiary, Molasses Products Corporation, in 1933, ensuring a supply of molasses as a fermentation base (Kelly 1936).

Molasses provided a nutrient medium for microbial production of riboflavin (vitamin B_2), first marketed in 1936. Human riboflavin consumption increased with the introduction of flour fortification in the 1940s, but it was initially sold for animal feed. This fermentation infrastructure was then turned to penicillin production by 1944. The CSC diversified into other agricultural products such as nitrogen and phosphate fertilizer in 1946 and resorcyclic acid lactones (estrogenic chemicals derived from fungi) in 1962. Throughout the twentieth century, using both high-pressure synthetic chemistry and fermentation, the CSC made substances for animal nutrition alongside pharmaceuticals, plastics, automobile tires, and all manner of other chemicals, from antifreeze to whiskey.

Pfizer tracked a similar course. Established in 1849, the company initially made compounds from whole flowers and fruits using direct-extraction processes, such as a plant-derived antiworm drug and citric acid from lemons. Shortages of lemons during World War I pushed the company to turn to harvesting citric acid from a mold, *Aspergillus niger*, with large-scale fermentation-based production transitioning the company from a small concern into a pharmaceutical giant. *Aspergillus* was grown on a sucrose solution, initially in long, shallow trays (for air exposure). By 1929 five thousand tons of citric acid valued at $4.5 million were being produced in the United States, as soft drinks and canning drove a growing market (Bud 2011). In 1929 the company developed a stirred-tank fermentation technology facilitating larger volumes of mold growth under aerated conditions. This brought Pfizer into the vitamin market, first for vitamin C, then B_2 in 1938 and B_{12} after the war. The stirred-tank fermenter—a "rarely acknowledged pillar of the modern age"—was essential to the establishment of penicillin production during World War II (Bud 2011, 325; Ginsburg 2008).

Intensification of animal agriculture was pursued via many avenues, including innovation in breeding, transportation, and marketing (Boyd 2001). Yet it was through microbial biochemistry that key bottlenecks to expansion were overcome, the most significant of which was the isolation of vitamin B_{12}. Overcoming vitamin and macronutrient deficiencies allowed for larger animals and better survival rates, but such animals ate more food. Increasing numbers in animal husbandry, particularly in poultry, produced an impossible demand for the very feed components farmers had been taught to rely on. Shortages of milk powder were remedied by using riboflavin, starting in the mid-1930s. Shortages of fish meal and tankage were exacerbated by the onset of World War II. Efforts to fill the gap with plant proteins such as soybean and cottonseed meal failed: they lacked amino acids such as methionine and lysine as well as an "animal protein factor"—"an unidentified principle so named because of its presence in animal tissues such as liver and muscle" (Jukes 1972, 526). Paradoxically, it was difficult to grow animals because there wasn't enough animal matter to feed them with.

Human medicine and bacterial nutrition research converged simultaneously on the animal protein factor question. Treatment of pernicious anemia in humans with liver extract, pioneered in the 1920s, provided a partial but imprecise fix for this debilitating condition, and a long pursuit of the "pernicious anemia factor" ensued. Quite separately, work on the nutritional needs of industrially salient microbes showed that *Lactobacillus lactis* Dorner (LLD), used for making sour cream and buttermilk, was for unknown reasons also dependent on liver extract. Mary Shorb, a microbiologist hired by the Dairy Board during World War II, worked with LLD, improving production of dairy food commodities. On being displaced from her position by a returning veteran in 1946, she joined the Poultry Science Department of the University of Maryland and was funded by a $400 grant from Merck to develop LLD as a bioassay for the active component of liver extract (Ahrens 1993). The bacteria indicated the presence of the "factor" by living or dying and helped pick the mysterious thing out of the complexity of biological fluids. It was isolated and crystallized in 1948 and named vitamin B_{12} (Shorb 1948).[5]

Shortly thereafter, it was discovered that some bacteria produce rather than require B_{12}. Thus, an enormous bottleneck to growth was overcome. By 1951 "feed manufacturers fortified 15 million tons of feed with 200 pounds of B_{12} additive. These 200 pounds replaced all of the natural B_{12} normally contained in approximately 1 billion pounds of meat and fish by-products" (Summons 1968, 311). On the strength of B_{12} production, Merck became the largest producer of vitamins in the United States by World War II, second only to Hoffman-La Roche worldwide (Chandler 2009, 179). It was an intensely competitive scene with high economic stakes; Pfizer, CSC, Glaxo, American Cyanamid, and many other smaller companies sent vitamins and minerals along the conduits established by the earlier manufactured feed industry centered on protein. By 1950 there were three thousand manufacturers of commercial feed in the United States, not counting midlevel operations combining commercial premixes with local grain or fodder material (Hillery 1952). Production of manufactured feeds had reached 35,000,000 tons a year by 1956, compared to 9,000,000 tons a year in the period 1930–34 (Scoville 1956, 123). An advertisement from Hoffman-La Roche proclaims "Vitamins by the Tons," showing trains and planes fanning out from their factory across the landscape (see figure 2.2). In this way microbial capabilities for turning grain or molasses into vitamins were plugged into animal processes at an unprecedented scale.

Vitamins led the way, but the excitement over microbial metabolism as a chemical factory for animal inputs extended much further. Fungal amylases (or "fungal spit," as I like to think of it) were used for predigestion of rough fodders. The production of amino acids was revolutionized using microbial cultures, replacing difficult processes for extracting them from grains, hair, and feathers with hydrochloric acid. Amino acids such as lysine were important supplements to corn-based diets, as corn has little of this essential amino acid, and animals must acquire it from their food because they have no metabolic capacity of their own to make it. With its high degree of targeted efficiency, the ability to add isolated lysine rather than relying on some expensive bulk material that contained a mix of amino acids would have made Henry Armsby proud.

In the same decade, Dow Chemical cultivated a flourishing market in urea supplements for cattle feed, a synthetic nitrogen product made with ammonia that was converted into protein by the microbes inhabiting the cow rumen. Company publications show a growth in sales from 500,000 tons of urea-containing feeds in 1946 to 4,500,000 tons in 1956 (Du Pont 1958). After World War II, techniques for cracking petroleum to make the amino acid methionine relieved another bottleneck to growth (Willke 2014). This amino acid was needed in chickens fed on corn or soy, because of the high relative proportion of methionine to other amino acids employed in the growth of feathers and the low availability of this amino acid in these dietary sources. Synthetic methionine was originally developed for humans, to treat postwar hunger edema resulting from chronic protein deprivation, but as this problem faded in acuity, the product found a much larger market in the targeted supplementation of animal feed, thus effectively opening a direct channel of material flow from petrochemicals to animals (Neubauer and Landecker 2021). In sum, for animal feed, the "practical chemical economy" meant new forms and scales of biochemical transaction between microbes and animals, between plants and microbes, and between petroleum and animals.

FIGURE 2.2 "Vitamins by the Tons," *Cereal Chemistry* 23 (1946).

"Meat in a Hurry": The Growth Promoter

Throughout the long history of scientific feeding, the calculation of feed efficiency was key. How much food (at what cost) did it take to raise how much animal matter (at what price)? At World War II's end, anxieties about food and labor costs sharpened. The Truman administration was troubled by public dismay over meat shortages and threats of a producer's strike just before the 1946 elections. Geopolitical considerations reared as agriculture became caught up in Cold War politics: "Farm conventions and journals began delivering the messages that Soviet spending on industrialization could outpace Americans', and that farmers needed to be vigilant of the possibility of enemies striking the nation's food supplies through bioterrorism"; the American role at home and in the world included providing more meat as part of "Freedom from want" (Finlay 2004, 242).

This scene is captured by "Meat in a Hurry," on the front page of the *Wall Street Journal* in 1952. "Farm-hand labor grows more costly," columnist Victor Hillery (1952) exclaimed. "And corn that sold for less than 50 cents a bushel just before World War II now brings $2.00. What's needed, say the animal-making wizards, are techniques to produce a given amount of animal with less grain and fewer hours of work." Vitamins and amino acids allowed the *intensification* of production, with larger animals or higher milk yields, but did not fundamentally change the ratio of food and labor input to product output. They also produced new problems in their own right. For example, vitamin D supplementation allowed year-round indoor growth of chickens, which triggered outbreaks of contagious intestinal parasites causing a disease called coccidiosis. In the words of one Du Pont representative, this meant that "economic considerations have put feeding and parasite control on the same production team" (Boughton 1956, 63).

Sulfonamides were the first drugs to demonstrate the ability to "literally feed away disease," but another drug developed to address the coccidiosis problem became the first medicated feed to significantly change the food-to-growth ratio while also accelerating the animal life cycle (Hedger and Manley 1956, 150). Arsenic-based medications proved to be effective against the coccidian protozoa—and to accelerate maturity. Over and above the effects of suppressing infection, even disease-free pullets fed with the medication reached physical and sexual maturity earlier, more of them survived to adulthood, food was converted to eggs and meat more efficiently, and hatchability and fertility seemed unaffected (Morehouse and Mayfield 1946). Significantly, careful analysis showed that arsenicals "when added to a commercial-type ration at a level of 0.01 per cent stimulated early growth and improved feed efficiency of chicks reared in batteries or floor pens, but not in birds raised on grass range" ("Arsenicals" 1956, 207). Dr. Salisbury's Laboratories' arsenic-based drugs for chickens were approved by the Food and Drug Administration in 1944 for the treatment of coccidiosis but also for weight gain, feed efficiency, and improved pigmentation (Couch 1954). This last category referred to the fact that the drug made the meat pinker and thus more appealing to the consumer.

Unlike vitamins and trace minerals, which corrected nutritional deficiencies, arsenicals pointed toward metabolic efficiencies (Landecker 2021). They accelerated life and therefore production. Treated pullets started laying fifteen days earlier than untreated birds, regardless of infection; treated birds reached market weight earlier. Where the vitaminists of the interwar era had been "guided by an essentially static model of health and growth," seeking to "itemize the ingredients that totaled up to the normal, proper diet," postwar medicated "modern feeding" was by contrast not concerned with natural limits but sought interaction between different ration components and animal metabolism for overcoming limits (Marcus 1993, 68). The message from both academic and industry quarters was that feed did not have to be, and in fact could no longer be, just food: "Modern feeding must take into account not only the balance of nutrients suitable for the ideal situation but anything and everything that in one way or another enhances feed efficiency under practical conditions. A growth promoter need not be an essential metabolite. It may, for example, speed up or slow down advantageously a critical metabolic process" (Boughton 1956, 61). This ability to speed and slow, augment and suppress, within the metabolic map of interlinked enzymatic reactions characterizes the postwar growth promoter.

The discovery of the growth-promoting effects of penicillin and arsenicals is often depicted as a fortuitous accident. Yet this was more than fortune favoring the prepared mind. The conventions for feeding and profit-ratio experiments were firmly in place, with every eye trained on feed-efficiency parameters. These substances were understood in light of a decades-long legacy of capitalizing processing wastes by feeding them onward into animal production systems (Landecker 2019). Animals, as already noted, had become consumers in their own right. Microbial metabolism was already firmly harnessed at scale to animal metabolism. Metabolites or medications could be immediately tested on model organisms of nutrition science, and knowledge circulated within a robust social and economic network among government, academia, and industry in which companies funded experimental programs or provided promising substances for testing. Agricultural scientists updated feed manufacturers on new supplements or medications through personal networks, written missives, and presentations at industry meetings; individuals moved from posts in industry to academia, or to government regulatory or research bureaus, and back (Marcus 1993). In other words, growth promoters did not make medicated feed possible but rather the reverse: the practices and logics of medicated feed were the conditions under which the "new" growth promoters emerged. Arsenicals were first; then antibiotics and hormones moved almost instantly from laboratory discovery to become the ubiquitously used staple of animal husbandry.

The growth-promoting characteristics of antibiotics were noticed in the late 1940s at American Cyanamid's Lederle Laboratories. Vat waste from aureomycin production was fed to chicks, with the aim of using the waste as a source for the recently discovered vitamin B_{12}. However, results outstripped those using B_{12} extracted directly from liver, indicating something else was at play, and growth effects were traced to antibiotics left over from the production process. For verification, American Cyanamid sent samples of aureomycin fermentation wastes to land grant colleges and experimental science station scientists to test on pigs, without informing the contracted researchers that they were testing for the growth-promoting effects of antibiotics (Finlay 2004). Growth promotion with antibiotics was immediately compared to arsenic-based medications and declared superior, but additive effects could be seen when using both; the latter increased feed efficiency, while the former pushed weight gains higher (Wallace et al. 1951). In a few short years, antibiotic-supplemented feeds dominated the market (Kirchhelle 2018).

These agricultural scientists and feed manufacturers were working on metabolism, not "food." Certainly they were attempting to make animal feed more nutritious or more disease preventing by adding things to it, but the measure of that success, and their means of assessing progress toward it, was in the parameters and quantification of feed efficiency. An assessment of medicated feed written in 1960 notes that "prior to the 1950s, the pounds of feed necessary to produce a given quantity of livestock had changed very little. Nutritionists had made improvements in meat output per animal and in rapidity of animal growth, *but these higher-producing animals always ate more*" (Summons 1968, 310, emphasis added). Now higher-producing animals that ate less and grew faster seemed possible. A 1952 photograph in *Fortune* beside "Antibiotics in the Barnyard" depicts feed efficiency. The fat pig is in a

FIGURE 2.3 "Antibiotics in the Barnyard," *Fortune* 45, no. 3 (1952).

pen stacked with 7 feed bags. The thin pig next door is in a pen stacked with 8.5 bags (see figure 2.3). The antibiotic supplement enabled the production of larger pigs using less feed. Arsenicals had indicated the way, and antibiotics followed.

It is also in this context that the first use of hormones as growth promoters occurred. Clover feed containing phytoestrogens had marked effects on ruminants, and intensive endocrinological research with chickens had made it clear that the transition to laying in hens involved a hormonally triggered shift in lipid metabolism; the thinking was that this could be artificially accelerated to shorten maturation and extend the laying period of the mature hen (Lorenz, Chaikoff, and Entenman 1938). Such manipulations became economically thinkable only when the synthetic estrogen diethylstilbestrol (DES) became available in 1938, because it was cheap and abundant, unlike the other estrogenic compounds or "pregnant mare urine" used in earlier lipid metabolism manipulation (Lorenz 1954). It was not enough to demonstrate effects in experiments; the right combination of chemistry, economy, and infrastructure had to be in place to bring a substance into wide use.

Inspired by observations of the effects of clover phytoestrogen, Wise Burroughs of Iowa State University and his colleagues showed in 1954 that weight gains of up to 35 percent could be attained in feedlot cattle given DES-supplemented feed, with up to a 20 percent reduction in feed cost. As with low-dose antibiotics, this was as much empirical tinkering in the terrain of feed efficiency as some kind of highly precise understanding of how DES affected growth at a molecular level. But it is clear that targeting metabolism was the framework for pursuing and understanding the effects of DES: "The fact that feed consumption is slightly increased but the economy of gain is greatly increased would point to the fact that protein anabolic processes are accelerated" (Clegg and Cole 1954, 109).

Burroughs, like other scientists of his generation, "saw no disjunction between hormonal and nutritive research.... [T]he endocrine and nutritive systems were plastic, subject to scientific manipulation to produce particularistic ends" (Marcus 1993, 79). Indeed, hormones seemed another variation on the drivers of particular metabolic processes, to be layered and combined with other agents preventing disease and accelerating enzymatic conversions while suppressing time-consuming maturation processes. Antibiotics and DES were cheap and plentiful. The infrastructure for distributing small quantities of medication through large quantities of animal feed was in place, as were the marketing and distribution systems of feed-manufacturing firms. When such substances were added to the feed bag, they were not the first of their kind. They joined the mix with vitamins, trace metals such as manganese and copper, growth-promoting medications such as arsenicals, nitrogen providers such as urea, concentrations of particular essential amino acids, and sweetening or odorant agents meant to induce animals to eat, such as magnesium oxide or butyric acid.

On the regulatory front, the surge in distribution of medications through animal feed spurred the Food and Drug Administration to open a veterinary medical branch in 1953—overseen by former or future feed-manufacturing executives. In 1956 a symposium on medicated feed opened with the comment that just one year after its introduction for use in cows, DES was now being used in half of the feedlot cattle in the United States, and three-quarters of all manufactured feeds contained antibiotics; the "feed manufacturers have, with reluctance, become drug manufacturers" (Durban 1956, 1). Eight years later, when the annual *Feed Additive Compendium* listed additives found in medicated feed and combinations found in various commercial feed products, the entries ran into the thousands (Animal Health Institute 1964). While antibiotics and hormones feature prominently, enzymes, antioxidants, minerals, vitamins, amino acids, fatty acids, antifungal medications, carotenoids, plant oils used as aromatics, and other less known substances also crowd the pages. So many additives were used to increase the palatability of feed to animals that the *Feed Additive Compendium* had a special section for them, and "stomachic appetizer" was a category of drug action. An advertisement from Dow Chemical aimed at feed manufacturers interleaved among the lists of food additives shows a variety of bags and barrels, the label underneath the offerings "Peep. Cackle. Oink. Moo." The ad's text continues: "If it makes

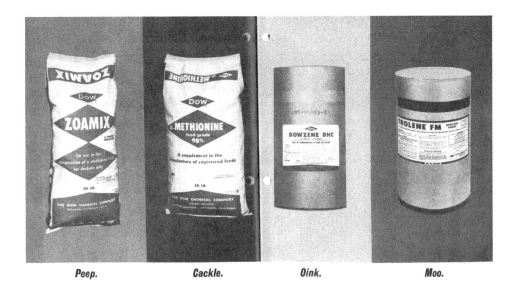

FIGURE 2.4 "Peep. Cackle. Oink. Moo." Advertisement for Dow Chemical feed additives, *Feed Additive Compendium* (1964), 362–63.

sounds like any of these, we have the feed additive to keep it healthy—and profitable" (362–63).

Conclusion: The Philosophy of the Butcher

In 1934, observing an unbridled enthusiasm for vitamins among pediatricians, the nutrition scientist Clive McCay and his colleague Mary Crowell criticized what they saw as an unthinking embrace of accelerated growth: "To-day research has tended to narrow into a channel of primary interest in the young, growing animal.... After it becomes an adult it is no longer an 'apple of the eye' of the nutritionist, but primarily a carcass that provides dissecting material for the pathologist. The nutrition student is too busy pouring vitamins, minerals and proteins into the young and growing to be much concerned with the grown" (1934, 405). Coming as it does from an observer of the 1930s scene, this rather anguished critique helps us understand the dominance of growth as both the object and the aim of vitamin science. Indeed, the relationship that McCay was critiquing in which the growth of meat animals became the model for human children without accounting for long-term consequences was seen by others as unproblematic, even a point of pride. "Chicks and Children," proclaimed a typical advertisement from one vitamin concentrate supplier, "need the same Vitamin D" (*Flour and Feed* 1932–33, 323). It was, McCay and Crowell wrote, a philosophy of the butcher that was leaving aside the question of the relationship among growth in youth, health in adulthood, and overall longevity, in both animals and humans:

> The healthy adult is a matter of little interest, even to himself, and the sick one usually rates as a pest. This philosophy belongs properly to the butcher. Every producer of meat animals wants to rear them rapidly because it is economical. These animals are killed as soon as they mature. What agricultural expert can tell the effect of the feeding during the growth period upon the milk-producing capacity of a cow during her entire life? What chicken specialist can tell the effect of the rate of growth of the chicken upon the egg production of the laying hen? Who can tell you the effect of the rate of growth of a child upon its susceptibility to disease during adult life? Who can give assurance that the child that matures rapidly will not die after a short life span? (1934, 405)

The lens of rapid growth left little room for other kinds of questions, for other experimental designs that might have explored possible adverse effects of accelerated growth, non-growth-related effects of vitamin use, or the environmental or ecological effects of increasing the relative presence of vitamins in the world through mass production and distribution. All of the knowledge being produced was about growth and about mechanisms enabling growth effects. McCay's own work on calorie restriction and longevity lay fallow for decades before being picked up again with the emergence of theories of the developmental origins of health and disease and concerns about rising rates of adult chronic disease related to overnutrition (Park 2010).

This chapter has set the stage for asking questions occluded by a profusion of knowledge framed only by growth. It is one thing to argue that metabolism has been industrialized; it is another to then begin to trace out the consequences of the biochemical remapping of conversion, scale, and time that has occurred with the dominance of medicated feed in animal husbandry. It is time to again pose McCay's question: Who can tell the legacies of childhoods fed on ideologies of maximum growth? What are the consequences of funneling arsenic into the American landscape through plants and animals, for decades? What are the metabolic legacies of producing a disproportionate amount of certain amino acids by using microbial fermentation or tapping into petroleum as a dietary input? What are the consequences of building an enormous extradigestive apparatus of fungal enzymes, mechanical grinding, and vitamin provision that encompasses our bodies and our animals' bodies?

While we may learn a great deal from focusing on any one of these substances and its particular legacies for human health, the environment, foodways, or the economy, there is also an important place for seeing the big picture in which chickens, milk, antibiotic resistance, growth hormones, or consumers are set. I opened this chapter by drawing on Tiago Saraiva's observation that the technoscientific practices of agriculture are not things that are shaped by context so much as world-making measures in their own right: here we see that the modernity constituted by feeding practices is a biochemical one, in which matter moves differently—at different scales and speeds, and through different metabolic relations than those that preceded metabolic industrialization. The world made thus is not confined to the animal body, nor to the eater of the animal body, but is the biochemical milieu for contemporary life.

NOTES

1. Marx himself did not use the term *metabolism*. He drew on his readings of nineteenth-century agricultural and animal chemistry, in particular those of Justus von Liebig and Jakob Moleschott, in using the German word *Stoffwechsel*. *Stoffwechsel* refers more narrowly to the chemical process of nitrogen turnover in muscular tissues than does the later term *metabolism*, which has come to encompass many more substances, tissues, organisms, and processes. Only after the end of the nineteenth century and after a synthesis of input-output physiology, cell theory, and fermentation studies (enzymology) in the rise of the new discipline of biochemistry is *Stoffwechsel* typically translated into English as *metabolism* (Landecker 2016). The word *metabolism* does not occur in English translations of Marx until the twentieth century. Marx could not have had the broader biochemical understanding of metabolism in mind that contemporary authors tend to read back into his work.

2. Armsby had earned a degree in chemistry in the first graduating class of the Worcester County Free Institute of Industrial Science in 1871 (which subsequently became the Worcester Institute of Technology) and sojourned in Germany as part of his graduate training in chemistry at Yale, spending a year at the Möckern Agricultural Experiment Station, where he was deeply inspired by feeding experiments that showed high-nitrogen "power feeds" such as rapeseed oil cake could increase milk production and thereby intensify farm output through the manipulation of animal diets (Matz 2015).

3. The story of manufacturing waste is also to a certain extent the story of the American corporate form. For an in-depth consideration of the story of food-processing waste in relation to animal feed, please see my "A Metabolic History of Manufacturing Waste" (Landecker 2019).

4. Economic historians Alan Olmstead and Paul Rhode (2008) offer these comparative figures as part of their argument that "biological innovation"—breeding and changes in animal husbandry—was more important than mechanical technologies in the development of this sector of agriculture during this period.

5. I discuss this story in greater length and in relation to tissue culture practices in "It Is What It Eats" (Landecker 2016).

REFERENCES

Ahrens, Richard A. 1993. "Mary Shaw Shorb (1907–1990)." *Journal of Nutrition* 123 (5): 791–96.

Animal Health Institute. 1964. *Feed Additive Compendium*. Vol. 1. Minneapolis: Miller Publishing.

Armsby, Henry Prentiss. 1917. *The Nutrition of Farm Animals*. New York: Macmillan.

Armsby, Henry Prentiss, and Charles Robert Moulton. 1925. *The Animal as a Converter of Matter and Energy: A Study of the Role of Live Stock in Food Production*. New York: Chemical Catalog Company.

Aronson, Naomi. 1982. "Nutrition as a Social Problem: A Case Study of Entrepreneurial Strategy in Science." *Social Problems* 29 (5): 474–87.

Atlanta Constitution. 1923. "Purina Mills Send Feeding Experts to Atlanta." January 21, 1923.

Bar-On, Yinon M., Rob Phillips, and Ron Milo. 2018. "The Biomass Distribution on Earth." *Proceedings of the National Academy of Sciences* 115 (25): 6506–11.

Bentley, Amy. 1998. *Eating for Victory: Food Rationing and the Politics of Domesticity*. Champaign: University of Illinois Press.

Biltekoff, Charlotte. 2013. *Eating Right in America: The Cultural Politics of Food and Health*. Durham, NC: Duke University Press.

Boughton, Donald C. 1956. "Antihelmitics in the Modern Feed Industry." In *Symposium on Medicated Feeds*, edited by Henry Welch and Félix Martí-Ibáñez, 61–64. Washington, DC: Medical Encyclopedia.

Boyd, William. 2001. "Making Meat: Science, Technology, and American Poultry Production." *Technology and Culture* 42 (4): 631–64.

Boyd, William, and Michael Watts. 2013. "The Chicken Industry and Postwar American Capitalism." In *Globalising Food: Agrarian Questions and Global Restructuring*, edited by David Goodman and Michael Watts, 192–225. London: Psychology Press.

Buchanan, R. E. 1945. "Microbial Metabolism and Agriculture." *Science* 101 (2623): 341–46.

Bud, Robert. 1994. *The Uses of Life: A History of Biotechnology*. Cambridge: Cambridge University Press.

Bud, Robert. 2011. "Innovators, Deep Fermentation and Antibiotics: Promoting Applied Science before and after the Second World War." *Dynamis* 31 (2): 323–41.

Canguilhem, Georges. 2000. *A Vital Rationalist: Selected Writings from Georges Canguilhem*. New York: Zone Books.
Carpenter, Kenneth. 1994. *Protein and Energy: A Study of Changing Ideas in Nutrition*. Cambridge: Cambridge University Press.
Chandler, Alfred D. 1977. *The Visible Hand: The Managerial Revolution in American Business*. Cambridge, MA: Harvard University Press.
Chandler, Alfred D. 2009. *Shaping the Industrial Century: The Remarkable Story of the Evolution of the Modern Chemical and Pharmaceutical Industries*. Cambridge, MA: Harvard University Press.
Clegg, M. T., and H. H. Cole. 1954. "The Action of Stilbestrol on the Growth Response in Ruminants." *Journal of Animal Science* 13 (1): 108–30.
Collingham, Lizzie. 2013. *The Taste of War: World War II and the Battle for Food*. New York: Penguin.
Couch, J. R. 1954. "New Experiments Indicate Pigmentation Aided by Arsonic Compounds." *Feed Age* 4 (1): 33.
Cronon, William. 2009. *Nature's Metropolis: Chicago and the Great West*. New York: W. W. Norton.
Cullather, Nick. 2007. "The Foreign Policy of the Calorie." *American Historical Review* 112 (2): 337–64.
Du Pont. 1958. *Digest of Research on Urea and Ruminant Nutrition*. Delaware: E. I. Du Pont de Nemours and Company Polychemicals Department.
DuPuis, E. Melanie. 2002. *Nature's Perfect Food: How Milk Became America's Drink*. New York: New York University Press.
Durban, Charles. 1956. "Opening Remarks." In *Symposium on Medicated Feeds*, edited by Henry Welch and Félix Martí-Ibáñez, 1–5. Washington, DC: Medical Encyclopedia.
Finlay, Mark R. 2004. "Hogs, Antibiotics, and the Industrial Environments of Postwar Agriculture." In *Industrializing Organisms: Introducing Evolutionary History*, edited by Susan Schrepfer and Philip Scranton, 237–60. New York: Routledge.
Fitzgerald, Deborah Kay. 2003. *Every Farm a Factory: The Industrial Ideal in American Agriculture*. New Haven, CT: Yale University Press.
Flour and Feed. 1932–33. Advertisement. *Flour and Feed* 33:323.
Fortune. 1952. "Antibiotics in the Barnyard." *Fortune* 45 (3): 108–37.
Foster, John Bellamy. 2000. *Marx's Ecology: Materialism and Nature*. New York: New York University Press.
Funk, Casimir. 1912. "The Etiology of the Deficiency Diseases." *Journal of State Medicine* 20 (6): 341–66.
Ginsburg, Judah. 2008. *Development of Deep-Tank Fermentation*. National Historic Chemical Landmarks Program. Washington, DC: American Chemical Society.
Guthman, Julie. 2011. *Weighing In: Obesity, Food Justice, and the Limits of Capitalism*. Berkeley: University of California Press.
Haber, Ludwig Fritz. 1971. *The Chemical Industry, 1900–1930: International Growth and Technological Change*. Oxford: Clarendon.

Haecker, T. L. 1903. "Investigation in Milk Production: The Food of Maintenance; Nutrient Requirements; Protein Requirements; Influence of Stage of Lactation on Nutrient Requirements." *University of Minnesota Agricultural Experiment Station Bulletin* 79:89–148.

Hedger, F. Howard, and Donald R. Manley. 1956. "Feed Control and Special Assay Problems for Diethylstilbestrol." In *Symposium on Medicated Feeds*, edited by Henry Welch and Félix Martí-Ibáñez, 150–88. Washington, DC: Medical Encyclopedia.

Hillery, Victor. 1952. "Meat in a Hurry; Feed Wizards Produce Broilers, Eggs, Hogs at Stepped-Up Tempo." *Wall Street Journal*, February 4, 1952.

Hobbs, Frank, and Nicole Stoops. 2002. *Demographic Trends in the 20th Century*. Washington, DC: US Department of Commerce, Economics and Statistics Administration, US Census Bureau.

Horowitz, Roger. 2006. *Putting Meat on the American Table: Taste, Technology, Transformation*. Baltimore, MD: Johns Hopkins University Press.

Jukes, Thomas H. 1972. "Antibiotics in Animal Feeds and Animal Production." *BioScience* 22 (9): 526–34.

Kelly, Fred Charters. 1936. *One Thing Leads to Another: The Growth of an Industry*. New York: Houghton Mifflin.

Kiechle, Melanie A. 2017. *Smell Detectives: An Olfactory History of Nineteenth-Century Urban America*. Seattle: University of Washington Press.

Kirchhelle, Claas. 2018. "Pharming Animals: A Global History of Antibiotics in Food Production (1935–2017)." *Palgrave Communications* 4: article 96. https://doi.org/10.1057/s41599-018-0152-2.

Kluyver, A. J. 1959. "Unity and Diversity in the Metabolism of Micro-organisms." In *Albert Jan Kluyver: His Life and Work*, edited by J. W. M. La Rivière, A. F. Kamp, and W. Verhoeven, 186–210. New York: Interscience Publishers.

Landecker, Hannah. 2016. "It Is What It Eats: Chemically Defined Media and the History of Surrounds." *Studies in History and Philosophy of Science Part C: Studies in History and Philosophy of Biological and Biomedical Sciences* 57:148–60. https://doi.org/10.1016/j.shpsc.2016.02.004.

Landecker, Hannah. 2019. "A Metabolic History of Manufacturing Waste: Food Commodities and Their Outsides." *Food, Culture and Society* 22 (5): 530–47.

Landecker, Hannah. 2021. "Trace Amounts at Industrial Scale: Arsenicals, Medicated Feed, and the 'Western Diet.'" In *Risk at the Table: Food Production, Health, and the Environment*, edited by Angela Creager and Jean-Paul Gaudillière, 187–213. New York: Berghahn.

Lipmann, Fritz. 1969. "The Biochemical Function of B Vitamins." *Perspectives in Biology and Medicine* 13 (1): 1–9.

Lorenz, Frederick W. 1954. "Effects of Estrogens on Domestic Fowl and Applications in the Poultry Industry." *Vitamins and Hormones* 12:235–75.

Lorenz, Frederick W., Israel Lyon Chaikoff, and Cecil Entenman. 1938. "The Endocrine Control of Lipid Metabolism in the Bird II: The Effects of Estrin on the Blood Lipids of the Immature Domestic Fowl." *Journal of Biological Chemistry* 126 (2): 763–69.

Lubbehusen, R. E. 1956. "Medicated Feeds, Some General Comments." In *Symposium on Medicated Feeds*, edited by Henry Welch and Félix Martí-Ibáñez, 9–14. Washington, DC: Medical Encyclopedia.

Marcus, Alan I. 1993. "The Newest Knowledge of Nutrition: Wise Burroughs, DES, and Modern Meat." *Agricultural History* 67 (3): 66–85.

Matz, Brendan. 2015. "Nutrition Science and the Practice of Animal Feeding in Germany, 1850–1880." In *New Perspectives on the History of Life Sciences and Agriculture*, edited by Denise Philips and Sharon Kingsland, 163–81. Dordrecht: Springer.

McCay, Clive. 1973. *Notes on the History of Nutrition Research*. Vienna: Hans Huber.

McCay, Clive, and Mary F. Crowell. 1934. "Prolonging the Life Span." *Scientific Monthly* 39 (5): 405–14.

McEvoy, John D. G. 2016. "Emerging Food Safety Issues: An EU Perspective." *Drug Testing and Analysis* 8 (5–6): 511–20.

Meiklejohn, Arnold Peter, Reginald Passmore, and Rudolph Albert Peters. 1932. "Pyruvic Acid and Vitamin B1 Deficiency." *Biochemical Journal* 26 (6): 1872–79.

Mendel, Lafayette Benedict. 1923. *Nutrition: The Chemistry of Life*. New Haven, CT: Yale University Press.

Mitman, Gregg. 1992. *The State of Nature: Ecology, Community, and American Social Thought, 1900–1950*. Chicago: University of Chicago Press.

Moore, Jason W. 2015. *Capitalism in the Web of Life: Ecology and the Accumulation of Capital*. London: Verso Books.

Moran-Thomas, Amy. 2019. *Traveling with Sugar: Chronicles of a Global Epidemic*. Oakland: University of California Press.

Morehouse, Neal F., and Orley J. Mayfield. 1946. "The Effect of Some Aryl Arsonic Acids on Experimental Coccidiosis Infection in Chickens." *Journal of Parasitology* 32 (1): 20–24.

Mudry, Jessica J. 2009. *Measured Meals: Nutrition in America*. Albany: State University of New York Press.

Neswald, Elizabeth. 2013. "Strategies of International Community-Building in Early Twentieth-Century Metabolism Research: The Foreign Laboratory Visits of Francis Gano Benedict." *Historical Studies in the Natural Sciences* 43 (1): 1–40.

Neubauer, Cajetan, and Hannah Landecker. 2021. "A Planetary Health Perspective on Synthetic Methionine." *Lancet Planetary Health* 5 (8): e560–69.

Nutrition Reviews. 1956. "Arsenicals as Growth Promoters." *Nutritional Reviews* 14 (7): 206–9.

Olmstead, Alan L., and Paul W. Rhode. 2008. *Creating Abundance: Biological Innovation and American Agricultural Development*. Cambridge: Cambridge University Press.

Park, Hyung Wook. 2010. "Longevity, Aging, and Caloric Restriction: Clive Maine McCay and the Construction of a Multidisciplinary Research Program." *Historical Studies in the Natural Sciences* 40 (1): 79–124.

Peters, Rudolph Albert. 1952. "Croonian Lecture—Lethal Synthesis." *Proceedings of the Royal Society of London B* 139 (895): 143–70.

Rabinbach, Anson. 1992. *The Human Motor: Energy, Fatigue, and the Origins of Modernity*. Berkeley: University of California Press.

Rahn, Otto. 1945. *Microbes of Merit*. Lancaster, PA: Jacques Cattell.

Roberts, Elizabeth F. S. 2017. "What Gets Inside: Violent Entanglements and Toxic Boundaries in Mexico City." *Cultural Anthropology* 32 (4): 592–619.

Roy, William G. 1999. *Socializing Capital: The Rise of the Large Industrial Corporation in America*. Princeton, NJ: Princeton University Press.

Saraiva, Tiago. 2016. *Fascist Pigs: Technoscientific Organisms and the History of Fascism*. Cambridge, MA: MIT Press.

Schrepfer, Susan, and Philip Scranton, eds. 2004. *Industrializing Organisms: Introducing Evolutionary History*. New York: Routledge.

Schwerin, Alexander von, Heiko Stoff, and Bettina Wahrig. 2013. "Biologics: An Introduction." In *Biologics: A History of Agents Made from Living Organisms in the Twentieth Century*, edited by Alexander von Schwerin, Heiko Stoff, and Bettina Wahrig, 1–31. London: Pickering and Chatto.

Scoville, Orlin J. 1956. "Medicated Feed as an Economic Factor in the Livestock Industry." In *Symposium on Medicated Feeds*, edited by Henry Welch and Félix Martí-Ibáñez, 121–26. Washington, DC: Medical Encyclopedia.

Shaw, Thomas. 1907. *Feeding Farm Animals*. London: Orange Judd.

Shorb, Mary S. 1948. "Activity of Vitamin B12 for the Growth of *Lactobacillus lactis*." *Science* 107 (2781): 397–98.

Smil, Vaclav. 2013. *Harvesting the Biosphere: What We Have Taken from Nature*. Cambridge, MA: MIT Press.

Snell, E. E., and F. M. Strong. 1939. "A Microbiological Assay for Riboflavin." *Industrial and Engineering Chemistry Analytical Edition* 11 (6): 346–50.

Solomon, Harris. 2016. *Metabolic Living: Food, Fat, and the Absorption of Illness in India*. Durham, NC: Duke University Press.

Summons, Terry G. 1968. "Animal Feed Additives, 1940–1966." *Agricultural History* 42 (4): 305–13.

Treitel, Corinna. 2008. "Max Rubner and the Biopolitics of Rational Nutrition." *Central European History* 41 (1): 1–25.

Wallace, Harold D, William A. Ney, and Tony J. Cunha. 1951. "Various Antibiotics and 3-Nitro-4-Hydroxyphenyl Arsonic Acid in Corn-Peanut Meal Rations for Swine." *Proceedings of the Society for Experimental Biology and Medicine* 78 (3): 807–8.

Wells, Jonathan C. K. 2016. *The Metabolic Ghetto: An Evolutionary Perspective on Nutrition, Power Relations and Chronic Disease*. Cambridge: Cambridge University Press.

Wherry, Larry. 1947. *The Golden Anniversary of Scientific Feeding*. Milwaukee, WI: Business Press.

Williams, Robert R. 1938. "The Chemistry and Biological Significance of Thiamin." *Science* 87 (2269): 559–63.

Willke, Thomas. 2014. "Methionine Production—a Critical Review." *Applied Microbiology and Biotechnology* 98 (24): 9893–914.

Yates-Doerr, Emily. 2015. *The Weight of Obesity: Hunger and Global Health in Postwar Guatemala*. Oakland: University of California Press.

processing

HANNAH LANDECKER /
ALEX BLANCHETTE

Here we turn from a story of feeding (food) animals over the twentieth century to feeding (pet) animals in the twenty-first. One chapter may feed another. Hannah's previous examination of the food of our food traces the history of medicated feed to think about how metabolism itself—rather than the qualities of a given food item, or those of a particular animal species—became an object of transformation for the sciences of animal feeding and nutrition. Alex's subsequent chapter on the food of our animal friends examines efforts to separate edible matter from taste sensations in domestic pet feeds, as a small group of companies competed to produce the flavorings that compel cats to eat slaughterhouse excess. The chapters share many concerns: the work and knowledge that underlies valuing industrial waste, the politics of feeding (as opposed to eating), and food capitalism's deep investments in, and reliance on, the senses and cellular processes of nonhuman beings. Both chapters ask what the anthropology, history, and cultural study of food might look like without the presumption that human eating and consumption is the primary or ultimate pivot on which the industrial food system coheres.

In this intercalary exchange between medicated and flavored feed, we think through what happens to *process*—specifically, what we mean when we say "processed food," when human eating and consumption is displaced from the center of analytic attention to become only one among other metabolic relations organized by industrialization. Arguably the form that defines the industrial food system for most readers, "processed" is generally understood as a quality that inheres in foodstuffs themselves, signifying edible matter that has been highly modified through labor and preservation technologies to augment consistency, durability, or flavor. Its iconic iterations include mechanically extruded corn, chemically preserved wheat snacks, chicken nuggets made of reconstituted flesh and cartilage slurry, oddly persistent "perishables" stabilized with preservatives, and artificial colors and flavors. As important as these qualities are to underpinning the standardized supermarket's negation of organic decay or seasonality, such properties are just one aspect of the chemical relations that unfold through the harnessing of the metabolisms and tastes of a whole host of beings that range from microbes to dogs. These chemical relations are increasingly the targets of many discretely developed processes and are subject to augmentation, diminishment, disembodiment, articulation, and rearticulation that can concatenate vital and synthetic components anew. In other words, processes are being modularized, pulled apart, and put back together before, in, and beyond food.

As such, a uniting thread across our two chapters is an effort to examine processing *not* as a material quality of foods themselves. It is, instead, about getting at the conjunctive relations that cohere eaters and eaten, the interspecies webs that manifest as concrete food items in grocery, pet, and farm supply stores. We trace the constitutive chains of distinct species' eating practices that make iconic forms of industrial food possible. The material qualities of contemporary meat are inseparable from animal diets, which in turn have come to depend on the metabolisms of microbes and plants. The price of supermarket hog flesh is inseparable from the profitable enlistment of dogs and cats to consume the lungs and bones that are infrequently served on dinner tables. These ramifying chains of eating also expand in other ways as processes of processing food unfold: diets are continuously becoming more complex with new wastes, additives, or geographies added in the form of drugs, recycled distiller's grains, or new minerals.

We use the language of webs or chains of eating to point to technical and vital systems through which processes become everywhere at once, rather than denoting discrete nodes whereby distinct ingredients and organisms come together. We find the ongoing industrialization of metabolism and taste processes suddenly spreading across alimentary systems. Within a decade or two, medicated feeds and the metabolizing body they entail suddenly appear at scale and across animal species. In a perverse inversion of *it all ends up in the same stomach*, all stomachs (and inhabitants of stomachs) end up enrolled in the same "it" of newly conjoined processes—such as when flavoring palatants simultaneously come to coat the surface of potato chips and most commercial animal feeds. Processes are about thresholds in terms of translating techniques of manufacture across species and domains. Tracking the processes that underlie food making today might lead us to tell stories of technical practices that emerge from efforts to manufacture a given thing and then immediately spread across others, rather than stories of discrete items organized by species—such as the now-ubiquitous histories and ethnographies of organisms such as tomatoes, corn, or cod.

We thus present an alternative to large-scale food systems signified by the chicken nugget by paying attention to industrialism as a matter of generating modular processes *and* rapidly expanding those techniques across domains of food manufacturing. *Processing*, it should be noted, is used to refer to slaughter in the lexicon of meat production. One might judge this a euphemism, a bloodless term behind which killing is hidden. Yet taken as an actor's category in light of the preceding analysis, it is an accurate term depicting slaughter as one key point among others in the endless imperative that characterizes the industry: to turn matter from one form into another. In tracing how metabolic and sensory processes both format and are formatted into new relations under conditions of industrial commodity production, we come to understand such processes themselves as the targets and means of commerce and innovation. Intercalating process between foodstuffs and eaters is intended here to expand the possibilities for empirical study of food and eating beyond individual bodies and ingestions.

chapter three

The Politics of Palatability

....

HOG VISCERA, PET FOOD,
AND THE TRADE IN
INDUSTRIAL SENSE IMPRESSIONS

ALEX BLANCHETTE

Visceral Monocultures

A squat white metal-and-concrete building sits in a barren, dusty Great Plains industrial park outside the town of Dixon.[1] It is unremarkable and is dwarfed by its two gargantuan neighbors: a slaughterhouse that kills more than nineteen thousand hogs per day and a factory that converts the ensuing harvest of 282,000 pounds of rendered fat into commercial biodiesel and glycerin for cosmetics. There are no signs or forms of branding that announce the building's ultimate purpose. A half dozen cars sit in its gravel parking lot. Two metal chemical storage cylinders poke out from the back. When I visited the facility shortly after it opened in the early 2010s, local residents were calling it the "kibble plant." But no one seemed to know what was actually being manufactured in its interior. Before meeting with its eight employees, I assumed it made small batches of designer pet food or dental treats. Instead, this building, along with a handful of identical others built next to the United States' largest slaughterhouses over the past decade, uses the chemically concentrated essences of hogs' lungs and livers to make a powdered or liquid flavoring substance that is called a *palatant*. This building is one stage of a quiet yet ambitious logistical process that promises to transform how all the world's domestic cats experience taste, while granting a small number of companies near-exclusive control over the feline species' gustatory sensations.[2]

This chapter develops some conceptual viewpoints onto the changing nature of American agribusiness through an ethnography of animal organs like lungs, tracing the multiplicity of eating practices that ripple through the modern industrial hog. Its premise is that pork corporations must develop new specialized sites of labor and value within each hog body *part* to sustain the broader project of industrialized animal life and death. Put differently, the factory farm as a massive monoculture—the specialized production of one organism—depends on the unending creation of distinct monocultures within individual hogs' bodies. The American pig is now worked as a collection of partible bodily substances even prior to its death. Moreover, the specific ways in which animals' bodies are killed and processed reverberate back through their lives.

Engineering the taste sensations of domesticated cats may appear an esoteric topic of study—perhaps even a flippant one given the well-documented environmental and moral detriments of modern meat. I would argue, however, that pet food palatants and their fixation on the minutiae of pleasurable feline feeling, as I describe in what follows, can help us think about changing forms of value and exploitation in monocultural agribusiness. Critics of factory farms have made interventions concerning the "meatification" of society, or how the unending march toward larger farms has outstripped demand and made it difficult for people of an average income to subsist in the Global North without consuming an ever-cheaper array of animal substances (see Weis 2013). This explosion in concentrated animal scale, in turn, is inseparable from economic strategies of capitalist slaughter that have made curious things like pet palatants into lucrative transnational corporate projects. As the sociologist Jen Wrye (2015) argues in an article on pet food and the ideology of nutritionism, the popular language of calling bones or organs *by-products* (in the sense of excess or waste products) to meat is misleading. Wrye calls them *coproducts*, indicating that the profits generated from these other carnal substances in the pig are part of what make muscles/meat cheap and ubiquitous. Indeed, since at least the 1890s, large meatpackers have largely broken even on meat products with the goal of undercutting competitors (see, for instance, Cronon 1992). The largest of industrialized slaughter facilities have long been distinguished by making their profit margins through building worth into hog physiologies beyond muscle and intramuscular fat—literally using "all" the pig in things like biofuels, fertilizers, brush bristles, or gelatins.

However, what palatants help us glimpse anew are the ways that the ever-increasing scales of American slaughter are tied, in part, to the search for unique carnal substances within hogs. Their manufacture further reflects how using all of the pig profitably is no longer just a matter of rendering nonmeat substances into generic slurries for pet food, gelatins, or bonemeal—but instead an ongoing, unendingly more fine-grained process of *by-production* (or coproduction).[3] Put differently, this is not simply a neutral matter of efficiency or waste reduction. Animal agribusinesses have been using all of the pig for over a century. Given this context and history, by-production is arguably the antithesis of efficiency: it is a capitalist diversion of scientific knowledge and social resources to find new uses for distinct porcine physiologies in the interests of agribusiness profitability and growth. The trick is that it makes little sense for a corporation to invest in a biodiesel factory to transesterify the fat of a few dozen hogs each day or to build a drug facility that uses the pancreatic materials of five hundred pigs (see Meindertsma 2007). Fur, blood, and stomach lining are more easily transmogrified—and their substances separated and worked on at finer chemical levels—when they are pooled in the thousands of pounds. One result is that most pigs in today's United States are raised and slaughtered in only eight locations, and more than 1,100 commodities are potentially carved out of every carcass—at least 400 of which are not edible muscle or meat products (see Blanchette 2020). We might say that the increasing scales of animal monocultures are actually a thresholding project in two conjoined ways, two versions of what Heather Paxson (this volume) denotes as moments when prior baselines are exceeded and new "normal" or standard systems emerge. That is, by-production aims to grow scales of slaughter until new sites of value within complex porcine bodies are made evident, and, in turn, it has the expansionary effect of converting the sustenance of more off-farm living beings and industrial processes into intensified relations of dependency with factory farms.

Recent scholarship in food and farming has started to arch beyond a long-standing ethical fixation on the brief moment of animal killing in slaughterhouses. Gabriel Rosenberg (2017, 2020), for instance, argues for more attention to the sexual and genetic politics of animal reproduction—or the often-violent and eugenicist ways that farm animals are brought to life. This chapter on processes of by-production extends this thinking *after* the moment when hogs' carotid arteries are slit—into the postdeath activities and labor that naturalize, justify, and make socially "necessary" the transcorporeal conditions in which farm *and* companion animals live. My gambit is that studying the remaking of pig biology to incorporate new kinds of eating can reveal this broader monoculture's fragility despite its growing dominance over many species—the lives of pigs, cats, and humans alike—and, in turn, provide new modes of political attention for promoting its abolition. Even more broadly, in some closing notes I argue that these palatants hint at how a century of by-production is resulting in the crossing of a pivotal threshold whereby the very value and capitalist nature of monoculture may no longer be the same. Palatants suggest how monocultures are no longer simply a means to the end of achieving greater yields or *quantities* of biology but instead are becoming prized by corporations for their *qualities*.

In this context pet food palatants suggest the need for a more expansive approach to both the phenomenological and political economic study of food. This chapter joins a host of scholars who illustrate how food studies' anthropocentrism—the sense that *food* is usually taken to mean "food that humans eat"—can make invisible the many parallel sites of pleasure and harm that follow in the wake of industrial alimentary systems.[4] What the fixation on the politics and ethics of human eating elides is that the industrial pig and its cheap meat are formed and subsidized via many modes of ingestion beyond those of human beings. The growing trade in feline sense impressions requires us to rethink how the spaces where industrial pigs are raised and killed extend far beyond farms or slaughterhouses and do not end at human stomachs, as corporate engineers invent foods that conjoin beings in new ways to monocultural agribusiness.[5] I do not mean this as a matter of nefarious corporate conspiracy. We will see that making palatants is partially a caring endeavor motivated by the desire to glimpse nonhuman sensory mechanisms and augment the well-being of other species (see Uexküll 2010). Instead, the rapid rise of animal palatants is a symptom of a striking but underdiscussed fact: human eaters alone cannot sustain the economic model of the factory farm and its mode of cheap growth cultivated through ever-deepening slaughter.

The pages that follow focus ethnographically on the labors and logistics that try to make industrial hog viscera become visceral: practices that attempt to manifest the feline species' deep-seated appetites, plug into them, and compel cats to act as sinks by eating the surplus of corporate food systems. In other words, rather than developing a generic ontology of food and eating—articulating a universal philosophy of the agentive vitality of things (e.g., Bennett 2010)—this chapter traces ongoing forms of (not-just-human) labor that are explicitly designed to cultivate a kind of food taste (and system) that becomes *more* agentive over time. Following the path of these increasingly potent palatants will take us from the recipes of migrant organ cooks in rural factories to the institutionalized labor of feline expert tasters in urban sensory labs. It will arch across how palatants emerge from the United States' historically unprecedented overaccumulation of uniform animal body parts, and pause to pay attention to the sciences of reduction—in terms of both culinary concentration and anthropological simplification (see Choy and Zee 2015)—that may augment the value of uniform monoculture itself. In some closing notes, this chapter details how critical interventions into monocultures might be made more potent by amplifying our focus from debates on eating animals into the politics of how animals are made to eat.

A Monopoly on Taste

In 2007 consumers in the United States were scandalized when they learned that most pet foods were made in one of two factories—regardless of cost or brand (Martin 2008). Following the infamous Menu Foods recall, when kidney-harming melamine was imported from China as counterfeit wheat gluten and mixed into pet foods, hundreds of companion animals died. As Marion Nestle (2008) details, pet foods from as many as nineteen brands (in addition to all of those brands' variations) were traced back to a single factory in Kansas that imported the melamine. This one production line was contracted to make them all using similar base ingredients that varied only in terms of textures or relative proportions of a recipe. This was perhaps only the tip of the iceberg. Despite an emerging array of specialty cat food products that vary in appearance, texture, ingredients, and smell—with differing labels and ethical claims (e.g., GMO-free)—the flavors of cat food have likely only become more identical over time. What I find striking is the rapid outcome of palatants: in just twenty years of use, the gustatory sensations of every cat (and dog) who lives in an industrialized country—or, at minimum, those who subsist on dry pet food purchased from commercial pet stores—are now designed by only a few companies.[6] Three companies compete to hold a monopoly on feline sense impressions; they are each working with pet food companies' mixes of kibble to develop their own designer tastes for all the world's cats.[7]

As a step in the broader process of making commercial pet food, manufacturers have long been cooking fatty flavoring liquid slurries of mixed hydrolyzed animal parts known as *digests*. Their purpose has always been an interspecies balancing act. Digests make extruded pellets or moist cans of foodstuffs sensorially appealing to both nonhuman eaters *and* their human feeders (Nestle 2008, 45). They mask the intense rendered stench that would be disagreeable to human noses, while enticing cats to ingest a host of processed and cheap grain meals, vitamins, and proteins that they might not otherwise grasp as edible (see also Overstreet 2018). These principles remained the same after the 1990s, when the industry shifted to palatants. But a palatant differs from a digest in at least four ways. First, as (typically) a powder, it is more intense than a digest and is used more sparingly to coat kibbles. It is closer to a material substance that is "pure taste" than a fat-slurry digest that carries additional nutritive qualities. This allows animal feed manufacturers more flexibility in their mixes that compose a kibble. For instance, the dozens of substances ground into hog feed pellets change alongside market prices, ranging from corn to expired Lucky Charms cereal and other detritus. Second, palatants are treated with amino acids to create chemical reactions—such as Maillard reactions, emphasizing meaty sensations—that intensify certain qualities of taste for a given target species (Nagodawithana, Nelles, and Trivedi 2010; Eiler 2015). Third, palatants are more selective than digests in their composition of material sources (livers, lungs, etc.) to create a uniform base. They appear to be a partial product of monocultures' large-scale uniformity in that they are made possible by highly consistent and concentrated pools of viscera. Finally, they require both logistical capacities to source pools of consistent viscera from factory farms and also a complex testing regimen using cat representatives to stand in for domestic felines as a whole. Palatants are, in other words, not only chemical products but also ongoing services provided to feed manufacturers that are rooted in mobilizing the labor of cats to work on their own species' taste sensations (see Paxson, this volume).

Put simply, palatants are commodified taste vehicles that compel nonhuman animals to eat. They are designed to encourage companion species to react in distinct ways, partially tied to the nature of their standard relationships to human beings: perhaps consuming quickly, or in large quantities, and in some cases while exuding affective signs of pleasure. In March 2016, for example, new palatants were introduced to industrial pig farms that chemically produce a smell and taste of sow milk and colostrum that is alluring to newborn piglets (National Hog Farmer 2016). These palatants would functionally enable hog farmers to more rapidly wean piglets from sows—and hence increase birthing and killing throughput—by reliably shifting babies to solid foods at a young age. Cat palatants are treated with, among a range of other chemicals, pyrophosphates that are believed to increase the sensitivity of feline umami taste receptors. This allows them to more profoundly experience an essence of protein and viscera that we humans cannot biologically perceive.[8] In the science writer Mary Roach's (2013, 44) playful tour of a palatant testing lab, an employee referred to pyrophosphates as "cat crack." But corporations' ideal is to develop a feline palatant that would do more than merely induce cats to rapidly ingest large quantities of food. The preferred palatant would indexically materialize taste (for the human caretakers) through feline behavior, inciting cats to run to the bowl at feeding time, purr, stretch, and emit signs of pleasure for their human companions (Beaton 2015).[9] In other words, palatants do not just chemically act on the target species but rather *operate on the target interspecies relationship*. They are transcorporeal technologies (Overstreet 2018; Paxson, this volume). They act to intensify and materialize preexisting qualities of a given bond of domestication, whether that relation is based on sentimental affection (for cats) or efficient exploitation (for pigs). Palatants act as conservative technologies even as they continually remake feline experience. They entrench and deepen preexisting species relationships in food systems.

Not for Human Consumption

"My bosses told me to tell you that they've completed their Bermuda Triangle around the competition," Jeff DeLong informed me, as we walked around BFG Essences' new facility. What he meant was that this building ensured that BFG Essences had unrestricted access to three major US pork packers, while at the same time geographically encompassing their competitors with organ-cooking stations. Jeff was in his mid-thirties, a jovial fellow who took pride in ably running buildings. He presented himself as an expert technician. He proudly walked me through each of his framed industrial certifications on the wall, though he maintained a sense of humor about his odd line of work. However, at the time that we met in the early 2010s, he also appeared a bit stressed. At that early juncture, a month into opening, there were still a lot of issues to work out. For one, the floors were overrun with cockroaches, and dense hordes of flies covered the back of the building. This had never happened at the other BFG facilities that Jeff had helped set up. He meticulously maintained the building's cleanliness, at one point even picking up a broom to dust some overhead pipes as we strolled around. But some odd combination of the Great Plains ecology and dense viscera vapors made insects "just throw themselves at us, at the building."

On the building's "hot side," boilers, reactors, and centrifuges run continuously for most of the day. There is a dry storage room with pallets of dozens of different chemicals that are used in the "cooking" process, and a laboratory for sampling the end product. The "cold side," a two-thousand-square-foot refrigerated concrete warehouse, is stacked with pallets of blue plastic bins that are the shape and size of oil drums. The bins are covered with warnings that the contents are not for human consumption. "Inedible" is stenciled in all caps with black spray paint on the bins' surface. Inside are hog lungs and livers that have been splashed with black food coloring to ensure that they are not accidentally ground up with muscle for human food.[10] The resulting reddish-white piles of inky black-stained viscera reminded me of squid. In this cold chamber, at any given moment, there are thirty thousand of these hog organs awaiting chemical processing into flavoring palatants.

This facility is officially called BFG Essences North. But when the company bosses flew in for a day from Europe and saw the flat Midwest surface, they informally renamed it BFG Essences Moon. The metaphor of a resource-extraction expedition to the moon felt fitting, for Jeff kept insisting that he's "just a stooge with a machine." He was a temporary transplant from North Carolina who had moved to Dixon for a few months to train some hired locals who would eventually run the factory. Following each "cook," he samples the substance and sends the raw data to Europe, where flavor scientists tell him what to adjust to try to match the flavor profiles of their other organ factories. Jeff and three other company operatives would stay until they were done tinkering with this viscera recipe. Then they would move to a different meatpacking town to set up another one.[11]

The logistical practices used by BFG Essences to try to standardize viscera give a striking portrait of how corporate hog production has reshaped the environments of select US rural places over the past twenty-five years, creating ecologies defined by large quantities of hogs. In this particular area of the Great Plains, some 7 million hogs are annually conceived, raised, and killed—largely by one corporation. Dover Foods (a pseudonym) has left in its wake a company town where human economic and social life is inseparable from industrial hogs in their distinct life stages and physiologies. It is one of perhaps eight to ten other global locations that contain so many hogs that transnational companies are now offshoring their facilities from Europe or Asia to the United States to "mine" porcine bodies that cannot be found at this carnal concentration elsewhere in the world.[12] Such places illustrate how a few select parts of the rural United States have become globally unique in their accumulation of animal biologies—akin, for instance, to Mongolia's underground deposits of rare earth minerals—as massive formations of body parts attract companies to relocate for access to these environmental deposits for chemical extraction.

What is remarkable about these companies relocating to concentrated porcine ecologies is how it reflects shifting capitalist valuations of large-scale, uniform monocultures. We might say that BFG Essences is pursuing a kind of industrial terroir—a reflection of environments in gustatory sensations, a "taste of place"—that, unlike wine or cheese cultures seeking regionally unique qualities in food, prizes uniformity (see Paxson 2013; Heath, chapter 7). This is partly a matter of quantitative scale: by having exclusive access to the largest pools of viscera, palatant companies can more easily create consistency across sourcing sites. But it is also tied to the standardized qualities of monoculture, revealing that the lungs and livers have been figuratively "cooking" through exposure to these environs long before Jeff DeLong puts them in a boiler. Indoor confinement's standardization becomes manifest in vats of lungs that have all breathed the same air ridden with ammonia and hydrogen sulfide, or livers that have all been processing similar rations of feedstuffs. The uniform qualitative atmospheres of monocultural environments in which pigs eat and breathe are, in a sense, what underlies and is being mined for palatants. This logistical process of setting up semiautomated extraction centers in large monocultures is part of the work of making livers into "the" liver; it is an attempt to manufacture not animals but generic animality. It is one step of making materials to create a single, uniform taste for the entirety of the feline species.

The Ongoingness of One Taste

While rereading C. Nadia Seremetakis's 1994 book, *The Senses Still*, I found her notes on industrial capitalist taste and sensory anesthesia to be prescient in terms of contemporary concerns about industrial food. She opens with a haunting description of mundane fruits that can no longer be tasted. Or, at least, of the incitement to nostalgia and discourse caused by memories of taste.[13] Seremetakis recounts her recollection of two stone fruits called the *rodhákino* and the *yermás*. Each differed palpably in texture, and their tastes summoned collective memories and solidarities for generations of Greeks. One day, on a return visit to Greece, she found that they had vanished from regional markets. New fruits such as kiwis were being sold, exciting a younger cohort of Greeks, but the cherished stone fruits of her own youth were replaced by some imported thing simply called "the peach." This peach tasted, at best, like a dulled version of the *rodhákino*. As Seremetakis frames the issue:

> In Greece, as regional products gradually disappear, they are replaced by foreign foods, foreign tastes; the universal and rationalized is now imported into the European periphery as the exotic [i.e., the kiwi]. Here a regional diversity is substituted by a surplus over-production.... Sensory premises, memories and histories are being pulled out from under entire regional cultures and the capacity to reproduce social identities may be altered as a result. Such economic processes reveal the extent to which the ability to replicate cultural identity is a material practice embedded in the reciprocities, aesthetics, and sensory strata of material objects. (3)

In Seremetakis's analysis, nations of human eaters are acting as sinks for the offloading of industrial agriculture's excess. The unique qualities of regional food are replaced by generic quantities of bulk peaches that do not even taste like peaches. Seremetakis evokes sensory experience's capacity to forge ties and communities through memory, juxtaposing it to industrial capitalism's modernizing tendency to constantly remake the material things that anchor generations (see Berman 1983). The human in this narrative is not an autonomous subject but is changing and becoming alongside the creative destruction of a more-than-human world. For Seremetakis and her generation, as I read her now, agricultural capitalism appears as a process of numbing of the senses. The senses, and with them collective experience, come to be dulled yet constantly changing in time as things like locally unique stone fruits—in retrospect, vessels for building generational meaning—are replaced by generic peaches.

This kind of narrative, besides being a recognizable romantic scholarly trope against rationalization, still feels compelling to me. I came of age at a moment when people felt industrialism had mass-produced the taste out of things, when it was quite palpable that human sense impressions were sites of cultural-economic struggle. After moving to a city for college in the early 2000s, I found my own return visits home to a rural Canadian community marked by friends' efforts to revitalize regional agricultures. This industrial evacuation of sensation helped create openings for other kinds of capitalist processes that (at least try to) prioritize local values, intensities of flavor, regional place, intimate connections to landscapes, and so forth (see Guthman 2006; Paxson 2013; Weiss 2016). But, alongside these resurgent regionalisms, replacing the lost tastes of things has, for some time, been solidifying as an (industrial) industry in itself (Khatchadourian 2009). The carcasses of corporate-raised chickens, now so lean that they can only be experienced as a texture, are coated and injected with liquid chicken flavor (Striffler 2005). Snack foods such as Cheetos are tasteless save for their powdered cheese-esque coating (Roach 2013). Since well before the 1960s, chemical flavor scientists have been devising and replicating a whole range of tastes and sense impressions to make processed foodstuffs edible (Schatzker 2015) or to give healthier foods flavors that appeal to current tastes (Butler 2020). However unhinged from the actual contents of food it may be—however "artificial," as some tend to say—industrial food science is releasing scores of new flavor and taste vehicles.

Perhaps unsurprisingly, flavor science has become essential to contemporary pet food. But, at least for cats, it has been developed differently. Rather than a range of new tastes and sensations—however compensatory—flavor scientists have been trying to refine one kind of taste for the world's felines. Perhaps it should not be terribly surprising that such processes, too, follow recognizable modernist ontological tropes: many human flavors are to culture as one feline taste is to nature (de la Cadena 2015). But the reason that I invoke Seremetakis's reading of the senses undergoing constant change is that it helps me think about the ongoingness of one taste. This is not a finished story, not some kind of completed project that perfectly compels all cats to eat. Each company is trying to expand their own feline taste device across broader populations of cats, and each company is refining their own taste profiles over time. Industrial creative destruction is here geared toward coming closer and closer to a pan-species taste, a sensation that sums up the desires of all felines. Cats are constantly experiencing changes to their taste sensations as recipes are refined and shifted. This project of a universal taste is ongoing. Paradoxically, it is perhaps interminable.

The Logistics of Feline Taste

The efforts of BFG Essences to secure ample pools of relatively uniform viscera are only part of their logistical program for remaking cat sensations. When I visited Jeff DeLong, our conversation centered on the urban laboratory sites where the organ recipe is designed, tested, and refined. The company's claim to distinction is its investment in, as Jeff put it, "a worldwide network of expert tasters." They "employ" (his words) over five hundred cats in three testing facilities across Europe and the Americas. These collections of feline workers—and they are collections, populations of animals that are carefully chosen—are designed to overcome the major hurdle of designing palatants: "The problem is that the cat can't tell us what it likes."[14]

Perhaps attuned to the controversies over animal testing, one of Jeff's colleagues quickly noted at the outset of this topic that "PETA [People for the Ethical Treatment of Animals] would love it there. They have to treat those goddamn cats like kings." This statement was partially an effort to underline that the cats are engaged in free employment relations featuring remuneration for their "work" on their own species' pleasure, as opposed to being the forced and sacrificial subjects of experimental testing (see Sunder Rajan 2007). But his words were more than defensive. Cultivating an interspecies practice that mimics a generic affect of domesticated love is part of keeping cats whose taste judgment qualifies as expert. One major palatant company touts how its testing facilities are designed to be closer than any other to the emotional environment of normative American domesticity. In turn, BFG Essences tries to one-up them by running in-home side trials through a network of US-based households, providing field conditions closer to where the cats actually eat. In her tour through a palatant testing facility, Roach (2013) seemed to witness this enactment of affect. All of the cats and dogs had been given cutesy names, the flavor scientists describing each in terms that highlighted their unique personality.

These testing sites for experimenting with variations on organ recipes were first initiated in the mid-2000s. They were deemed necessary when recipes came to be more refined for a given company's specific mixture of kibble. The palatant companies turned into providers of research services that monitored the changing range of cat flavors in a market, and they offered sites for demonstrating the efficacy of a taste. If, for example, a company such as Hill's Science Diet chooses to source its palatants from BFG Essences, then the latter uses its tests to determine the correct palatant recipe and intensity for the given kibble. But they are also sites of comparison: BFG Essences tests its contracted manufacturers' products against other brands—for example, Friskies or Meow Mix—that are aligned with a different palatant company. This is to see how competitors' tastes are changing over time and whether they are starting to "outperform" (as they call it) one of BFG Essences' contracted brands that was previously dominant. In this manner a given company's taste (allegedly) becomes more "agentive" and "catlike" over time in its ability to make felines consume, and consume in particular ways.

What makes a cat an expert taster is its consistency. Each cat is slightly (or starkly) different—palatant companies acknowledge that—but what they want are cats that are individually predictable regardless of their quirks or preferences. They cultivate such feline differences within the "worldwide network": cats with certain allergies, for instance, are useful for some trials concerning niche pet foods. The basic trial—the "Gold Standard," as it is called—is the two-bowl test. A cat is given two bowls of kibble, one with BFG Essences' palatant and another with a competitor's palatant, and various parameters are measured. These include which food the cat eats in greatest total quantity, the speed at which it eats, the first bowl it approaches, and the first bowl from which it eats. Another company measures what they call "emotional palatability." These are the bodily signs given off by cats that, based on survey data, US-based pet owners currently deem significant—such as stretching in front of the bowl. As this company puts is, "To make meal time a shared enjoyable moment, pet food manufacturers not only need to satisfy pets' appetite, they also need this satisfaction to be clearly perceptible by the owner" (quoted in Beaton 2015).

I want to underscore that this is a mode of mass-produced palatability. One thing that unites the long logistical chains transforming modern hog organs is scientific practices of reduction and complex ways of "making the same" (Hayden 2012). Complicated sourcing networks are enlisted to make lungs and livers appear interchangeable, measures of feline pleasure are reduced to durations of licking or stretching, and chemical cooking aims to create a pure essence of viscera.[15] Indeed, the factory farm's efforts to produce a uniform organism at a large scale—to manufacture "the pig" rather than a diverse array of individual pigs—is refracted into palatant tasting panels. The diverse collection of cats employed for tests in BFG Essences' multisite, so-called worldwide network is used by the palatant company to claim that it knows what the cat (in general) prefers. As AFB International (n.d.), one of the three major flavoring companies puts it in some advertising literature about its tests, "some variations include the number of pet participants, the environment, the feeding length, the 'normal' diet of pet participants, the breed of the pet participant, and even the region where the test is run." Palatant companies offer quite a striking portrait of attempting to use cats' work to operate at the level of a species—to identify a taste that drives all of a species' earthly manifestations or individual tokens to consume—by conducting tests across breeds, geographies, and facilities that simulate the everyday lives of cats. They are trying to produce an interspecies universal out of the intersection of immense quantities of standardized swine coupled with cats that are enacted through tests as indexical representatives of the entire global feline population.

You Are with Whom You Eat

The making of palatants is equal parts amusing, insidious, and inspired in ways that defy easy judgment. This is a curious political economy of pleasure, inseparable from the state of modern pet culture in Euro-America. It reflects, for better or worse, how being a caring companion to nonhuman selves has become legible as a mark of one's refinement and ethics (see Nast 2006; Tsing 2012). From one angle, given the long history of lax regulation and corner cutting underlying pet food manufacture (recall the section, "A Monopoly on Taste"), it is easy to see this concerted attention to feline feeling as a laudable expression of intervention against widespread social logics that make animals' lives negligible. From another, it is an instance of modern biopolitics flitting across hierarchies of organisms (Wolfe 2012). The deepening immiseration of hogs intensifies the pleasures of cats; the food of our friends tells a vastly different story from the food of our food (Landecker, chapter 2). Granted, there is a silliness to all of this, one even glimpsed in tongue-in-cheek asides in taste-industry publications. It should partially defy the weighty tones of most academic analyses, including this one. For these companies are mobilizing histories of scientific knowledge and statistical technique to make flavors that humans cannot biologically perceive—and building high economic stakes and transnational corporate competition into rates of feline stretching.

If palatants are challenging to slot into well-worn analytic grooves, however, it is perhaps a symptom. At their broadest, I want to argue that palatants entail the need to alter how we grasp the *qualities* of capitalist agribusiness and its monocultures in the first place. Sarah Besky (2019) examines labor on Indian tea plantations to argue against the tropes that many scholars tend to use to analyze monocultural agriculture. Too often, she claims, anthropologists and geographers treat monocultures such as factory farms or Iowa cornfields as terminal projects that have reached the apotheosis of their logic and are now approaching the verge of collapse owing to their ecological unsustainability. While helpful in underlining that other modes of agriculture are possible or desirable, these perspectives fail to account for the dogged durability of monocultures across the planet—and, more important, they elide ongoing forms of action and evolution that occur within sites of monoculture. Besky instead proposes that we pay more critical attention to the active and diverse work of *monoculturing*: the ongoing and evolving labor of maintaining these kinds of formations as active, expanding sites of capitalist value and global agricultural norms. Monoculture is not a fixed ecological state, she suggests, but rather a labor- and imagination-intensive process constantly shifting in time.

Insofar as most critical theory treats agribusiness as a nonstatic place where (new) things happen, the ongoing reduction of complex landscapes and interspecies interactions to simplified monocultures is usually framed as a means to an end. It is about gradually increasing yields of a given life-form and, in turn, decreasing both production and commodity costs to more cheaply "feed the world" (see Moore 2015). But by-production and the capitalist traffic in feline sensory experience is useful for expanding what we might mean by monoculturing as an active process—not only in terms of increasing quantities of yield and output but also in terms of transforming the very qualities and value of uniform industrial animality. The rise of things like palatants reflects how monoculture may not be at a logical terminus but instead be evolving as a social and biological form of capitalist agriculture.

Large-scale monocultures leave new monocultures in their wake as companies come to specialize in a single muscle, organ, or dimension of bodily chemistry.[16] Monocultures beget monocultures, and hog organs are neither economically or biophysically what they were even a decade ago. Moreover, this is not just some kind of automatic structural logic but instead one that takes concerted and layered practices of ongoing reduction in terms of both concentration and simplification. It requires acts, sciences, and cultures of by-production and monoculturing. This chapter has outlined an array of acts of monoculturing in the form of simplifying a pig's environment and diet to materialize animals in uniform ways, the concentration of those resultant organs into intense and consistent essences, and their use to engineer a single and uniform taste for all of the world's cats. As such, examining factory farms from the perspective of organs rather than muscles (or meat) illustrates how it is not just the copious quantities of flesh originating from monocultures that are valuable. Instead, in the rise of devices like palatants, we are seeing the emergence of investments aiming to augment the value of monocultures' large-scale, standardized, and uniform qualities themselves. The manufacturing of industrial cat taste is a small example of how monoculture is still crossing thresholds as it enlists new practices, values, aesthetics, and participants. The corollary is that the factory farm remains in flux: expanding the world's dependence on its biological substances but always needing to generate novel outlets for its pig bodies. It is necessarily a project and mode of transcorporeal capitalism—one that must continually expand how others species' lives are entangled with those of its pigs.

At the same time, this begins to suggest how animals eating is as important a political and ethical issue as eating animals. With many exceptions, food studies tends to boil down to following substances that are cultivated and processed to fulfill human needs and desires. But a vast amount of industrial agriculture—perhaps the majority—is not organized around human nourishment. Much agricultural and crop development is geared around making biofuels (McMichael 2010). Nutritionists have accumulated as much funded knowledge of, and society has invested as much worth into, industrial chicken nutrition as it has human nutrition (Boyd and Watts 1997). Geographies are shaped through animal metabolism (Hetherington 2020). From the commodity cornfields of the American Midwest to the soybeans that are clearing out Amazonia, swathes of agricultural terrain and practice are directed toward feeding nonhuman animals. While it is tempting to skip over the steps of making meat to arrive at the telos that it all leads to our stomachs, human beings ingest only 50 percent of those industrial animals' bodies through eating. The United States' 163 million pet cats and dogs alone consume more than 25 percent of all animal-derived calories (Okin 2017). If these American critters constituted a whole country, there would be only four others in the world with human populations that eat that quantity of animal substances (Brulliard 2017). Even this shocking figure does not account for the food animals eaten by food animals, with large amounts of beef fat underlying swine diets—and much hog blood being recycled to nourish baby piglets in the form of processed plasma.

This chapter has taken up a small piece of such a project by tracing how companion animals' sensory impressions have entered into industrial dynamics. Taste is being made into a separate and lucrative site of industrial logistics, its powdered vehicle sold to pet food manufacturers who now specialize in cheaply creating nutrition profiles, textures, and branded appearances. What I have been describing in these pages is arguably a shift in degree rather than kind. For at least eighty years, cats and dogs have been fed from the nonmeat substances of industrial slaughterhouses (Grier 2010). These companion animals have long subsisted on rendered mixtures of fur, hooves, bonemeals, and organs mixed with various grain meals and vitamins to compose a (purportedly) "nutritionally complete" diet for a given species (see Wrye 2015). Cats and pigs have long been industrially conjoined, but how the feline species dwells in the world—how it experiences taste—is shifting alongside the kinds of cramped and concentrated lives that modern pigs lead. Industrial hog lungs, all breathing in abysmally uniform air, compel cats to more uniformly and rapidly ingest muscles. It can be tempting to grasp this as a story of totality, one of human mastery in authoring the biologies, senses, and lived lives of others. Or as a story to be celebrated, of a progressive capitalism that has reached certain new ethical plateaus whereby it becomes caring to some nonhumans and not purely anthropocentric. But, following Marianne Elisabeth Lien's (2015, 107) push against all "too-smooth account[s] of industrial success," it also points to the fragility, unpredictable entanglements, and unintentionality of monoculture. So many beings must work and live to maintain the factory farm; so many lives (and an ever-expanding array of lives) are recruited to handle its surplus biologies and maintain the cheap meat that is fed to populations of humans.

The point here is that we cannot understand how most humans are made to eat within an industrial food system without attention to nonhuman practices of ingestion. There is the line attributed to Jean Anthelme Brillat-Savarin that "you are what you eat," perhaps framing the consumer as an agentive shape-shifter of sorts who makes herself up through things she chooses to eat (see Brillat-Savarin [1825] 2011, 15). Michael Pollan (2006) negated any such ideas, arguing that you are what is eaten by the beings that you eat. For US-dwelling meat eaters, most of whom only have access to food at major grocery stores and restaurants, that essentially means they are composed of corn and drugs. Thinking with palatants suggests we need an additional take: you are with whom you eat, with those who join you at the table. Cats' eating is one small but significant factor shaping American meat today.

ACKNOWLEDGMENT

Some passages and paragraphs from this chapter originally appeared in a truncated section of my book *Porkopolis* (2020).

NOTES

1. All company names and place-names in this chapter are pseudonyms.

2. I take the word *logistical* from Deborah Cowen's 2014 book, *The Deadly Life of Logistics*. Among Cowen's many important contributions is an effort to theorize how production processes are no longer confined in spaces such as factories. Instead, they are stretched and made across logistical distribution paths—taken apart, containerized, segmented, and designed for reassembly (see also Tsing [2009] on supply chain capitalism).

3. The historian Eric Slauter suggested the term *by-production* to encapsulate this process during a 2020 seminar on American history at the University of Chicago where I workshopped this chapter. I thank him for this term, along with Andrew Seber for organizing that venue.

4. See Mullin (2007), Paxson (2013), Lien (2015), Wrye (2015), Overstreet (2018), and Landecker (chapter 2) for exceptions that develop more-than-human studies of food and eating practices.

5. They also, of course, extend beyond the many other ways that industrialization of animals ripples through the planet in the forms of antibiotic resistance, dead zones in oceans from manure runoff, deforestation for soy, and so forth.

6. This merits some qualification. The very cheapest pet foods likely still use digests rather than palatants (see discussion later in this chapter). Conversely, the highest-end pet foods—Orijen brand in the United States, for instance, or a foodie-targeting raw-food brand (see Mullin 2007; Martin 2008)—typically use "human-grade" ingredients that would not include these kinds of concentrated organ extracts. The Menu Foods recall did spur some real alternatives to cat food being endless variations of the same factory-farm slurries of protein. In between those two poles, however, lies the vast majority of commercial dry pet foods in most of the world. My understanding is that this is truer for dry (kibble) pet foods than for wet/canned foods, which use palatants at a lower frequency.

7. This chapter focuses on cats rather than dogs, partly because this was the palatant that was being manufactured in the factory where I did ethnographic research. All three of the major palatant companies produce flavors for both cats and dogs, however, in addition to other products for "livestock." That said, cat and dog palatants are not the same. Corporations organize their production around the assumption that cats "taste" relatively more with their tongues, while dog palatants are more designed around smell. Similarly—and this is quite consequential for this chapter—the practical assumption of these companies is that cats prefer monotony: that it could be possible to achieve a limited array of flavors that would appeal to all cats (Roach 2013). Some studies have found, for instance, that kittens will eat greater quantities more consistently if they are fed the same flavor over time (Jojola 2016). There is a more diverse range of dog flavors, in addition to a wider range of protein sources for dog palatants (chickens, kangaroos, etc.), since they are understood to eat more consistently if they have access to a wider range of tastes and foods.

8. In a brilliant analysis of animal taste centered on dairy herds in Wisconsin, Katy Overstreet (2018) examines how Midwestern farmers and veterinarians use their own cultural and physical experiences of food ingestion to interpret and relate to cows' gustatory desires. The situation is slightly different with respect to cat palatants because the scientists who develop these commodities assume that they cannot biologically experience the same sensations as felines. In Roach's (2013) tour of a palatant lab, she sipped a vial of pyrophosphates and perceived only an off-tasting water.

9. Brad Weiss (2016), writing of heritage-breed pigs, thinks about the ephemerality of taste and efforts to stabilize it as outward expressions to build connections and relations through such sensations (such as discursive practices, a classic example being wine-tasting descriptions).

10. Hog lungs, or *lights* (as they were once called in the English-speaking culinary world), have been banned for sale for human consumption by the US Department of Agriculture owing to the difficulty of removing bacteria from their inner surfaces. In other places they are still consumed for food (think, for

example, of Scotland and haggis—a traditional preparation that is illegal in the United States).

11. One can imagine a whole array of factors that could make industrial pig lungs and livers starkly distinct across sites: breeds and genetic stock, the typical kill age of a given corporation's hogs, different feed ingredients and regimens, and perhaps even barn building and fan construction styles that circulate air and chemical vapors from pooled feces differently.

12. This is with the exception of one province in Canada and a few regions in Denmark. China raises the most pigs in the world by a good margin, though until recently the majority were on relatively small farms. It is undergoing industrialization as versions of the US factory-farm model are exported and remade in light of China's ecology and history (see Schneider 2015), and palatant companies appear to be following in their wake. A half dozen companies, in addition to BFG Essences, have relocated to this area of the Great Plains for unrestricted access to unique pig parts.

13. Brad Weiss (2016, 190) notes that, despite the text being about the taste of a peach, there is actually only a sentence or two that actually tries to describe what the *rodhákino*, or Breast of Aphrodite, tasted like.

14. This turns out to be a fascinating problem in ways we might not expect. Companies use electronic nose and tongue technology to try to get an "objective" sense of the taste of palatants and as a means of being able to describe tastes to owners (Beaton 2015). But the machines have been designed alongside human testing panels and perhaps do not pick up the same sensations as cats. The latter cannot biologically perceive sweetness, for instance (Roach 2013).

15. Moreover, they merge with the long history of pet food manufacturing, as a new chapter in what Molly Mullin (2007) has identified as a tendency to build value through appeals to the "wild" or evolutionarily ingrained qualities that remain "within" domesticated animals.

16. This is by no means unique to animal agribusiness. Think, for example, of the dizzying arrays of goods currently produced with various dimensions of wood or corn (Prudham 2005; Pollan 2006).

REFERENCES

AFB International. n.d. "Principles of Pet Food Palatability." Accessed October 4, 2021. https://afbinternational.com/wp-content/uploads/2019/03/Principles-of-Pet-Food-Palatability-re-brand-only-for-print-v3.pdf.

Beaton, Lindsay. 2015. "Palatability Technologies in the Pet Food Industry." Petfoodindustry.com, September 1, 2015. https://www.petfoodindustry.com/articles/5349-palatability-technologies-in-the-pet-food-industry.

Bennett, Jane. 2010. *Vibrant Matter: A Political Ecology of Things*. Durham, NC: Duke University Press.

Berman, Marshall. 1983. *All That Is Solid Melts into Air: The Experience of Modernity*. New York: Penguin.

Besky, Sarah. 2019. "Exhaustion and Endurance in Sick Landscapes: Cheap Tea and the Work of Monoculture in the Dooars, India." In *How Nature Works: Rethinking Labor on a Troubled Planet*, edited by Sarah Besky and Alex Blanchette, 23–40. Albuquerque: University of New Mexico Press.

Blanchette, Alex. 2020. *Porkopolis: American Animality, Standardized Life, and the Factory Farm*. Durham, NC: Duke University Press.

Boyd, William, and Michael Watts. 1997. "Agro-Industrial Just-in-Time: The Chicken Industry and Postwar American Capitalism." In *Globalising Food: Agrarian Questions and Global Restructuring*, edited by David Goodman and Michael Watts, 192–225. London: Routledge.

Brillat-Savarin, Jean Anthelme. (1825) 2011. *The Physiology of Taste: Or Meditations on Transcendental Gastronomy*. Translated by M. F. K. Fisher. New York: Vintage Classics.

Brulliard, Karin. 2017. "The Hidden Environmental Costs of Dog and Cat Food." *Washington Post*, August 4, 2017. https://www.washingtonpost.com/news/animalia/wp/2017/08/04/the-hidden-environmental-costs-of-dog-and-cat-food/.

Butler, Ella. 2020. "Producing Taste: Food Science and the American Sensorium." PhD diss., University of Chicago.

Choy, Timothy, and Jerry Zee. 2015. "Condition—Suspension." *Cultural Anthropology* 30 (2): 210–23.

Cowen, Deborah. 2014. *The Deadly Life of Logistics: Mapping Violence in Global Trade*. Minneapolis: University of Minnesota Press.

Cronon, William. 1992. *Nature's Metropolis: Chicago and the Great West*. New York: W. W. Norton.

de la Cadena, Marisol. 2015. *Earth Beings: Ecologies of Practice across Andean Worlds*. Durham, NC: Duke University Press.

Eiler, Brooke. 2015. "Digest versus Palatant: What's the Difference?" Palatants+, December 2, 2015. https://web.archive.org/web/20170821060722/http://palatantsplus.com/blog/digestvspalatant.

Grier, Katherine. 2010. "Provisioning Man's Best Friend: The Early Years of the American Pet Food Industry, 1870–1942." In *Food Chains: From Farmyard to Shopping Cart*, edited by Warren Belasco and Roger Horowitz, 126–41. Philadelphia: University of Pennsylvania Press.

Guthman, Julie. 2006. *Agrarian Dreams: The Paradox of Organic Agriculture in California*. Berkeley: University of California Press.

Hayden, Cori. 2012. "Rethinking Reductionism, or, The Transformative Work of Making the Same." *Anthropological Forum* 22 (3): 271–83.

Hetherington, Kregg. 2020. *The Government of Beans: Regulating Life in the Age of Monocrops*. Durham, NC: Duke University Press.

Jojola, Susan. 2016. "Flavor Variety: Does It Stimulate Intake in Kittens?" Palatants+, June 6, 2016. http://web.archive.org/web/20170916214434/http://palatantsplus.com/blog/flavorvariety.

Khatchadourian, Raffi. 2009. "The Taste Makers." *New Yorker*, November 23, 2009.

Lien, Marianne Elisabeth. 2015. *Becoming Salmon: Aquaculture and the Domestication of a Fish*. Oakland: University of California Press.
Martin, Ann. 2008. *Food Pets Die For: Shocking Facts about Pet Food*. Troutdale, OR: NewSage.
McMichael, Phillip. 2010. "Agrofuels in the Food Regime." *Journal of Peasant Studies* 37 (4): 609–29.
Meindertsma, Christien. 2007. *Pig 05049*. Amsterdam: Flocks.
Moore, Jason. 2015. *Capitalism in the Web of Life: Ecology and the Accumulation of Capital*. New York: Verso.
Mullin, Molly. 2007. "Feeding the Animals." In *Where the Wild Things Are Now: Domestication Reconsidered*, edited by Rebecca Cassidy and Molly Mullin, 277–304. London: Bloomsbury.
Nagodawithana, Tilak W., Lynn Nelles, and Nayan B. Trivedi. 2010. "Protein Hydrolysates as Hypoallergenic, Flavors and Palatants for Companion Animals." In *Protein Hydrolysates in Biotechnology*, edited by Vijai K. Pasupuleti and Arnold L. Demain, 191–207. New York: Springer.
Nast, Heidi. 2006. "Critical Pet Studies?" *Antipode: A Radical Journal of Geography* 38 (5): 885–1098.
National Hog Farmer. 2016. "New UltraCare Pig Creep Formula Supports Young Pig Performance." March 15, 2016. http://nationalhogfarmer.com/nutrition/new-ultracare-creep-feed-supports-young-pig-performance.
Nestle, Marion. 2008. *Pet Food Politics: The Chihuahua in the Coal Mine*. Berkeley: University of California Press.
Okin, Gregory S. 2017. "Environmental Impacts of Food Consumption by Cats and Dogs." *PLoS ONE* 12 (8): e0181301.
Overstreet, Katy. 2018. "How to Taste like a Cow: Cultivating Shared Sense in Wisconsin Dairy Worlds." In *Making Taste Public: Ethnographies of Food and the Senses*, edited by Carole Counihan and Susanne Højlund, 53–67. London: Bloomsbury.
Paxson, Heather. 2013. *The Life of Cheese: Crafting Food and Value in America*. Berkeley: University of California Press.
Pollan, Michael. 2006. *The Omnivore's Dilemma: A Natural History of Four Meals*. New York: Penguin.
Prudham, Scott. 2005. *Knock on Wood: Nature as Commodity in Douglas-Fir Country*. New York: Routledge.
Roach, Mary. 2013. *Gulp: Adventures on the Alimentary Canal*. New York: W. W. Norton.
Rosenberg, Gabriel. 2017. "How Meat Changed Sex: The Law of Interspecies Intimacy after Industrial Reproduction." *GLQ: A Journal of Lesbian and Gay Studies* 23 (4): 473–507.
Rosenberg, Gabriel. 2020. "No Scrubs: Livestock Breeding, Eugenics, and the State in the Early Twentieth-Century United States." *Journal of American History* 107 (2): 362–87.

Schatzker, Mark. 2015. *The Dorito Effect: The Surprising New Truth about Food and Flavor*. New York: Simon and Schuster.

Schneider, Mindi. 2015. "Wasting the Rural: Meat, Manure, and the Politics of Agro-Industrialization in Contemporary China." *Geoforum* 78 (1): 89–97.

Seremetakis, C. Nadia. 1994. *The Senses Still: Perception and Memory as Material Culture in Modernity*. Boulder, CO: Westview.

Striffler, Steve. 2005. *Chicken: The Dangerous Transformation of America's Favorite Food*. New Haven, CT: Yale University Press.

Sunder Rajan, Kaushik. 2007. "Experimental Values." *New Left Review*, 45:67–88.

Tsing, Anna. 2009. "Supply Chains and the Human Condition." *Rethinking Marxism* 21 (2): 148–76.

Tsing, Anna. 2012. "Unruly Edges: Mushrooms as Companion Species." *Environmental Humanities* 1 (1): 141–54.

Uexküll, Jakob von. 2010. *A Foray into the Worlds of Animals and Humans*. Translated by Joseph D. O'Neil. Minneapolis: University of Minnesota Press.

Weis, Toni. 2013. *The Ecological Hoofprint: The Global Burden of Industrial Livestock*. London: Zed Books.

Weiss, Brad. 2016. *Real Pigs: Shifting Values in the Field of Local Pork*. Durham, NC: Duke University Press.

Wolfe, Cary. 2012. *Before the Law: Humans and Other Animals in a Biopolitical Frame*. Chicago: University of Chicago Press.

Wrye, Jen. 2015. "Deep Inside Dogs Know What They Want: Animality, Affect, and Killability in Commercial Pet Foods." In *Economies of Death: Economic Logics of Killable Life and Grievable Death*, edited by Patricia J. Lopez and Kathryn A. Gillespie, 95–114. London: Routledge.

(in)edibility

ALEX BLANCHETTE /
MARIANNE ELISABETH LIEN

What is edibility?

We propose an ontological and political claim: human edibility is not a baseline feature of the material world. Based on Alex's interpretation of the industrialization of American hog lungs that precedes this interlude, and Marianne's ethnographic reflections on transformations from animal to edible that follow, we suggest that edibility—along with its allegedly constitutive opposite, inedibility—is a thresholding project: classificatory, social, cultural, physiological, and digestive. Hence, edibility is not an inherent property of things as such but the outcome of a heterogeneous process in which a substance's status as food and an organism's status as eater are mutually realized.

Edibility and inedibility are never given from the outset. As Alex's chapter shows, what is classified by the US government as inedible to humans (hog lungs) opens up as edible to cats (and is perfectly edible to human eaters in other countries, such as Norway). Then there are things that in themselves, or in their manner of cooking, become inedible to some but not to others. (In)edibility, then, is a situated, more-than-human sociality reflecting the minute details of proper relating, slaughtering, cooking, sharing, and consuming—which, in turn, mirror species-specific digestive systems as well as cultural distinctions.

In defining the nature of food, the commonplace contrast between edibility and inedibility is no minor distinction. The implicit assumption that "food" is defined as being edible *to humans*, we contend, frames the entirety of the world in terms of human appetites and can make all organic matter that is *not* consumed by humans appear to be a matter of unrealized potential. Consider, for example, the classic anthropological notion of food taboos. Its invocation tends to presume that *not* consuming some particular thing must reflect a concerted practice of avoidance. The avoidance of certain foods by certain people becomes an anomaly that merits ethnographic explanation. In this tradition the *in*edible becomes the locus of explicit thought and practice, while the multitude of subtle practices involved in making-edible are effectively concealed. Focusing on thresholds helps us notice how edibility is a constant and ongoing social achievement.

Rather than presume edibility/inedibility as a generalizing binary that encompasses all things, we also wish to make room for that which is neither one nor the other: we mobilize the notion of *nonedibility*. Many things in the world do not a priori register as either edible or inedible; they simply are—quite apart from consideration as food fit for humans. Glue (another by-product from pigs) would be an example, as are reindeer moss, haworthia plants, and fish pellets. Evoking nonedibility, we wish to call attention to a world of "food-in-the-(un)making" in which the vast majority of flora and fauna are, in fact, entirely overlooked, dismissed as irrelevant to the realm of human ingestion.

In the chapter on intensifying cat food flavorings (chapter 3) and in chapter 4 on making social persons through everyday forms of eating in the rural landscapes of North Norway, we trace the coemergence of the edible and the inedible. Banning human ingestion of lungs opens up the pig to relations with new kinds of eaters, such as house cats. In a reindeer corral, the muscles and fat of an injured, dying calf are made into desirable meat by the skilled process of separation from stomach acids, bile, and excrement. The edible and the inedible are made together; edibility carries inedibility as its shadow companion, and vice versa—while both require concerted effort to be summoned from the unremarkable mass of things in the world overlooked as nonedible, not registering as potentially ingestible at all. Such processes invariably involve hegemonies of power that define the world. Examples include recent mass-market efforts to expand the category of "meat" protein to encompass the bodily tissues of insects or lizards—or, conversely, agribusiness-driven legal efforts to ban the label for plant proteins or laboratory-grown mammal cells. They can involve concealment, fraud, and choice as well as persuasion, belonging, and celebrations of identity. Our cases exemplify these possibilities, and they show how the making of (in)edibility is social, even when it is done in your own kitchen and even when it involves other-than-human species, such as reindeer, cloudberries, cats, or hogs.

While we insist that edibility is a multispecies achievement, subtly accomplished during every act of eating, this should not be taken as a celebratory gesture. A fully edible world, where everyone consumes everything in its totality and there is no "waste," is not the ideal that some would insist. First, although edibility, as we have argued, is a social achievement, it is not as if anything goes. Digestive tracts display their own kinds of thresholds, by expelling what has been served or failing to properly transform it into life-sustaining nutrients. Hence, when farmed salmon are now fed pellets made of soy, there remains a threshold determining how far the soy/fish balance can be pushed before compromising the salmon's health. Second, as we may ask in relation to industrial pig lives: How problematic is a world where every gram of substance is given some kind of value and consumed in some way, where nothing is marked off as simply being? While the Finnmark landscape is productive and not at all scarce, it is still a landscape that is maintained by what is *not* consumed, as that which does not pass through social circles and stomachs.

We should not regard the world as all latent substance just waiting to be made edible. Such a voracious ontology would imply that everything that is not productively consumed in a way that is legible to humans would count only as a waste of lost calories, nutrients, and dollars. Instead, we should be attentive to the potentials of edibility's apparent others: the inedible, the weedy nonedible—and all of the many things that people, for whatever reason, refuse to consume, or even fail to notice as potentially edible, as well as the work it takes to make other such items cross the threshold of edibility. In this way, we may avoid Eurocentric assumptions about what passes for food and might even learn to better appreciate multispecies relations that do not have human consumption as their ultimate end.

chapter four

Becoming Food

EDIBILITY AS THRESHOLD IN ARCTIC NORWAY

MARIANNE ELISABETH LIEN

ACTS OF EATING NOURISH RELATIONS, MATERIALIZE SOCIAL DIFFERENCES, and maintain cultural norms, as foods are effective vehicles for negotiating the boundaries of what is acceptable. These are well-known insights from food studies, yet the implications of such axioms remain underexplored, as the study object "food" is often taken for granted. How does food emerge in the first place? How do entities recognized as food come into being in the lively fabric of life?

This chapter explores a set of moments when entities become food, or when they shift from being food to becoming something else. As I pay attention to these shifts, I also invite the reader to let those generative moments linger, because it is precisely at such moments, when things are not yet edible or edible no longer, that significant transformations occur. Such moments highlight food and eating as sites of interspecies encounters, heterogeneous assemblages through which various sets of relations are stabilized and reaffirmed. Analyzing such moments as *thresholds* allows us to consider how food comes into being in situated and relational practices and helps bridge the gap between approaching food as a social signifier and approaching food as a material substance.

Anthropological studies of food and eating are drenched with meaning as a topic of scholarly concern. One implication of this is that one may easily overlook how a conceptual category, such as food, is itself the outcome of situated practices and specific ways of shaping worlds. In this chapter I suggest that food is itself an arbitrary way of stabilizing worlds so that, once it is done, it renders the process of coming into being invisible (Blaser and de la Cadena 2019). Hence, while interpretative approaches to food and meaning provide important insight, they rarely question food as such, what it is and how it comes into being. This chapter is an attempt to pay attention to the latter by drawing on interpretative ethnography as well as on material semiotics (Law 2004).

This chapter starts from the premise that food does not exist outside the practices that make it so. Rather than looking for the meaning of terms, or objects, I draw attention to the situated practices through which they come into being (Yates-Doerr 2015, 319). I approach practices involving food and eating not merely as the representation of a taxonomic essence (ethnicity, gender, occasion, and so on) but as processes through which the very categories of "food," "eater," "relation," and "social person" take form and are enabled, challenged, and maintained.[1] The status of food as edible and the status of a person as an eating subject are thus mutually constituted through practices of eating. The concept of *thresholds* is mobilized to discern the various practices that are involved in stabilizing and negotiating boundaries, such as that between edible and inedible.

A common concern in culturally oriented food studies is how sensual experiences of taste become public (e.g., Counihan and Højlund 2018). I shift the attention to how the boundaries between insides and outsides are negotiated and maintained between private and public, edible and inedible, or in the maintenance of social groups, and how such boundaries are enacted through practices of, for example, slaughtering, eating, giving, and receiving (see also Vialles 1994; Weiss 1996; van Daele 2018).

Thresholds, as Amy Moran-Thomas notes (this volume), call bodies into question. Similarly, they call food into question and draw attention to the transformation of "animal to edible," the fleshy practices transforming, as I will elaborate, a reindeer calf into an evening snack, or a leftover filet of cod into an inedible substance. Meat is of particular interest in this context, because, as anthropologist Noëlie Vialles (1994) has elaborated, it is shaped in moments that conjure thresholds of living and dying and in relations of one body being "given over" to another. The notion of being given over serves here as a reminder that life and death are shifting states that unfold in various relations to each other. Hence, "given over" facilitates a shift from the Maussian gift exchange to relations that are not so clearly reciprocal and less reliant on circuits of return (Cohen 2013; see also Solomon, chapter 5). The purposeful slaughtering of an animal with the intention of producing meat creates one such relation, but it is not the only way in which the occurrence of death in one body sustains life in another. Hence, as we shall see, the making of meat—and the making of relations such as kin—can involve enactments that vary from that of being "given over" to that of "giving away."

The ethnography that follows is from Varanger, a northeastern peninsula in Finnmark, North Norway, and spans three decades of ethnographic engagement.[2] Finnmark is both part of Sápmi, denoting the Indigenous parts of Fenno-Scandinavia, and part of the Norwegian nation-state. At the latitude of northern Alaska, and characterized by permafrost and low summer temperatures, parts of this region are also considered to be Arctic. The population has historically been diverse, with many languages spoken (Sámi, Norwegian, Finnish, Russian, and Kvæn), and with migratory patterns of subsistence. During the late nineteenth and much of the twentieth century, Indigenous minorities (Sámi, Finnish, and Kvæn) were subject to harsh measures of Norwegianization, including stigmatization of the Sámi and the denial of Sámi ancestry, widely recognized today as a political and cultural scandal (Østmo and Law 2018; Lehtola 2019; Lien 2020). The recognition of the Sámi as an Indigenous people and the creation of the Sámi parliament in 1989 are a political response to that scandal, but "continued state-mediated pressures on Sámi land-related practices" still persist (Østmo and Law 2018, 358).

I am interested in how the circulation of fish, cloudberries, and reindeer flesh—as well as culinary advice and acts of eating—constitute relations between people as well as between people and landscapes. The culinary materials are affordances of the local landscape and seascape that can be harvested, picked, fished, or caught (Lien 2001). Attentive to how edibility is performed, I focus on eating, sharing, and naming, asking how such practices can make or unmake food as a category. I detail moments when (in)edibility is performed, as dead bodies, plant material, and living beings are constituted as food through practices that engage thresholds of accessibility, of identity, and of edibility and thresholds of life and death. These are often intertwined, but I will describe them separately, starting with access and accessibility.

Thresholds of Accessibility: The Cod on My Doorstep

February 1985. The wind from the Barents Sea was ice cold, and darkness still filled most hours of the day. I had arrived in Båtsfjord, a fishing village on the Varanger coast, a few weeks earlier. From my window I could see trawlers approaching the harbor with catch for the processing factories. But the only fish accessible in local stores was frozen fish sticks mass-produced by Findus. "You get your [fresh] fish at the factories," people told me. "But give them a call first, to make sure they have it ready for you."

I began to make phone calls, but there was always a problem. Sometimes the trawler had just arrived, and they were too busy. Other times they had just left. After a couple of weeks, I told a woman I had just interviewed about my bad luck. She got up and made a quick phone call. When I returned to my flat, I found a bucket full of freshly gutted cod at my doorstep, expediently delivered by taxi from one of the processing factories where her husband happened to work.

The cod at my doorstep became my entry into a network of food exchange that was unfamiliar to me as a Norwegian "southerner." I was grateful for this sign of social recognition that the fish might imply, and analytically intrigued by this gesture toward a world of food reciprocity so strikingly Maussian (Mauss [1954] 1991). What sort of relations might this cod speak to, and what sort of community had I, by this token of generosity, been included within? What was expected in return? The cod at my doorstep became my dinner but also an ethnographic moment inviting further analysis. I learned that giving and receiving food are key modes of sociality in Finnmark but also a practice that differentiates, enacting subtle boundaries and hierarchies (see Lien 1989, 2001; Kramvig 1999).

Much analytic effort has been spent decoding the category of the gift at the expense of materials themselves, their temporalities, and the more-than-human relations they embody or from which they emerge (Ingold 2011, 20). Fresh cod is highly perishable and must be dried, salted, frozen, cooled, or otherwise preserved, or find its way to somebody's kitchen more or less immediately. Sharing the catch of the day with kin and neighbors made a lot of sense when small-scale fishing was common and industrial processing less developed than it is today. It can also be seen as a social investment in a situation of precarity. Access to food is a way to secure access to a good life.

In hindsight, I think that my attempts to make the cod in the bucket "speak" were too insistent. Today I would rather see the cod as *an enabler*, a gesture that would allow me to begin to play, if I was so inclined, like a first dealing from a deck of cards when the rest is open ended. As for relations, the woman hardly knew me. This was not the beginning of a long-lasting friendship, and I think it was never meant to be.[3] But over the years other relations have emerged and become stronger. Food gifts are still abundant and are an important part of the social interaction in Båtsfjord.

Cod is caught at sea; its availability depends on fishing boats and hence on one's relations to those who work onboard or in the local fish-processing industry. In this way, while it is abundant at sea, cod is also experienced by some as a scarce resource. Cloudberries, on the contrary, are mostly available to anyone who is willing and able to pick them during the summer season. Picking berries is time intensive but generally does not require any special gear other than an able body. How, then, does gifting berries differentiate? What do *they* speak to?

Thresholds of Accessibility: "God's Chosen and Those Worthy in Need"

I never left Hanna's house empty-handed. Even when she was old and frail, she insisted on giving me something. Usually it was a tin of frozen cloudberries. I knew that someone would have picked them for her and that her regifting might gradually deplete her precious supply. When, on one of my last visits, she fetched yet another tin of berries from her freezer, my first impulse was to suggest that she should save them for another occasion. Cloudberries are precious gift items. As a local saying goes, "Cloudberries are for God's chosen and those worthy in need" (Herrens utvalgte og verdig trengende). But I had also learned that the gift of cloudberries was not so much about our relation as about her, a woman still capable of passing cloudberries on to a guest. Rather than a gift with an obligation to return, the cloudberries were more like a relay item, situating both of us in a network of food gifts that has woven people and places together across differences and across generations. They are orange-red and bittersweet, and their taste evokes the warmth of the sun and the abundance of marshes in the mountains nearby. The only appropriate thing to do with Hanna's cloudberries was to be grateful and accept, which I did.

There were many women like her in the village, women whose persistent eagerness to share became a key marker of their way of being in the world.[4] Some "had elderly" whom they gave to. The recipient would typically be seen as "worthy in need," but their neediness was tactfully silenced. Often the gift was disguised, by transforming it into a request for a favor: "My husband caught such a lot of pollock this morning, can you please take some?" or "I had so much leftover cake yesterday, could you help me out so it doesn't go to waste?" Such practices of giving reflect differentiated access and affordances, and express how people's lives have been intimately connected to food-procuring practices at land and at sea. For women of the older generation, cloudberries, haddock filets, and fresh-caught fish weave people together, performing *their* way of belonging through local affordances. Skilled practices of procurement are themselves enacted as the food is given away. Thus, when Hanna gives me cloudberries, she inscribes herself—and me—in a landscape that she knows well but that she can no longer sense directly. References to marshes and hillsides are not explicit, but it is as if they linger in the gift itself, as a haunting or a longing, reflected in our shared appreciation of the berries' preciousness. This is not an instance of "making taste public" but a subtle and highly gendered mode of being in the world that is recognizable across much of this region and that cuts across ethnic distinctions, so that what Hanna does, as a Norwegian-speaking woman, is not very different from what a Sámi-speaking woman might do.

Thresholds of Identity: Shifting Notions of Being Sámi

When I first conducted fieldwork in Båtsfjord in the mid-1980s, none of my friends identified as Sámi, and I was told that there were practically no Sámi-speaking people in Båtsfjord (see also Eidheim 1969). I later learned that some of those who identified as Norwegian when I met them would have spoken Sámi when they grew up (for details, see Lien 2020).

Around the turn of the twentieth century, state policies of colonization erased Sámi place-names from maps and silenced Sámi speakers so that many of the postwar generation learned to be monolingual, without access to the Sámi language that their parents or grandparents spoke (Helander 2004). During World War II, Norway was occupied by the Nazis. As a result of the Nazi military tactic of scorched earth toward the end of the war, in 1944, and the annihilation of entire villages along the North Norwegian coast, fifty thousand people were forcefully evacuated. This brutal uprooting of an entire population caused a serious setback in the region but paradoxically also created opportunities for stigmatized Sámi to "remake themselves" as Norwegian when they returned and to take part in the rebuilding of villages according to Norwegian ideas of progress (Lien 2020). Hiding traces of Sáminess, many people stopped speaking Sámi and never taught their children their mother tongue.

Can practices of knowing exceed the words that capture them? Might the practices of picking and sharing cloudberries offer a way of belonging that transcends the rupture, and the muting of a mother tongue? Whether Hanna grew up as Sámi is something I will never know. But many others did, and many would engage in coastal subsistence practices that were more or less the same across ethnic distinctions. Perhaps it is not so surprising, then, that the Sámi language enacts realities that are, in some ways, more appropriate than the Norwegian words that we actually spoke.[5]

One such Sámi term is *meahcci*, a concept that is related to place, movement and use, seasons, and affordance in the landscape. It is described as "a landscape where the natural resources are found" (Schanche 2002, 163) but also as "a densely textured and changing network of identity sustaining and respectfully negotiated long-term movements and encounters between lively, morally conscious, and often powerful human and nonhuman actors" (Østmo and Law 2018, 358). Various prefixes specify *meahcci*'s affordances so that, for example, *luomemeahcci* refers to the place you pick cloudberries, *guollemeahcci* is where you may fish, and *muorrameahcci* is the place you chop wood (Rybråten 2014, 81; Schanche 2002). In this way, *meahcci* captures the landscape not as passive foil but through the active engagement of knowing people and animals that together constitute the land as resourceful. The Norwegian vernacular variably denotes such areas as wilderness, nature, or *utmark* (literally, "outfields"), in contrast to *innmark* ("infields"), which denotes the fields of the sedentary farmer. But the Sámi term *meahcci* exceeds such distinctions. It bears witness to entanglements of persons, animals, stories, and plants that constitute the landscape as valuable at any given moment, in a place where the division between nature and culture makes little sense. Hence, *meahcci* cannot be disentangled from practices and affordances that secure viability for humans and nonhumans; it is fluid and multilayered (for details, see Ween and Lien 2012; Joks, Østmo, and Law 2020).

Meahcci also points to various thresholds of accessibility that are at work simultaneously. With this in mind, we may see how it is precisely the practices of procuring-receiving-giving that constitute certain food items as precious, and how relational practices that facilitate their mobility constitute persons as well as food. The following ethnographic example adds further nuance to accessibility through its focus on thresholds of life and death. We move from the coast to a mountain plateau, an area designated as and for a reindeer-herding *siida*, and to people who mostly identify as Sámi.

Thresholds of Life and Death: Enacting Meat through Practices of Separation

The sound of reindeer hooves against the sand fills the air, and occasionally we hear the deep murmur of a female reindeer calling out for her calf. We are outside the wooden fence of the reindeer corral where people have gathered to help mark the calves. Such annual gatherings include those who are reindeer owners through kinship relations to this particular *siida*, and sometimes their children or immediate family.[6] Inside the corral, female reindeer and their calves run around in large circles. A dozen people are gathered in the middle, the owners of distinct "reindeer marks" and their family and friends. They are here to identify their calves and to provide them with an earmark (a distinguishable cut) and a green tag with a number, signifying the calf's relation to a specific human owner and its registered identity in relation to the Norwegian state.[7] Calves are being grabbed by the horns and held until someone else arrives and helps push them to the ground, squatting over their backs, to hold them still so that they can perform the cut and tag the mark on the calves' ears. Some days earlier, the calves were equipped with number plates around their necks, and their mothers were spray-painted with a colored number. Since then, people have spent many hours observing the calves' and their mothers' bonding behavior in order to identify their respective parental relations. Such observations are noted on a written list that then connects calves and their human owners (the owner of a female reindeer that gives birth is also by default the owner of its offspring). Hence, every time a calf was caught in the corral, a person called out its number and the first name of its proper owner, who would then immediately step in and mark his or her new calf.

But the operation can be harmful. Occasionally, the calf is held too forcefully, and the horn breaks. If the fracture is close to its head, the calf will suffer and is therefore slaughtered on the spot. One day when I was watching, this occurred twice. Each time, Anders, the leader of this *siida*, was called on to remove the calf from the corral. Once outside, he cut its throat immediately, left it to bleed, and performed an emergency slaughter soon after. I had brought a camera, and as things happened quickly, I switched to video. The snippets of film were no more than a few minutes each, but they have allowed me to notice details that constitute the transformation of lively animal into edible meat in some detail.

Below is a description based on these film snippets. The people involved are Anders and two boys aged approximately ten and fourteen, whom I refer to here as the younger and the older boy. Anders left it to the two boys to take care of the calves and to ensure that they bled out properly. I describe the unfolding events in detail, because they display a set of interrelated practices at the threshold of life and death, of animal and edible.

SCENE 1: BLEEDING THE CALF AND CUTTING THE HEAD OFF

A reindeer calf lies on its side, bleeding from its throat, occasionally kicking its feet while one of the boys pushes its rib cage and shoulders to the ground. Blood runs slowly onto the grass. The boys take turns holding it steady until the spasms subside and the pool of blood grows bigger. The other boy calls out, "Look! Shall I show you how to get more [blood] out?"[8]

He lifts the calf's head, and more blood is released from its throat.

A few minutes later, Anders returns with a small knife. He squats by the calf's head and makes a cut along the length of the throat, down to the chest, and then he cuts the windpipe and esophagus at the throat, pulls them out, and hands them to the older boy, saying, "Hold this!" Meanwhile, the young boy touches the ribs while he comments on the possibility of poo inside the calf's stomach, giggling at the thought. Anders makes a cut from the calf's nose toward its ear. As the calf's neck is cut open, a greenish substance appears, and the young boy shouts, "What is that yucky stuff there?" The older boy explains that it is the stomach acid, stomach contents, adding, "Isn't it, uncle?" while the young boy repeats that it is disgusting!

Anders ignores his comment, continues to cut around the throat of the animal, and explains, "I just have to stop this stuff getting into the meat, you see." The young boy responds, "Yes. Since we want meat, don't we!" When the calf's head is released, Anders bends its jaw backward, picks up the knife, and makes a precise cut that releases the tongue. He places the tongue on top of the calf's head and returns to the corral.

During the course of just a few minutes, several thresholds are engaged. First, there is the uneasy transition from life to death. The calf's throat is already cut, but spasms require that the boys hold it down while they ensure that it bleeds properly; and with this bleeding, life ebbs too. As they perform this task, they experiment with the forces of gravity. They calmly watch the blood cover the ground while the kicking subsides. The moment of death is neither marked nor mourned.

Discomfort occurs when the young boy notices the green substance. It is not until the contents of the calf's stomach are exposed that he shouts out that this is yucky. But the sense of disgust is partly settled when the older one names the substance, offering a more precise term (stomach acid, stomach contents). Anders's additional explanation that he is trying to stop the green substance from getting into the meat seems to settle the matter, and these two moves of classifying and then naming the purpose of the ongoing separation (performed by the knife) are significant here. Anders performs an act of physical separation, and it is at this very moment—when the green stomach contents are physically separated from the rest of the carcass—that the calf's flesh is verbally designated as meat. At this point, the young boy's feeling of disgust is replaced by acceptance, and he exclaims, "We want meat, don't we!" With the expression "*we* want meat" he associates the meat not only with his uncle but with an unspecified group. The reference to people wanting meat comes almost as a release; through his verbal enacting of the animal's purpose as food, the preceding acts of bleeding and cutting and exposing disgusting substances make sense to him. But what sort of "we" is enacted?

SCENE 2: RELEASING INTESTINES—NEARLY BECOMING MEAT

A few minutes later, another calf has been bled, and Anders is back with a much bigger knife. He has turned the other calf over on its back and opened its hind legs so that the lower part of the stomach faces upward. Squatting over it, he makes a cut around the anus and genitals. Then he sticks the tip of the knife carefully into its abdomen just below the ribs and slowly makes a straight cut through the hide and skin toward the anus. The older boy sits next to him, holding the calf's hind leg. Anders cuts again around the genitalia, releasing muscles and tendons so that the hind legs open up more, and the skin is pulled back, revealing grayish intestines. Then he places the knife on the animal's hind leg and reaches into the animal's stomach with both hands and grabs hold of the intestines. Anders notices the knife resting on the calf's leg and hands it to the young boy, who takes it, but then the older one takes it away from him. The young boy turns around and says to the older one, with a smile, "I know how to hold a knife!"

In the meantime, Anders has released the intestines from the body and placed them on the ground next to the calf. He grabs one of the hind legs and says to the young one, "Here, hold the foot!" whereupon the boy picks up the calf's hind hoof, pulling it slightly so that the cavity opens up again while his uncle continues to cut tendons and skin around the hind legs. The young boy looks at his uncle's big knife and says, "Look at that slaughter knife!" whereupon the uncle replies, "It is a Finnkniv, this one."

As the knife passes from the young boy to the older one, a certain hierarchy is established between the boys, but not without some resistance from the young one, who insists that he knows how to hold a knife. Anders asks him instead to help hold the calf's hind leg. As the boys admire the slaughter knife, Anders names the knife as is commonly done in Finnmark: "Finnkniv," or "Sámi knife." In this way, he also instills a sensibility in the young boys about a certain categorical identity, a Sáminess.

In the next scene, the designation of the dead calf as meat becomes solidified, and the reindeer is transformed into food. Through acts of sharing and through culinary evocations, the calf passes the final threshold from inedible to edible.

SCENE 3: ENACTING MEAT THROUGH SHARING

Suddenly another voice is heard; a young woman has arrived, and she asks Anders, "Can I take a head?" Anders responds, "Yes! It is best when it is boiled. You can ask uncle. He likes to boil heads. Just take it."

The young woman asks if she should take the tongue as well, and Anders replies that, yes, she can take it. The woman responds, "I fried tongues yesterday. This one is so small. It is just enough for a piece of bread. An evening snack."

In the meantime, Anders has separated membranes from the inner organs, and reaching inside, he releases another large, red chunk of offal. Then he calls out again to the young woman, who is here with a friend: "Would you like to try liver? Liver is the best."

Meanwhile, the older boy gently touches the foot of the calf, placing his hand in the cleft between its two toes and cuddling them slowly. Anders cuts the remaining membranes that connect the liver to the body, lifts up the liver, and hands it to the woman and her friend, saying, "Here, take the liver, and then you can cook it on sticks over the fire."

The young woman, who has been standing behind him, watching, with the calf's head in her right hand, now receives the liver with her left hand, while Anders turns back toward the calf. Another woman says that she has seen her dad do that, and Anders adds, "I have done that many times. On a fire." The woman giggles and says, "OK!"

Still busy cutting the calf, Anders suggests that she should throw it on the barbecue, and the young woman then calls out to the group that has gathered around them: "Shall we make a fire tonight and do that?"

Anders adds, "Sliced! Finely sliced!"

While Anders gives culinary instructions, he lifts up another chunk of offal; cuts it apart, letting the remains fall onto the ground; and says to a man who has just arrived, "Here, hold this." The young boy asks, "Is that the heart?" Someone confirms, and the boy responds, "Aren't you going to dry the heart?"

There is no answer, and in the meantime, Anders lifts the calf's hind legs, while the older boy takes the front legs, and together they carry it over to the side and lay it down, gently. Someone inside the corral calls out the name of the man who is currently holding the calf's heart, and asks him to come over to help out. He replies, somewhat reluctantly, "Robert is not doing anything. I am doing something!"

The young boy shouts, "It is something. It is a heart that he is holding!"

The last scene shows how separate chunks of flesh and offal are distributed to various people and thus repurposed as food. Until someone asked to have it, the tongue and the liver were part of the calf's dead body lying on the ground, not yet distinguished from what would soon be discarded as waste. But as soon as a woman expressed an interest and related having fried a tongue the night before, Anders proposed other culinary practices, such as barbecuing liver over the fire and slicing it thinly. Together they enacted the dead calf, not only as generic meat but as a culinary delicacy. In this way, the animal became edible, literally, as Anders grabbed ahold of various inner organs and identified them by name.

Shortly afterward, we see the young woman smiling, liver in one hand and a calf's head in the other. It appeared that this was not a trivial experience for her but an occasion to be incorporated within a setting and a kind of commensality that was slightly out of the ordinary, hence the culinary instructions. Not unlike the cod on my doorstep, the liver in her hand can be seen as an invitation to engage in relational practices that weave a sense of community in and around what we may think of as *meahcci*.

Anders is happy to share these delicacies with her, but he is also concerned that relatives who have inherited the right to own a reindeer mark through their *siida* family relations are properly socialized. They may be somewhat inexperienced in relation to life in the reindeer corral, but they should at least learn what it is about and learn to appreciate and respect this way of life. The reindeer marking can be seen as a semipublic event that offers ample opportunities for this kind of "passing over" of knowledge and skills. Anders appears to be mindful of this and performs his role well.

The unexpected casualty at the reindeer corral offers a glimpse into the becoming of food at the threshold of life and death. It also introduces a third and final dimension, which concerns the practices of separating animal from edible.

Food is enacted through practices. These may be material acts of separation, such as when intestinal content is separated from muscles, or a when liver is released from an injured calf's body. But they may also be verbal expressions, speech acts, that perform the substance as a potential food gift or a delicious snack when barbecued over the fire. The transition is not inevitable: it takes work, it calls for manual as well as classificatory and culinary skills, and it is a collective endeavor involving mutual confirmation at each step. In this way, it can be interpreted as an example of "making taste public," in the sense that taste is produced "in our communication, through our hands and craftsmanship, in our sharing of values and activities" (Counihan and Højlund 2018, 3). Through these examples we see how the threshold between inedibility and edibility is indeed ambiguous and negotiated, and continuously enacted and acted on.

Unlike common slaughter, this instance of killing was hardly planned. The dead animal was a casualty, and the act of killing was justified by reference to the animal's anticipated suffering. Its transformation to meat was not obvious; instead, the meat emerged almost as an afterthought, as a way to ensure that the animal would not be wasted. The following day, when I visited Anders in his summer camp, two calf hides were nailed to a wall to dry, while meat had been hung inside the *lavvu* (a temporary dwelling supported by several wooden poles; these structures are often placed next to houses and used for various activities such as smoking meat), where a fire made with salix branches had been burning for hours. Over the next few days, several visitors would be offered a piece of smoked calf meat to take home. The unplanned slaughter and the subsequent transformation from animal to edible allowed new connections to be made, as the various parts of the calves' bodies were distributed across a wide geographic area.

Industrial slaughter typically occurs out of sight, invisible, characteristically escaping the attention of consumers and eaters (Vïalles 1994; Blanchette 2020). The process is a linear logical chain of intention, action, and effect, and its destined eaters are anonymous. In the case described here, the meat was enacted through relations of sharing, relations of the *siida* and of the *meahcci*. The calf literally became edible as it was given away, and simultaneously, by that token, it enacted Sámi relations and traditions.

The two final examples concern how edibility can be negotiated through modes of preparation and through the act of eating. Let us return to the coast and a meal that took place many years ago.

Culinary Thresholds: Preparation as (Failed) Enactment of Edibility

It was a sunny afternoon, and we had made a bonfire behind an old farmhouse in the abandoned village Syltefjord that now served as a recreational home for weekends and holidays. We barbecued sausages over the fire, but as the refrigerator also contained boiled cod from the day before, I suggested we could wrap it in tinfoil and heat it over the fire, so that it would not go to waste. My friend thought it was a good idea. But when her elderly father realized what we were about to do, he objected. This was clearly not how cod should be prepared, in his opinion. We argued that there is nothing wrong with heating cod over the fire, just as we would with char, trout, or fresh salmon. But the old man was skeptical, and as we began to eat, he dismissed the fish with an expression of disgust.

"*Ufesk*," he said.

"*Ufesk?* This is not *ufesk*; it is cod," his daughter insisted.

But the old man refused to even taste the tin-wrapped parcels of cod from the barbecue. Clearly, to him the content was inedible.

Ufesk is a term in North Norway that refers to all the fish in the sea that one would not want to eat and was commonly used in the 1980s (less so today). Literally translated as "unfish," it stands in opposition to the fish species that are edible, which are also referred to by specific names (cod, haddock, pollock, salmon, and charr). When something unexpected is caught, categorizing it as *ufesk* is a way of saying that it is inedible. It does not need to be named or classified according to any species taxonomy. It just needs to be disposed of.

In the 1980s the boundaries of *fesk* and *ufesk* were frequently negotiated. Some people had begun to name a few of the species previously referred to as *ufesk*, and their potential edibility had become a matter of conversation. The two most common were catfish (*steinbit*) and monkfish (*breiflabb*), which had recently made their way onto the menus of fish restaurants in cities such as Tromsø. But for most people in Båtsfjord, these were still *ufesk*.

In the preceding example, the transformation from edible cod to inedible *ufesk* was not about species categorization but about modes of preparation. While *ufesk* is a generic category for all species of fish that are seen as unsuitable as food, my friend's father mobilized the term to mark what he saw as an unacceptable way of *preparing* this particular fish. For him, barbecued charr would be acceptable, whereas cod should be steamed. It does not belong on a barbecue. The example shows how species categories are fluid and depend on divisions and practices other than conventional taxonomic schemes. As

Emily Yates-Doerr (2015) shows in her ethnography from highland Guatemala, meat can take ontologically diverse forms. The preceding example underscores her more general point: that species classification does not refer to a naturally ordered essence but is rather "an occurrence of coherence situated amid ever-transforming divisions and connections" (309). Hence, for a cod to remain cod after death (and not become *ufesk*), certain culinary practices are called for. My suggestion to place it on the barbecue was clearly not among them.

In the example from the reindeer corral, acts of separation followed by anticipated culinary transformation, and the act of giving away, enacted the dead calf as meat. In the case of the reheated cod, it is precisely the culinary preparation that *strips* the fish of its edible potential and thus of its identity as fish (*fesk*). It is reverted to the category of the unnamed, the "unfish" that are, by definition, inedible.

The final example introduces a further nuance to the thresholds of edibility, suggesting that edibility can also be enacted nonverbally through the act of eating.

Thresholds of Consumption: Eating as Enactment

The soup was made with broth from the head of a freshly caught salmon and seasoned with garlic, chives, a few carrots, and cream. I thought it was delicious, and so did my friend. I had prepared it in her kitchen; as a young ethnographer and frequent houseguest, I was often referred to as "the housemaid." Fish soup was usually not made this way in Båtsfjord in the 1980s, and salmon would not normally find its way into soup. But today it was dinner, and my friend, her husband, their two children, and I had gathered around the table. We chatted but not about food. Then my friend asked, "So how do you like the soup?"

The question was for her husband, who was more reluctant to try new things than the rest of us. Perhaps it was also a way of bringing some explicit appreciation to the table, an acknowledgment of my efforts to cook them a meal.

There was no answer, just the sound of spoons full of soup lifted, then swallowed. Her husband continued to eat, while she repeated the question. He remained silent, continued to eat, and then reached for a second helping. Once again, my friend posed the same question, adding that he "could at least say something."

Slowly, almost reluctantly, her husband began to form a sentence: "It is," he said. "It is . . ." We waited while he searched for the right word. "It is edible" (Den er etandes).

And then he looked down and continued to eat.

The vernacular phrase *etandes* (edible) is a colloquial term in the North Norwegian dialect that captures not only digestibility but also a sense of quality in a context in which the taste of food is often not subject to much verbal elaboration (Lien 1989). His response was not a dismissal of the soup, nor was it impolite. I see it now as the awkward encounter between two modes of valuating, or qualifying, food: one that relies on a verbal repertoire of descriptive signifiers, another enacted nonverbally through bodily practices, such as eating. The former was my way; the latter was his, but also the way in which most families, and especially men in this region, would acknowledge their appreciation of food in the 1980s: appreciation in the act of eating, but no words, no further gestures than what the embodied performance of appetite can reveal.

Talk happens, of course, and especially among women with a special interest in food, such as my friend and me. For months we had enjoyed cooking together, and she had taught me difficult things like making savory fish cakes, baking lefse, and salting a leg of lamb. Gradually, she had also become familiar with my more verbalized approach to food and adopted it, to some extent, amid our practical tasks. But her husband was not very interested in our kitchen practices. Suddenly pushed to express appreciation in a mode he was not used to, he was reluctant to respond. With his final response, "It is edible," he gave in to his wife's expectation that he would "say something," and yet his statement was only an affirmation of what he had enacted all along (and emphasized through his second helping): the soup was edible—it was *etandes*. It was, quite simply, food. Whatever we had done in the kitchen was less important than the result: it was edible, and his act of eating was his preferred mode of confirming this and thus of enacting edibility at that moment. His brief verbal response ("It is edible") can be seen as a way of meeting us halfway: a compromise that recognizes the social need to acknowledge the cooking skills of the visiting anthropologist-housemaid but that simultaneously refuses the ontological shift that any other verbal response would imply.

The word *edible*, *etandes*, can be seen as a gatekeeping device, policing the threshold of what is acceptable as food and what is not. Such boundaries shift; new items have been gradually added to the domain of edible food. My point is that in addition, and only *partially connected* to such changes in food habits, another shift was taking place: a shift between different modes of acknowledging, or valuing, food, that is, from nonverbal to verbal modes of acknowledgment (Lien 1989; see Heuts and Mol 2013 for a related discussion).[9] The difference is related not only to which items get classified as food but also to the modes through which food is enacted ontologically.

In an analysis of connections between taste and place in Sámi food activism, Amanda Green (2018) draws attention to how the taste of reindeer fat, although highly appreciated, is only vaguely articulated among her research participants. She points to what she calls a "fat-vocabulary vacuum" (2018, 174) and cites Amy Trubek, who argues that "taste evaluations must occur through language through a shared dialogue with others" (Trubek 2008, 7, quoted in Green 2018, 174). She then suggests that the notion of terroir, a notion clearly recognized among her interlocutors, though only vaguely articulated, could be strategically deployed in asserting Indigenous (Sámi) rights to their lands. While I sympathize with her intention, I disagree with the stated premise that taste evaluations must occur through language. If food is habitually enacted through nonverbal practices that simultaneously perform a range of *other* socially and culturally significant relations, there is a risk that increased verbalization, rather than enhancing the valuation of reindeer meat, could imply an ontological shift that would in fact weaken the assemblage that such meat relies on in order to come into being. Indigenous rights are not only about rights to territory and clever marketing but also about ontological sovereignty.

In Båtsfjord in the 1980s, a small emergent "chattering class" of local urbanized foodies were already quite adept at verbalizing local taste distinctions. But beyond this fairly small group, a different mode of ordering was (still) at play, one that was hardly verbal at all. Eating and sharing meals were rarely associated with verbal descriptive appreciation or valuation of food, as this seemed unnecessary or inappropriate. How, then, were judgments shared? How was "taste made public" (Counihan and Højlund 2018)?

As I have suggested, food was enacted through the act of eating. A few times, when some kind of qualification had to be made in advance and at a distance—such as when preparing for a trip to the Canaries, for example—the word *edible* (*etandes*) was mobilized.[10] As a proxy for the act of eating, the term *etandes* ensured that friends and family would navigate successfully through the confusing isles of Spanish grocery stores, accessing what was needed to enact a proper meal. As edibility defines food, it also orders the lively world of living beings that occasionally end up on a plate. These examples speak to how edibility is enacted at the threshold of eating; more precisely, they concern edibility as relational practice, through a nonverbal medium of bodily ingestion.

Concluding Remarks

A study of food and eating practices can be epistemological and interpretative, with "food" as a category defined a priori, questioning how shifting connections between "food" and "people" affect the cultural dimension of both, asking, for example, how different people know, perceive, or attach meaning to various foods. But it can also be ontological, in which case the very category of food is unstable from the outset. This approach facilitates an understanding of how eating both transcends *and* marks boundaries between food and self, and between the inside and the outside of human bodies and social persons. While the ethnographic snippets in this chapter lend themselves to both modes of analysis, I have leaned toward the latter. Rather than assuming that food exists a priori as an element that may transcend cultural boundaries, I have argued that both food and persons are constituted through the act of eating. I have focused on how the act of eating and the process of becoming edible enacts food as an ontological entity.[11]

Our reliance on a language that distinguishes humans from nonhumans, landscapes from their affordances, and human identities from practices makes it hard to avoid an analysis in which agency is distributed beforehand, skewed toward the human as an acting subject. It makes it hard not to imagine landscapes' affordances as if they were already there for the taking, ready to be mobilized for various life projects. But there are other options.

In Finnmark, where many food gifts are procured from and through what Sámi speakers might call *meahcci*, the local valuation of gifts reflects an appreciation of skills involved in their procurement and the effort it takes to bring things home. Perhaps, if we consider the act of giving and receiving in light of the fluidity and flexibility inherent in this concept of *meahcci*, we might be able to shift our analytic habits too, transcending the sharp separation of giver and recipient and of *meahcci* and food. Perhaps we may consider the possibility that the frozen cloudberries, the codfish in the bucket, and the freshly cut reindeer tongue are not first and foremost "food" that is subsequently "gifted" by and to certain "persons" but rather practices of procuring–receiving–giving away that constitute these "foods" as edible *and*, simultaneously, the "givers" and "recipients" as socially significant persons. We may notice how the relations that allow things to travel constitute people as significant beings in a world where boundaries among people, things, landscapes, and affordances are less sharp than conventional analysis tends to make them.

Just as *meahcci* cuts relations differently, we may imagine that the acts of eating, giving, and receiving cut worlds differently too. "Enacting food through eating" is a way of pointing to *other* relations than those conventionally associated with culinary valuations. Instead, we may notice relations that seamlessly connect the practices of procurement, preparation, and digestion in ways that weave together the land; the people involved in the making, giving, or receiving; and the foods thus performed. Just as the act of giving and receiving can confirm or dismiss relations as socially significant, the act of eating (or refusing to eat) confirms or dismisses some things as edible while implicitly validating, or acknowledging, the many relational practices that brought them to the table in the first place.

As we have seen, the process is not smooth: barbecuing the wrong fish, failing to separate stomach contents from the reindeer meat, or refusing to receive a tin of cloudberries may disrupt relations, stop the flow, or rearrange the order of things in ways that undercut edibility and thus unmake potential mutual relations of valuing and sharing. In this perspective a local culinary repertoire that may seem somewhat narrow to an outsider turns out to be not narrow at all. Instead, it draws attention to relations other than mere taste, to the rich unfolding of the many connections and relations that include *meahcci*, relations, and seasonal affordances. Food emerges, then, neither as "tradition" nor as "eating habits" but as heterogeneous assemblages through which the world and "nearly everything" in it may be negotiated, enacted, performed, or dismissed.

ACKNOWLEDGMENTS

I wish to acknowledge the generosity and creativity of participants at the panel at the Oslo Food Conference in 2016, where these ideas were first presented. Special thanks go to Wim van Daele for convening the conference and to Heather Paxson for her leadership of our panel and for very valuable comments to an early draft. As always, I am grateful to people in Finnmark for generous sharing of all kinds, including food, friendship, knowledge, and ideas.

NOTES

1. The argument in this chapter draws on material semiotics. Another way of saying this is that if a statement about something (naming bread as food, for example) seems straightforward, then this is "because most of the assemblage within which it is located has been rendered invisible" (Law 2004, 88).

2. My first long-term fieldwork in this region was in 1985. Except for recent ethnography from the reindeer corral, most of the ethnography is from the 1980s. All persons are anonymized.

3. Later I learned to access fresh fish myself. I skipped the phone call that would reveal my Oslo dialect and walked directly to the factories. As I tried to ignore subtle sexual remarks from fishermen outside the factory building, I learned the emic term for fishing luck that was said to follow sexual intercourse (*hail*) but also learned always to bring a plastic bag (how else can you carry the fish back home . . .). I further learned that such skills were not shared by everyone. The obstacles experienced by newcomers in acquiring fish locally were significant.

4. Hanna sent parcels of fish filets to visually impaired people. She had met them at the regional hospital, where she had learned of people who have to eat fish with their fingers for fear of swallowing a fish bone. Having worked at the fish-processing factory, Hanna took pride in her excellent bone-picking skills. Now retired, she purchased haddock and cod from local fishermen, carefully removed every tiny bit of bone, froze parcels of filets, and sent them by mail to recipients all over Norway.

5. There are many terms that resist translation, including *siida* and *meahcci*. I am thankful to Solveig Joks, Liv Østmo, and Mikkel Nils Sara for discussions. For a discussion about Sámi words and translations, see Østmo and Law (2018); Joks, Østmo, and Law (2020).

6. According to the Norwegian Reindeer Husbandry Act, the *siida* is defined as "a group of reindeer owners that practice reindeer husbandry jointly in certain areas" (Sara 2011, 138). However, as in the case of *meahcci*, *siida* is also a concept that transcends English and Norwegian distinctions between the social and the natural. According to reindeer herder and Sámi scholar Mikkel Nils Sara (2009, 2011), *siida* can refer to a specific area, a corporate group, a set of family relations, a form of governance, a way of engaging specific affordances, and a migratory herd of reindeer. Reindeer herding is characterized by active engagements in relation to their reproduction and seasonal migration across great distances. In short, a *siida* can be thought of as a territorial, economic, and social unit, or as a socio-ecological system associated with nomadic and seasonal reindeer herding. According to Sara, a significant dimension of the *siida* continuity is the knowledge that can be transmitted from one generation to the next through the *siida* processes of adaptation to local surroundings, anchored in practices *in place*.

7. The information partly overlaps, as everything can be found in the state registry. But earmarking is also traditional Sámi practice, and even though the physical cut may seem superfluous, reindeer owners I spoke to insisted that an earmark was necessary in case the green tag got lost.

8. Anders speaks Sámi fluently, and the boys are fluent too. On this occasion many people who did not speak Sámi were present, and Norwegian and Sámi were spoken interchangeably. The verbal exchange surrounding the slaughter was spoken mainly in Norwegian.

9. Frank Heuts and Annemarie Mol (2013) touch on this when they describe eating as one of the many different performative formats that valuing (food) can take. The point I wish to push here is slightly different: I suggest that the different formats that are presented (and that constituted a more general shift in Båtsfjord at the time) were not about differences in "valuing food" but speak to *different ontological enactments of food as such*. The soup, in other words, was not established as food prior to being consumed. Contrary to Heuts and Mol, who based their study on interviews about tomatoes in the Netherlands and who suggest that the act of valuing tomatoes through eating simultaneously "finishes them off," I argue that rather than "finishing it off," the act of eating constituted the soup as food in the first place.

10. The word for edible—*etandes*—was also used when confronted with strange and unfamiliar items. For example, when planning a trip to the Canary Islands (a common tourist destination), women in their fifties and sixties would advise less experienced travelers through references to the food available there in relation to its being "edible." Potatoes, they said, were *etandes* in the Canaries. Certain cuts of lamb would be *etandes* too. Fish, on the other hand, was questionable and often not edible in this part of the world. Some planned their holiday menu in advance and brought nonperishable ingredients in their suitcases, such as *bokna fesk*, a semidried cod that can easily be transported and stored. The idea that one might see the experience of culinary difference as an additional attraction seemed irrelevant.

11. That it simultaneously enacts people as sociable, or reluctant, participants around the table, or the reindeer corral, and thus confirms relations of affinity and belonging, is a point that is made repeatedly in studies of food and eating. These enactments take place in my examples too, but I have chosen not to elaborate on these aspects here.

REFERENCES

Blanchette, Alex. 2020. *Porkopolis: American Animality, Standardized Life, and the Factory Farm*. Durham, NC: Duke University Press.

Blaser, Mario, and Marisol de la Cadena. 2019. "Introduction: Pluriverse: Proposals for a World of Many Worlds." In *A World of Many Worlds*, edited by Marisol de la Cadena and Mario Blaser, 1–23. Durham, NC: Duke University Press.

Cohen, Lawrence. 2013. "Given Over to Demand: Excorporation as Commitment." *Contemporary South Asia* 21 (3): 318–32.

Counihan, Carole, and Susanne Højlund. 2018. "Making Taste Public: An Ethnographic Approach." In *Making Taste Public: Ethnographies of Food and the Senses*, edited by Carole Counihan and Susanne Højlund, 1–11. London: Bloomsbury.

Eidheim, Harald. 1969. "When Ethnic Identity Is a Social Stigma." In *Ethnic Groups and Boundaries: The Social Organization of Culture Difference*, edited by Fredrik Barth, 39–57. Bergen: Universitetsforlaget.

Green, Amanda S. 2018. "Reindeer Fat and the Taste of Place in Sámi Food Activism." In *Making Taste Public: Ethnographies of Food and the Senses*, edited by Carole Counihan and Susanne Højlund, 169–84. London: Bloomsbury.

Helander, Kaisa R. 2004. "Treatment of Saami Settlement Names in Finnmark in Official Norwegian Place Name Policy." *Diedut* 30 (3): 102–19.

Heuts, Frank, and Annemarie Mol. 2013. "What Is a Good Tomato? A Case of Valuing in Practice." *Valuation Studies* 1 (2): 125–46.

Ingold, Tim. 2011. *Being Alive: Essays on Movement, Knowledge and Description*. London: Routledge.

Joks, Solveig, Liv Østmo, and John Law. 2020. "Verbing *Meahcci*: Living Sámi Lands." *Sociological Review* 68 (2): 305–21.

Kramvig, Britt. 1999. "Ære og verdighet, kvinnelighet og mannlighet i et fiskerisamfunn" (Honor and dignity, femininity and masculinity in a fishing village). In *Globale Kyster: Liv i endring, kjønn i spenning*, edited by S. Gerrard and R. R. Balsvik, 63–77. Universitetet i Tromsø, Norway: Kvinnforsk.

Law, John. 2004. *After Method: Mess in Social Science Research*. London: Routledge.

Lehtola, Vela-Pekka. 2019. "Evasive Strategies of Defiance—Everyday Resistance Histories among the Sámi." In *Knowing from the Indigenous North: Sámi Approaches to History, Politics and Belonging*, edited by T. H. Eriksen, S. Valkonen, and Jarna Valkonen, 29–47. London: Routledge.

Lien, Marianne Elisabeth. 1989. *"Fra bokna fesk til pizza": Sosiokulturelle perspektiver på matvalg og endringer av matvaner i Båtsfjord, Finnmark* ("From *bokna fesk* to pizza": Sociocultural perspectives on food and changes of food habits in Båtsfjord, Finnmark). Oslo Occasional Papers in Social Anthropology 18. Oslo: University of Oslo.

Lien, Marianne Elisabeth. 2001. "Likhet og verdighet: Gavebytter og integrasjon i Båtsfjord" (Equality and dignity: Food gifts and integration in Båtsfjord). In *Likhetens Paradokser*, edited by Marianne E. Lien, Hilde Lidén, and Halvard Vike, 86–109. Oslo: Universitetsforlaget.

Lien, Marianne Elisabeth. 2020. "Dreams of Prosperity—Enactments of Growth: The Rise and Fall of Farming in Varanger." *Anthropological Journal of European Cultures* 29 (1): 42–63.

Mauss, Marcel. (1954) 1999. *Gaven: Utvekslingens form og årsak i arkaiske samfunn* (The gift: Forms and functions of exchange in archaic societies). Oslo: Cappelen.

Rybråten, Stine. 2014. "'This Is Not a Wilderness. This Is Where We Live.' Enacting Nature in Unjárga/Nesseby, Northern Norway." PhD diss., University of Oslo. https://www.duo.uio.no/bitstream/handle/10852/40947/PhD-Rybraaten.pdf?sequence=1&isAllowed=y.

Sara, Mikkel Nils. 2009. "Siida and Traditional Sámi Reindeer Herding Knowledge." *Northern Review* 30:159–78.

Sara, Mikkel Nils. 2011. "Land Usage and Siida Autonomy." *Arctic Review on Law and Politics* 3 (2): 138–58.

Schanche, Audhild. 2002. "Meahcci—den samiske utmarka" (Meahcci—the Sámi outfield). In "Samiske landskap og Agenda 21: Kultur, næring, miljøvern og demokrati," edited by Svanhild Andersen. Special issue *Diedut* 1:156–70.

Trubek, Amy S. 2008. *The Taste of Place: A Cultural Journey into Terroir*. Berkeley: University of California Press.

van Daele, Wim. 2018. "Food as the Holographic Condensation of Life in Sri Lankan Rituals." *Ethnos* 83 (4): 645–64.

Vialles, Noëlie. 1994. *Animal to Edible*. Cambridge: Cambridge University Press.

Ween, Gro, and Marianne Elisabeth Lien. 2012. "Decolonization in the Arctic? Nature Practices and Land Rights in the Norwegian High North." *Journal of Rural and Community Development* 7 (1): 93–109.

Weiss, Brad. 1996. *The Making and Unmaking of the Haya Lived World: Consumption, Commoditization, and Everday Practice*. Durham, NC: Duke University Press.

Yates-Doerr, Emily. 2015. "Does Meat Come from Animals? A Multispecies Approach to Classification and Belonging in Highland Guatemala." *American Ethnologist* 42 (2): 309–23.

Østmo, Liv, and John Law. 2018. "Mis/translation, Colonialism and Environmental Conflict." *Environmental Humanities* 10 (2): 349–69.

giving

MARIANNE ELISABETH LIEN /
HARRIS SOLOMON

How might one access a gift? In Marianne's preceding chapter, we are struck by how things left at the doorstep (fish) or in the hands of others (berries) offer no easy clues about either giver or receiver nor any clarity about food's translation between obligations and offerings.

Lawrence Cohen, in an essay titled "Given Over to Demand," writes of circulations of flesh and body parts, via blood transfusions and organ donation, for which ideas about exchange, in India and elsewhere, might require a shift from "the gift" to "the given over":

> To write of a gift places the subject in some kind of elementary structure, *pace* Mauss and Lévi-Strauss, an erotic triangle (Sedgwick 1985) with an inevitable return, in several senses, to the donor. To write of that which is given over is to acknowledge that we are often confronted, as we work to specify situations in the world, with a particular genre of ethical scene (Cohen 2010): a body is given over, to another, in a way that remakes its being or horizon. One is asked to attend less to a position or relation than to a kind of release. (Cohen 2013, 319)

Cohen's framing of the given over challenges us to inquire about the moral and value economies of edibility rather than to assume we know their terms in advance. If animals and humans are given over, then it is more difficult to track circulations from eater to eaten, or from feeder to fed. This is a productive uncertainty, we think, because it challenges us to ask what kind of releases might be happening, materially and ethically, as food moves.

We see imprints of such releases in our own work. We notice this as meat becomes available in butchering, in the context of relations of Sámi worlds that connect reindeer herds, their people, and the areas they cross through migration. In Marianne's analysis, a sense of given-over reindeer bodies appears as accidents happen, horns get broken, and wounded calves get their throats cut. As a calf bleeds and life ebbs out, the act of giving over repurposes its heart, liver, and flesh so that instead of a life being wasted, a dying body becomes food. Marianne describes how various organs are offered to relatives so that "the calf literally became edible as it was given away."

The calf is not killed to be eaten. It is killed to be saved from pain, but the moment is not defined by one purpose only. There are multiple outcomes. This connects to the Mumbai trauma ward, where Harris watches ventilators move and halt between seriously ill or wounded people. Here one person's death while attached to a ventilator becomes the possibility of another person's potential move away from death toward recovery and more life. This is because in India's public hospital intensive care units, a steady supply of working machines is not guaranteed. Ventilators concentrate the ways a person is given over to life, even though skirting death entails so much more than the ventilator, in terms of medicine and all the other inputs that trauma demands.

The ventilator and the reindeer calf might seem to be odd interlocutors, but in thinking them together we discover shared themes of presumed relief and the transmutation of life toward different purposes. In their juxtaposition the examples invite us to slow down as ethnographers and to appreciate the multiple outcomes of any given moment. Putting things to use *for someone else, for something else*—giving life over to demand—does not mean, necessarily, that the actions that land someone or something at a transitional threshold always have giving over in mind as an aim. Facilitating someone else's life through one's own death is rarely in anyone's personal script, just as the accidental injury of a reindeer calf has nothing to do with dinner. But accidental incidents and unanticipated moments might change the course of events, suggesting new possibilities or potentials, new "ethical scenes," as Cohen suggests. This means that we cannot easily assume that giving over is a celebratory or redemptive move, that feeding someone else with a dead animal, or resuscitating person B with now-dead person A's ventilator, is the sign of a fractured world's piecemeal realignment. We remain deeply ambivalent about access to things given over. We also remain compelled to think more openly through passages through life that may not appear purposive or heroic or conservational.

Referring to the patients in the Mumbai trauma ward, Harris quotes Alphonso Lingis: "Death appears as a deliverance from dying—from the suffering of dying" (2000, 111). These words also capture the human feeling of relief as the throat of the reindeer calf is cut, relieving the animal's pain. Yet its legs occasionally move, in spasms, while a boy cuddles its tiny hooves. We are reminded that death is not an obvious moment but rather that it unfolds as a sequence of events, often in irreversible order, anchoring the temporality and performativity of death and dying. Worlds apart, a Mumbai trauma ward and a reindeer corral come together in shared human concern over death and dying and for the insights offered about the threshold between life and death.

Our materials further invite us to consider thresholds between bodies and their surrounding media—air, as in breathing, and food, as in eating. The life-sustaining actions of breathing and eating are closely intertwined, reminding us of how life is sustained by and through substances (food, air) that mediate between the inside and the outside of living bodies. If we view these substances as media, we see how they channel between worlds. We notice their dual capacity as both a means of transmission and mediators between worlds (inside, outside). Following Cohen, channeling can remake ethical horizons. This perspective draws our attention to the fragility of life, and to death as an ever-present possibility, a potential threshold of being given over.

REFERENCES

Cohen, Lawrence. 2013. "Given Over to Demand: Excorporation as Commitment." *Contemporary South Asia* 21 (3): 318–32.

Cohen, Lawrence. 2010. "Ethical Publicity." In *Ethical Life in South Asia*, edited by Anand Pandian and Daud Ali, 253–74. Bloomington: Indiana University Press

Lingis, Alphonso. 2000. "To Die with Others." *Diacritics* 30 (3): 106–13.

Sedgwick, Eve Kosofsky. 1985. *Between Men: English Literature and Male Homosocial Desire*. New York: Columbia University Press.

chapter five

On Life Support

....

HARRIS SOLOMON

THE PRESENCE AND THREAT OF DEATH MAKES LIFE SUPPORT DISTINCT from more everyday forms of feeding meant to cultivate life-force qualities and banal pleasures (Farquhar and Zhang 2012). Surely, death is forcefully pedagogical (Parry 1985; Copeman and Quack 2015). But so, too, are the acts that precede and evade death. I take a cue from ethnographers who discuss how death is *in* life (Chua 2014; Stevenson 2014) and who work through threshold moments between the two domains. Resuscitation acts, their ethics, and their materializations as feeding shed light on broader issues about the connections between food and life.

This chapter takes up the problem of life support in the context of an emergency trauma ward in Mumbai, India, in moments of tracheal intubation and mechanical ventilation. I demonstrate how being on life support is a form of being on life thresholds, and I explore this form of medical resuscitation across both its successes and its failures in trauma cases caused, largely, by traffic accidents. The chapter engages breath as a critical substance and examines the acts of feeding and withdrawal that mechanical ventilation demands. In what ways do the substances of life and life itself overlap, and to what ends? To answer this question, the chapter makes two key claims. First, I explain how breath is a critical feature of embodiment, which renders ventilation a process of interest to food studies scholars interested in ways the body is "both enfolded in and enacted by encounters between food and care" (Abbots, Lavis, and Attala 2015, 10). I have argued elsewhere that the grounds of metabolic life are realized as the politics of absorption (Solomon 2016). The case of ventilation shows us that in addition to absorption, processes of resuscitation—and their embodiment—are equally crucial to metabolic politics.

Second, and related, I show how breath is part of death's possible approach and how life's valuation takes shape through breath at its limits. This effort is in conversation with Didier Fassin's (2015, 770) discussion of the need for "the anthropology of lives." Fassin explains the need to conceive of life "that is not biological but physical": "from life as an object of science to life as the matter of existence, delimited by birth and death—life as it is lived by human beings" (772). He poses an anthropology of living, an endeavor beyond an anthropology of life as rendered through the biosciences. The explanatory distinction of this shift, Fassin suggests, is a biopolitics that better accounts for craggy social landscapes wherein moral equipoise is often/always made impossible and the hills and valleys of life's valuation take shape as disparities in health and viability. For Fassin, it is crucial to apprehend "how physical life has been apprehended as social life" (772). How can ethnography find analytic and narrative mooring in "physical life" in situations where it is possibly at its end?

This chapter takes up an examination of *breath* as such a mooring, considering it through different formations: of dying (one's final breath), of breathing (an indication of having life), of resolving mysteries or letting them just be, of the chest rising and falling. At stake is the challenge of working outward from dioramas of injury that appear in the hospital ward—through the wounds, through their experience, and through dying and resuscitation and thriving as they are shot through with those fields we gingerly separate out as physiology, political economy, ethics, and intimacy. Between the ventilator and the person it supports, certain questions emerge: What kinds of constrictions and expansions of life does breath make evident? When inhale and exhale would seem to mirror each other in some moments and blur in others, does ethics materialize in the flow of the breathing tube (Abrahamsson et al. 2015)?

The principal argument of the chapter is that scenes of resuscitation are instructive for addressing these questions when artificial ventilation is the grounds for life. I begin by situating the problems and possibilities of ventilation in the broader contexts of injuries that make life support necessary. I then turn to the trauma ward's intensive care unit (ICU), where scenes of ventilation unfold. I describe the processes and substances entailed in intubating patients, that is, what it takes to *produce* ventilation. In the section that follows, I analyze the problems involved in *removing* ventilation, in the case of weaning patients from artificial life support, and the politics of euthanasia that this process conjures up. The chapter's conclusion reflects on these findings in light of broader questions about the relationships between care and life.

Feeding across Lifelines and Deathlines in Mumbai

Resuscitation as a medical term has a constellation of everyday and textbook meanings. Its primary semantic force derives from the meaning of its Latin root: "to rise again." Or, to make alive what was close to death. It can align with a sense of inflation: to lift by means of air. In the air, through the breath, resuscitation brings someone away from death and toward life. Breath is given *and* taken away. Throughout, life support creates present and future problems of care—this even as it most certainly edifies life and can right some of the physiological wrongs of injury. On a ventilator the mechanisms of a traumatic injury's cause and redress settle into context and can sometimes quiet a bit. The accident that brought a patient to the ward can recede from view, and in the foreground each breath matters. In the ICU, breath stages that context for patients, their families, and the medical staff circulating around them.

A dense set of material metaphors about food string across the utter normalcy of the injuries in the trauma ward in Mumbai. When I tell neighbors or friends in the city that I study traffic accidents, they express little surprise. Death and injury from traffic accidents are banal matters and are integral to public cultural forms like films, songs, and jokes. Food glues together some of these everyday sensibilities about death and injury. Food also offers semantic resources to reconcile death and injury with the social rhythms of daily life. A motorcycle enthusiast recalled witnessing a motorbike skidding on the pavement and tumbling the driver along with it, the driver's face skidding for hundreds of meters on the asphalt and "becoming like *kheema*," or minced meat. Faces can be erased in the moment of accident, dissolved into meat. This example is hardly exceptional in the space of the public hospital casualty ward. And metaphors of meat are hardly exceptional as ways of bodily knowing. Cuts of meat, as Emily Yates-Doerr and Annemarie Mol (2012) have detailed, have a capacious semio-material force. The grotesque and the culinary are often in close relation, and the trauma ward—a place where amputated hands and feet make a regular appearance—is shot through with these relations too. Humor and trauma go hand in hand (Nelson 1999). To ask about feeding in the context of breath is to ask about what obligations substances create, how obligations form, and how they devolve.

Mumbai is a city both famous and infamous for its gridlocked traffic and has the highest number of "accidental" injuries in India. Intense vehicle-to-vehicle collisions are low because of slower speeds, but the number of vehicles colliding with pedestrians and motorcycles is very high. Consequently, injuries are the primary cause of death for men ages fifteen to twenty-four in India (Roy et al. 2010, 2011). Traffic as gridlock relates directly to traffic as movement. Clogged streets compel many residents to take the aboveground train system, which offers faster transit times but at considerable bodily risk. Mumbai's municipal and suburban railway system is among the busiest globally, carrying 7.6 million passengers daily (Mumbai Railway Vikas Corporation 2013). The railways are known as Mumbai's *lifeline*—an English word used across vernacular languages. It is a material metaphor that describes well how the north-south rail line moves life through the island city; further, this appeal to vitality helps us understand how Mumbai folds into India's broader history of colonial and postcolonial development through the railways (Kerr 2003; Bear 2007; Prasad 2013).

In Mumbai, as in many settings in India, to move through space is to move across thresholds of living and dying. Movement (such as commuting or, in longer arcs, migration) is necessary for life for many. But movements can overlap in the form of collision. On the street or train platform and into the hospital ward, collision can be labeled as an "accident" (*hadsa* in Hindi, *apghat* in Marathi, *aksident* in Mumbai's colloquial Hindi dialect). Once an injured person is in the hospital, oxygen is a critical substance for understanding how severe a trauma case might be. A person's systemic blood oxygenation levels and systolic blood pressure help medical staff assess a case. If the patient cannot breathe properly on their own, they will be ambu-bagged: a manual ventilation bag mask will be applied to their mouth to supplement necessary oxygen. It is often the relative accompanying the patient who does the compression and release of the Ambu-bag, or, sometimes, it is the orderly. The anesthetist will take over in moments, but she is often busy preparing for the next alternative to establish an airway: intubation.

Resuscitation is not just one thing; it is many different kinds of movements—movements made in a distinct political economy of resources. In this ward the shuttling back and forth of air, from bag to lungs, occurs in the context of restricted resources. The ward has fourteen beds but only (at last count) nine mechanical ventilators that work. A young man from the company that manufactures the ventilators is constantly in the ward, opening up the bodies of the machines and rewiring them. Despite his efforts, it is one of the basic tenets of the ward that there is not enough supported breathing to respond to the demands of trauma cases. The death of one patient on a ventilator means the possibility of giving ventilator support to another person. These movements from the dead to the still living, and from giving up hope to providing it, can all happen quickly in the ward's complex ventilator economy. And there are in-betweens: if a ventilator is not available and a patient needs support, ambu-bagging will certainly be done. There is a time-frame issue, though. India's present euthanasia laws require that once placed on a ventilator, a patient must stay on until she is able to breathe on her own, or until doctors assess that the person is dead. Even if the family wishes for life support to be withdrawn, doctors cannot dial down the oxygen unless the patient is understood to be clinically dead, with multiple careful protocols followed to assess brain stem inactivity in place. Put simply, doctors cannot make a ventilator available to another patient if it is already connected to a breathing person. Only a dead or recovered patient can make it available. If the mechanical ventilator's offerings of recovery and life are to be understood as a form of nutritive power, the machine's economies raise the issue of availability—and unavailability—in thinking about what sort of biopolitics emerge in their presence (L. Cohen 2001, 2004; E. Cohen 2009; Cooper 2009; Crowley-Matoka 2016).

Air also sets the terms of resuscitation's failure. When a patient dies in the trauma ward in Mumbai, a doctor often tells the next of kin, "He expired" (expire *ho gaya hai*). There is a medical and colonial holdover here, semantically; the British English utterance of *expire* here means death (Latin *ex-*, "out" and *spirare*, "to breathe"). Colonial medicine's lasting imprint in India has kept the word *expire* in vernacular languages, most certainly so in Mumbai, where a negotiated combination of Hindi and Marathi with a peppering of medical English glues together everyday communication in the hospital ward. It can cause confusion at times. Once, a trauma resident told a woman that her husband "expired ho gaya hai," that he had expired. "Expired, matlab dead?" (Expired, meaning dead?), she asked. For the woman, both words, *expire* and *dead*, meant death, but in that moment of absorbing its truth, one English word borrowed into Hindi cemented the reality of another.

Veena Das (2015) has detailed at length the indelible imprints of the clinical in urban Indian everyday family life. I observed these imprints in the municipal government hospital too, because the movements of cases in the municipal trauma ward are made up of kin relations, formal and informal. For patients, the presence of relatives in the ward causes certain reverberations of home life. For example, mothers and elder siblings can exert enormous influence by reminding nurses that the IV drip is finished or that their charge is still waiting. Their advocacy is its own demand for motion. The division between home and clinic can thereby be rescripted. At the same time, makeshift or fictive kin relations can emerge in the ward among extended kin, friends, neighbors, and iconic community figures such as police. These figures by no means stand in equal positions of authority. Police have vested forms of power, and among patient relatives, power works through gendered and kin structure lines. Kinship has force well beyond patients and families. Among ward staff, kin categories name and give structure to hierarchies of power. Male orderlies (ward boys) are called *mama* (elder maternal uncle); female sweepers (janitors) are called *maushi* (maternal aunt); female nurses are called *sister*, and male nurses *brother* (a colonial holdover).

Doctors may determine when death is certain, but it is the nurses who certify a death for the hospital because they are in charge of patients' paperwork. The nurse will enter a death into the ward's "Death Book" in red pen, along with standardized data: time of admission, time of expiration, the putative cause of the injury, the presence or absence of relatives at the moment of death, and confirmation that doctors have sent the body for postmortem (which is required by law for trauma cases, which are medico-legal cases). In the trauma ward, the cause of death, marked in the Death Book by the Greek letter delta, is almost always one of three types: RA (Railway Accident), RTA (Road Traffic Accident), and Fall. Such causes of death appear in all forms of records: in the Death Book of the ward, in the ward's registry, in the hospital's central medical record, in the ledgers of the mortuary, and on pink index cards that are tied to the crossed wrists of a dead body once it has been cleaned by staff and nurses in the ward. Technically, this conflates the mechanism of injury with the cause of death. A penetrating trauma to the chest from a road accident is the mechanism of injury, and hemothorax (the accumulation of blood in the pleural cavity) is the cause of death. But in the Death Book and, importantly, in conversation and discussion, the accident itself is likely to be the cornerstone of death. *Expiry* is generally the last word, from the hospital's standpoint and indeed from the standpoint of the state.

Staff and doctors often return to matters of breath when they engage patients. If a patient had undergone surgery in the emergency operating theater (as many did) before lying in the ICU and then dying, doctors would have urged them to breathe in moments of induction (the beginning of surgical anesthesia for paralysis and sedation) and also when the surgery is complete and the patient comes to. One anesthetist was known for his "calming" approach: "Take a good long breath" (acchha lamba sans le lo), he'd coo to the patients like a parent attempting to usher a baby toward sleep, except this was in order to usher the patient out of the sleep of anesthesia and toward the threshold of recovery in the awake world. Before the final expiration of death, then, many exhales have occurred, but they occur in a landscape of uneven possibilities for taking the next inhale.

Feeding Time

It is feeding time in the trauma ward ICU. Trauma patients cannot survive on breath alone. Solid nutrients must also be fed to them. The ICU is attached to the resuscitation area of the ward ("resus") and to the emergency operating theater. In the ICU a nursing student doing her practicum pulls at a nasogastric tube, a tube that goes into a person's nose, down the throat, and into the stomach for mechanical feeding. The end of the tube outside the body is attached to a syringe. She pours a yellow goop, mostly liquid, down a small funnel, into the syringe barrel. She holds the tube vertically to allow gravity to do its work. She feeds according to orders. A nutritionist has visited this ward and for each patient has scribbled out a concoction of nutrients. Other nursing students will collectively do this work five times a day for the patient, feeding him a mixture of buttermilk, salt, albumen powder, coconut oil, sugar, and the water that results from soaking *dal* (lentils) and rice. Air has previously dried the raw materials; now they will be rehydrated in water. The nutritionist has totaled the amount of calories, protein, fat, and carbohydrates that the "prescription" entails; if ingredient substitutions have been made, the nursing student will recalculate the formula. The powders come from a medical shop, procured by a relative of the patient. If, as is often the case, the patient has no available relatives, a small supply of protein powder and other nutrient supplements are available in the ward's stock area. This patient, a fifty-year-old man, watches the nursing student's gravity work. Down the well it goes. He gurgles a bit.

Next to him, another fifty-year-old man in the ward owing to a traumatic accident begins with a similar gurgle, but his sound is sharper than his neighbor's. Beeping drowns it out. His ventilator has sounded an alarm. He is gurgling for air. He cannot breathe. He coughs, bucks. The endotracheal tube that connects him to the ventilator is coming up, out of his trachea, out of his throat, out of his mouth. Its ends have been taped to his face with bandages; this is how you keep the tube in place. But he is extubating, for reasons unknown. The alarm alerts an anesthesia medical resident. This is her first week in the trauma ward, one of numerous rotations she will do throughout the hospital's varied ICUs. She looks at the vitals monitor attached to the man—the digitalization of his life signs. The concentration of oxygen in his blood (SpO_2) is dropping. He cannot breathe. The thing that was supposed to feed the man air, the ventilator, is no longer properly connected, now that the endotracheal tube is not where it should be. The circuit of resuscitation has been broken. Airways are channels constrained or enabled and become a problem of affordances (Keane 2014; Abrahamsson et al. 2015).

How might we understand the synergies and disjunctures of these two forms of substance provision, one called *feeding* and the other called *ventilation*? One way is to assess the act of provision itself. As Margaret Lock (2002) has detailed, the development of artificial respiration ("breathing machines") entailed different types of machines and, in turn, different types of bodily envelopment and force over time. First there was the iron lung of the 1930s that encased the body and allowed the lungs to expand by applying negative pressure to the chest. Later iterations in the 1950s and their descendants today are called *ventilators* and stand as bedside monitors. A tube down the trachea has replaced the body in the machine. Positive pressure replaces negative pressure. The machine forces air into the breather, rather than the other way around. Lock traces this history to set the stage for her own study of the onset of organ transplant technology, for it was the development of a category of persons diagnosed with "irreversible coma" that helped cement twentieth-century transplant technology. Lock observes, "Technology is indispensable not only for supporting the respiration of critically ill patients but also for feeding them, administering medication, and monitoring body functions" (2002, 61). In the North American settings studied in *Twice Dead*, feeding and technology connect metaphorically and materially.

The anesthetist attempts to reestablish that circuit. She must intubate the man again. She yells for the orderly to bring an intubation tray equipped with a laryngoscope for visualizing and opening the airway. The alarm continues to beep; the *mama* flicks off the ventilator. The warning sign on the screen reads "circuit fault," but that fades to black as the machine powers down. It is a distraction in this moment. The job of the anesthetist is to establish an airway, a path between the world outside the body and the body's interior. This pathway is not a given in trauma patients. It is made. She stands behind the man's head, her eyes on his throat and chest. She takes a laryngoscope and inserts it slowly into the man's throat. He is still bucking, gagging, fighting for air/breath. The scope has a light. She angles its blunt blade to visualize the man's epiglottis. Now she can see. With her other hand, she guides in a fresh endotracheal tube, inching it down... mouth, pharynx—past the vocal cords, into the trachea. The light on the laryngoscope and her angle of entry help ensure this pathway... she must get the tube down the trachea and not the esophagus. Inflating the stomach with air would kill the man. Sometimes, intubation causes collateral damage to eating: in the process of establishing an airway, the metal laryngoscope can break teeth if the scope hits and pulls incorrectly.

The tube is in. She moves it to the corner of the old man's mouth, and the *mama* connects the fresh tube to the tubes coming from the ventilator. He turns the machine back on. It reboots. The resident configures the machine. Its beeps resume, but this time they are pulsing, regularly, with each breath taken. This time, she tapes the tube to his face twice over, as if an *x* marks the spot of breathing. The man reboots, inasmuch as the ventilator's sensors stand in for him and his being. His oxygen saturation returns to normal. His blood pressure approaches normal.

Thus, one way that feeding and ventilation might be compared is through *process*. Another is through *substance*, that is, the material forms that flow and are at stake in each effort to support life. In the case of feeding, it is food (solid or liquid). In the case of ventilation, it is oxygen from the atmosphere, rendered as breath in the body. But there are other substances important to ventilation too. In the case of the patient just described, the man will be under the anesthetist's watch as she makes rounds through the ward. If she has time, she will perform suction on the tracheostomy tube, something that everyone working in the ward knows to be incredibly painful for patients. A small tube is inserted into the tracheostomy, and it is connected to a vacuum pump that pulls the secretions out of the body's interior, through the tubes, and into a large bell jar on a cart that will later get emptied and shifted to another patient's bedside. The jars contain breath's undesirable liquid obstacles.

The patients cannot speak, but they tear up when the tube is cleared with vacuum suction. Secretions accrete and can cause secondary infection—indeed, ventilator-assisted pneumonia is a common occurrence and a constant concern (another way that air becomes a problem for life: this time, "dirty air"). But suction also happens when relatives come. The strain on the workforce in the ward means that numerous tasks are offloaded onto willing relatives. So if the patient has family, and they are present, it is quite possible that they will be guided by the *mama* in suctioning the tube, just as they will also help with rolling bodies over to prevent bedsores and thumping on patients' chests to loosen secretions there. A resident instructs a patient's wife that the way to loosen secretions is to pretend she is eating with her hand. She is to feign the hand position of scooping up rice, thumb pressed against forefingers. That's the hand position for thumping against her husband's chest, nothing to be scooped up but certainly something to be tamped down. Only the chest X-ray will show the effects of the secretions in situ; one must gauge it otherwise through auscultation—listening closely through a stethoscope—and by eyeing the volume of secretions sucked out into the bell jars at the tail end of the vacuum pump. The materiality of ventilation can be as dangerous as it is vitalizing.

This is ordinary grunt work in the ward: intubating, extubating, thumping, suctioning. It is resuscitation in a very ordinary sense. Yet it is extraordinary work, for in one moment the man described here approaches suffocation, and in a moment that follows, suffocation is averted. He is *already* on a ventilator, meaning that at some point ahead of this moment, another anesthetist performed the same steps: scope, tube, ventilator. He wasn't breathing on his own in a life-affirming way, but then once on the ventilator, he could breathe again. Mechanical ventilation forms the threshold between living and dying, and the supply of air keeps that threshold moored.

This elision of ventilator and vitality poses a problem for a patient's kin too. As this is a municipal public hospital, it principally serves the city's poorest population. Relatives possessed a basic knowledge that a machine was helping the breathing for their patient, deemed "serious." Either they knew this already or doctors would explain that the patient was not breathing on his own and that a machine was now breathing for him. This did not always stick as an explanation, not because relatives misunderstood owing to lack of education, but rather because the ventilator worked somewhere in between machine and medicine. Relatives would sometimes ask if the ventilator was making "the body" better. The anesthetist would explain that the purpose of the machine was to breathe. But in the context of traumatic injury, and, more specifically, polytrauma—meaning that patients often have head injuries, orthopedic injuries, surface-level injuries, and deep internal organ injuries—the ventilator was often a point of confusion. For some relatives, it was of course breathing for their injured kin, but it seemed to do so much more. It healed. It breathed life. Not only into the lungs but into the body's capacity to regenerate too. On the thresholds of life, the ventilator feeds vitality.

Weaning Time

A resident talks to the professor of anesthesiology who is currently overseeing the ICU. "Can't you just reduce [the ventilator support]?" she asks the professor. The subject of her concern, of the reduction, is an elderly man in the corner of the ICU named Mr. M. He is on a ventilator, and his prognosis is very poor. Mr. M's brother has visited him constantly since his admission and has explained to the doctors that Mr. M *wants* to die. He insists on this, to them and to me. We have heard this several times, the ward staff and I. We heard it just yesterday, in fact. By asking, "Can't you just reduce?" the resident means to ask the anesthetist, "Can't you just reduce the oxygen?" Can't you just dial it down? Can't you just temper the air, so he will die? The anesthesiology professor replies quickly, "No, no." Not allowed. He summarizes: That would be euthanasia. Euthanasia is not legal in India. It is tantamount to killing. And so it is not done.[1] If Mr. M's condition were more stable, they would slowly reduce the assistance that the ventilator provides. In that hypothetical situation, his own respiratory system would take over. He would breathe by himself again. But that is not the situation at hand: his physiology and its assessment by doctors suggest that he would code if removed from the ventilator. He does not currently meet the hospital's clinical benchmarks for persistent vegetative state or brain death. Everyone must wait and watch.

As for Mr. M, he will stay on the ventilator until his life signs deteriorate or he recovers. He cannot be removed from the ventilator, which is called *weaning*. *Weaning* is a common medical term (Lock 2002; Kaufman 2005), and it is employed in the ward's vernacular as well: *usko wean kar do*, "wean her." It implies calibrating the ventilator's set levels of oxygenation, air volume, and pressure. There is the metaphor here of slowly withdrawing a substance, of taking away in order to encourage a person to self-regulate. As with food, so with air. The idea of weaning off a ventilator is that a patient will be weaned from artificial, assisted ventilation in order to resume breathing on her own. Recall how the ventilator is understood to be fundamentally as damaging as it is necessary, for besides a breathing tube's own mechanical damage (to internal tissue, to teeth), there are the downstream risks of infection and even "addiction." A ventilated person may become too accustomed to assistance to be able to go on without it. And so ventilation can become damaging, even addicting.

Professors reminded their residents to consider a strategy for weaning after a patient has been stabilized on mechanical ventilation. Stability is the first order of business, but once stable, the person hooked to the ventilator should eventually come off of it (preferably alive). This takes time. Oxygen levels and the tidal volume of ventilation must be carefully calibrated according to the patient's vital signs. Weaning is often nonlinear; life support may be reduced, and the patient's breathing strengthens, only to falter again a few hours later. The machine's support will then be amplified again. The process will be repeated, with the hope that the body detaches for good at some point that the tube can come out, and that breath can become "normal" again.

But there is no weaning in sight for Mr. M. The anesthesiology professor tells me that this is tragic, that the man will die on the ventilator, for he was "a just man," a man of principles and goodwill, according to the man's brother who speaks for him. Mr. M's brother, Mr. G, had explained to me the tally of good deeds; he must have spoken to the anesthesiologist too. What the patient ate and drank—and, more specifically, what he did *not* eat and drink—made him into what the brother said was "a pious man": he was not a drinker; he did not eat nonvegetarian food. He is a Hindu, and in this context, his past ingestions will in part affect his future—because he followed a vegetarian diet, he caused no harm to animal forms of life, and as a result accrued karma.

This is actually Mr. M's *second* admission to a trauma ICU. Almost a decade ago, he was hit by a motorbike while walking on the street. He required numerous metal plates in the surgical reconstruction of his face (plates that, Mr. G asserts, came from Germany and thus were exceedingly expensive as a medical device import). Eventually, though, Mr. M recovered and was discharged from the hospital. But his injuries precipitated severe depression. He lost his job in computing, leading to further depression. Mr. G wonders if these were symptoms of a possible brain injury that was never understood or treated. His brother would speak loudly and get easily disturbed ("Maybe it was the pressure on the brain?"). His digestion was impaired. He would wash cooking vessels again and again, even after they were clean. There was not much life to recover in this current instance, no resuscitation possible. "He wanted to die," Mr. G says of his brother. The injuries of the past (being hit by a motorcycle as a pedestrian) inflect the impasse of ventilation now. If Mr. M wanted to die before, surely he wants even more to die now, his brother explains. Nonetheless, he is being constantly fed air, and as the anesthetist has determined, Mr. M must keep breathing it.

There may be love in wanting someone to die, according to philosopher Alphonso Lingis. "When someone we love who has been suffering dies, we feel a sense of relief. We feel a loosening of tension, a repose. Death appears as a deliverance from dying—from the suffering of dying," he writes (2000, 111). There is a contrasting wish that someone may live, that they fulfill our desire for more time, "time for her to flourish," according to Lingis. He notes, though, "One can doubt the straightforwardness of our wish that the other live: is our wish that the other live a wish for her or for ourselves?" (111). There are proportions of dignity and desire at work here. For Lingis, dignity is something that emerges as a "side effect" that strikes us only when we observe a loved one dying. We project dignity "back over the whole life" of the dying person (112). So it was, in part, with Mr. M. "Let him have a peaceful death," his brother says by the man's bedside.

The ventilator breathes life into narrative too, but selectively so. People are fed news of a patient's prognosis, (well-)being, bits here and there. And kin share news that may or may not further contextualize, or give shared meaning to, technologically mediated information. Mr. G's assertion that his brother wants to die is not taken for granted. Some nurses in the ward believe it. Others are more hesitant to accede so easily. After all, one points out, the patient himself cannot talk, because he is intubated and because he is not awake. As with many patients in the ward, illness narratives come secondhand. The tube deflects any easy collection of a first-person narrative. Information is often adjuvant. Is the brother's wish to remove Mr. M from the ventilator a matter of compassion? Or is there some property, money, or other kind of inheritance at stake? Ward staff don't know, don't *want* to know. That is reaching too high toward the story's float. It's not in the job description, and it is only because of the privilege I have as an observer that I can take the time to consider these angles. The rest of the workers in the ward have to keep tending the cases that continue to come in, for the injuries do not stop. As for Mr. M, the ventilator tells the staff what they must know in their rounds: his vital signs (degrading). His body offers signs like spontaneous movement or response to pain stimulus that doctors will repeatedly calculate and write in the record of his neurological abilities. These abilities seem to be diminishing. The ventilator is still beeping.

The accident that brought Mr. M to the ward this time occurred between 5:30 and 6:00 p.m. He was out walking and was hit by a motorcycle. The motorcycle sped off. "He was lying in a pool of blood. Lots of people stood around but did nothing," Mr. G said. A local politician brought him to the hospital. Mr. G himself "broke down" when he saw his brother again in this situation, but he pulled himself back together in order to deal with things. "The days are numbered," he says of his brother's life. "If the Lord wants to take him, let him take him in his whole form." He emphasized again that *he*—Mr. G—does not want his brother to undergo the surgeries that the ward's doctors insist would, in a standard protocol of treatment, extend his life. (He was, however, keen to donate his brother's organs.) He, Mr. G, wanted reduction in intervention.

Several staff in the ward commented on Mr. M's condition by centralizing the ventilator. One nurse said to the trauma resident, "Just turn the ventilator off" (venti off kar ke). She did not say this out of not-knowing, for she was not new to the ward and therefore knew the protocols. She knew what the doctor would say: We cannot do that. There are protocols. One cannot simply turn the ventilator *off*; it is the patient who makes that happen, not us. We are not God. She says it, I think, as a wishful but impossible end to the impasse at hand. In the ICU, a place where so much talk is about what *should* be done (orders, protocols, rounds), it can be tricky to hear the reverberations of the ethics of life support.

"He's going, today" (jaata hai, aaj), another nurse observed. It remains unclear if Mr. M's death was peaceful, for who could answer such a question? But the nurse's predictions of his death's timing were nearly correct: he died a day and a half later, likely of systemic organ failure. The day following his death, I rounded with the residents. The one whose shift was ending gave an update on each patient for the incoming shift resident. He pointed to the empty bed previously occupied by Mr. M. No words, just a gesture to the empty space and the powered-down ventilator. "Good, he had to go," the other resident said. By this she meant that Mr. M's death was not good, but it was good that he was no longer breathing in *this* room. To linger on life support in the ICU is a form of pain that no one should endure. Her eyes glanced upward, directing us to the expanse of the airy realm that encompassed all that the earthly realm could not. "Honewalla," she said. "That's where he's going." The impasse of life support was over. In death, Mr. M could move again. Released from the bonds of breath, to venture elsewhere, and opening up space for more breathers here.

Conclusion

Air may indeed be a form whose substantiation matters to anthropologists (Choy 2011). In the cases described here, air and body are momentarily interchangeable. In the public hospital trauma ward, you can rely on a ventilator to breathe into a person, in theory, but in practice the economy of ventilation can change that trust. The machine will continue on, regardless. In this sense, the withdrawal of the machine from a (dead) person confirms death and promises the possibility of life for another who needs it. But to linger for a moment on the dead, we can see that economies of breath may appear to be hydraulic—one machine for one body, always substitutable in an ideal ventilator economy—but these substitutions are less movable when it comes to reckoning with sorrow and with the tough choices of whom to ventilate mechanically and whom to ventilate manually. To remove the machine is to remove the thing that even for a moment promised hope of recovery, the temporal horizon that follows resuscitation, even as the machine stands by the bedside and marks death's strong possibility.

Feeding can be taken away as much as it is offered. This dynamic of care and withdrawal is another insight that the ventilators offer for studies of food's realization as life. The cases presented here show that withdrawal and weaning are already built into the consumption of the supplement on offer. This feature deserves more attention in critical studies of metabolic processes. Feeding certainly is care, but it is also a form of distribution (Mol and Mesman 1996; Weiss 1996; Gewertz and Errington 2010). With breath, its distribution sits uneasily in the ward. The feeder—human and/or machine—is invested with a twofold form of power: control over the body itself and an investment in a system of rationing sustenance. A critical reading of food that is awash in affective modes of surplus economies cannot account for contexts of tensely distributed economies. In contexts of surplus, the "choice" to feed one person is not at another's expense. Yet in the contexts described in this chapter, the decision to make one person breathe mechanically is often at odds with the possibility to do so for another.

At the edges of ventilation, breath is required for imminent resuscitation yet immediately poses problems of weaning, addiction, and withdrawal. The act of life support creates future possible acts on a body and a person who has *too many* attachments to the feeding of life. Breathing is ethical work. The commonsense model of the ventilator in the Mumbai trauma ward is that it is a machine that breathes for the person who cannot. That very model is shot through with inequalities and ethics. Such ethics often emerge at moments of attachment to and withdrawal from the machine. Resuscitation is a process done *to* someone, *for* someone, and therefore entails a life politics of feeding that arcs across multiple persons and that rarely leaves the technology out of the moral shockwaves of injury and death. The breath, at the threshold of the "natural" and the "artificial" (and, in fact, somewhere between those two scripted domains), plots the arc of life politics. It moves between biological and physical life; humans are thresholding projects in this way. The arc moves from machine to body and back again. It moves from death to life and back again.

ACKNOWLEDGMENTS

I wish to thank the patients, families, and caregivers in the trauma ward who face ventilation's affordances and struggles every day. My gratitude goes to participants in the Oslo workshop that deepened my understanding of these materials, and especially to Heather Paxson for her mentorship and editorial acumen. My fieldwork and writing was supported by a National Science Foundation Cultural Anthropology Program CAREER Award (number 145433). In Mumbai, I am deeply grateful to Drs. Vineet Kumar, Sanjay Nagral, Nobhojit Roy, Kalpana Swaminathan, and Ishrat Syed. Siddharth David provided incredible research assistance, and Gabriel Rosenberg sharpened the ideas and writing at every step.

NOTE

1. While "euthanasia" may be regarded in this scene as a form of killing, it is critical to situate its discussion in terms of (1) its different possible categories, such as active and passive euthanasia, that derive from bioethics and are cited in jurisprudence; (2) legal distinctions between murder and homicide not amounting to murder in the Indian Penal Code; and (3) the way that euthanasia crystallizes through certain high-profile cases in the Supreme Court of India, notably *Aruna Ramachandra Shanbaug v. Union of India and Ors* (2011). See Gursahani (2011) and Nair (2016). I am sometimes asked if I ever saw doctors take someone off a ventilator without a weaning stage in cases that did not meet brain death or persistent vegetative state standards. The answer is unequivocally no. See Kaufman (2005) on the ways that US hospitals can produce seemingly infinite options in the face of persistent vegetative states.

REFERENCES

Abbots, Emma-Jayne, Anna Lavis, and Luci Attala. 2015. "Introduction: Reflecting on the Embodied Intersections of Eating and Caring." In *Careful Eating: Bodies, Food and Care*, edited by Emma-Jayne Abbots, Anna Lavis, and Luci Attala, 1–24. London: Routledge.
Abrahamsson, Sebastian, Filippo Bertoni, Annemarie Mol, and Rebeca Ibáñez Martín. 2015. "Living with Omega-3: New Materialism and Enduring Concerns." *Environment and Planning D: Society and Space* 33 (1): 4–19.
Bear, Laura. 2007. *Lines of the Nation: Indian Railway Workers, Bureaucracy, and the Intimate Historical Self*. New York: Columbia University Press.
Choy, Timothy K. 2011. *Ecologies of Comparison: An Ethnography of Endangerment in Hong Kong*. Durham, NC: Duke University Press.
Chua, Jocelyn Lim. 2014. *In Pursuit of the Good Life: Aspiration and Suicide in Globalizing South India*. Berkeley: University of California Press.
Cohen, Ed. 2009. *A Body Worth Defending: Immunity, Biopolitics, and the Apotheosis of the Modern Body*. Durham, NC: Duke University Press.
Cohen, Lawrence. 2001. "The Other Kidney: Biopolitics beyond Recognition." *Body and Society* 7 (2–3): 9–19.
Cohen, Lawrence. 2004. "Operability: Surgery at the Margins of the State." In *Anthropology in the Margins of the State*, edited by Veena Das and Deborah Poole, 165–90. Santa Fe: School of American Research Press.

Cooper, Melinda. 2009. "The Silent Scream—Agamben, Deleuze, and the Politics of the Unborn." In *Deleuze and Law: Forensic Futures*, edited by Rosi Braidotti, Claire Colebrook, and Patrick Hanafin, 143–62. New York: Palgrave Macmillan.

Copeman, Jacob, and Johannes Quack. 2015. "Godless People and Dead Bodies: Materiality and the Morality of Atheist Materialism." *Social Analysis* 59 (2): 40–61.

Crowley-Matoka, Megan. 2016. *Domesticating Organ Transplant: Familial Sacrifice and National Aspiration in Mexico*. Durham, NC: Duke University Press.

Das, Veena. 2015. *Affliction: Health, Disease, Poverty*. New York: Fordham University Press.

Farquhar, Judith, and Qicheng Zhang. 2012. *Ten Thousand Things: Nurturing Life in Contemporary Beijing*. New York: Zone Books.

Fassin, Didier. 2015. "The Value of Life and the Worth of Lives." In *Living and Dying in the Contemporary World: A Compendium*, edited by Veena Das and Clara Han, 770–83. Oakland: University of California Press.

Gewertz, Deborah, and Frederick Errington. 2010. *Cheap Meat: Flap Food Nations in the Pacific Islands*. Berkeley: University of California Press.

Gursahani, Roop. 2011. "Life and Death after Aruna Shanbaug." *Indian Journal of Medical Ethics* 8 (2): 68–69.

Kaufman, Sharon R. 2005. *And a Time to Die: How American Hospitals Shape the End of Life*. New York: Scribner.

Keane, Webb. 2014. "Rotting Bodies: The Clash of Stances toward Materiality and Its Affordances." *Current Anthropology* 55 (S10): S312–21.

Kerr, Ian J. 2003. "Representation and Representations of the Railways of Colonial and Post-colonial South Asia." *Modern Asian Studies* 37 (2): 287–326.

Lingis, Alphonso. 2000. "To Die with Others." *Diacritics* 30 (3): 106–13.

Lock, Margaret M. 2002. *Twice Dead: Organ Transplants and the Reinvention of Death*. Berkeley: University of California Press.

Mol, Annemarie, and Jessica Mesman. 1996. "Neonatal Food and the Politics of Theory: Some Questions of Method." *Social Studies of Science* 26 (2): 419–44.

Mumbai Railway Vikas Corporation. 2013. *Annual Report 2012–2013*. Mumbai: Mumbai Railway Vikas Corporation.

Nair, Sreelekha. 2016. "Aruna Shanbaug and Workplace Safety for Women: The Real Issue Sidestepped." *Indian Journal of Medical Ethics* 1 (1): 47–52.

Nelson, Diane. 1999. *A Finger in the Wound: Body Politics in Quincentennial Guatemala*. Durham, NC: Duke University Press.

Parry, Jonathan. 1985. "Death and Digestion: The Symbolism of Food and Eating in North Indian Mortuary Rites." *Man* 20 (4): 612–30.

Prasad, Ritika. 2013. "'Time-Sense': Railways and Temporality in Colonial India." *Modern Asian Studies* 47 (4): 1252–82.

Roy, Nobhojit, Vikas Kapil, Italo Subbarao, and Isaac Ashkenazi. 2011. "Mass Casualty Response in the 2008 Mumbai Terrorist Attacks." *Disaster Medicine and Public Health Preparedness* 5 (4): 273–79.

Roy, Nobhojit, V. Murlidhar, Ritam Chowdhury, Sandeep B. Patil, Priyanka A. Supe, Poonam D. Vaishnav, and Arvind Vatkar. 2010. "Where There Are No Emergency Medical Services—Prehospital Care for the Injured in Mumbai, India." *Prehospital and Disaster Medicine* 25 (2): 145–51.

Solomon, Harris. 2016. *Metabolic Living: Food, Fat, and the Absorption of Illness in India*. Durham, NC: Duke University Press.

Stevenson, Lisa. 2014. *Life beside Itself: Imagining Care in the Canadian Arctic*. Oakland: University of California Press.

Weiss, Brad. 1996. *The Making and Unmaking of the Haya Lived World: Consumption, Commoditization, and Everyday Practice*. Durham, NC: Duke University Press.

Yates-Doerr, Emily, and Annemarie Mol. 2012. "Cuts of Meat: Disentangling Western Natures-Cultures." *Cambridge Anthropology* 30 (2): 48–64.

transgression

HARRIS SOLOMON /
EMILY YATES-DOERR

A transgression is a breach, something where two fields/zones/spaces/things cross. It is also an invitation to push our thinking and writing about inter- and intra-actions in novel directions. A threshold, as this volume's introduction suggests, is where transmission and transformation come together: a space of ex/change. We write from two connected cases of threshold, where things—the breath and the placenta—contravene normative orders of knowledge and embodied experience. We bridge them via a museum exhibit that we visited together while in Amsterdam, using the conversation that ensued as a provocation for reworking thresholds as a form of transgression.

After a seminar in Amsterdam one day, we headed to the city's modern art museum, where the Indian artist and feminist Nalini Malani's work was featured. We did not expect to come across small images of a child with a tubelike umbilical cord running from its mouth. But there it was, a ballooning placenta-figure connected to a tube that extended outward from the child into the surrounding air (see figure 5a.1). The placard below the piece read: *The Rebellion of the Dead Will Be the War of the Landscapes*. The image uncannily fuses our chapters: Harris's preceding chapter on ventilators "feeding life" in trauma wards, Emily's, which follows, on the eating and feeding practices of the human placenta.

The exhibition room featured quotes by Julia Kristeva and Arjun Appadurai—both scholars have been cited in our chapters. Kristeva, on one side of the room, advises museumgoers (her French has been translated into English) that "the maternal body transforms violence into tenderness." Appadurai, on the other side, explores nonviolence as political action. Looking at the life getting sucked into or blown out of bodies in the picture and in our chapters, we wonder about other kinds of give and take, and what forms of violence make our material thinkable in the first place.

Emily, nodding to the Kristeva quote, cannot help but wonder about the effects of using the English words and problems of a continental philosopher—even a feminist philosopher who did not write in English—to frame the work of an Indian artist. Why not use the words of an Indian philosopher to analyze Malani? Harris responds by saying that it is not as though Malani's collaboration with Appadurai means that no boundaries are crossed. Here is the thing: English is a language of poetry, of power, of tragedy, and of compromise. Blockage and production go together: *but/and*. Both Kristeva and Appadurai pose transformations of the imponderable (violence into tenderness, nonviolence into politics), *but/and* these transformations also leave unfinished business behind.

After taking in the image of breathing placentas, we step into *Transgressions*, the largest Malani installation. The museum's catalog entry describes it as "a unique combination of painting, video, and moving shadows, termed by Malani as 'video/shadow play.' The work is created out of four cylinders of Mylar plastic that the artist painted from the inside (the so-called 'reverse painting' technique). Moving slowly at a rate of four rotations per minute, the cylinders are traversed by three video projections on the wall."[1]

The images and sounds conjure up themes of loss and its incorporation: colonialism's enduring mark. A child's voice, twisted with electronic interference, sings through the loudspeaker. She reads a poem, written by Malani, that evokes how the body's connectivity—signified by "airtime rupees" purchased to operate cellular phones—grounds ways to survive and how to succeed (again, *it's about English*).

> It was the best of times
> We had everything before us
> We were all going direct to heaven.
> Vada pav rupees 3, Airtime rupees 1.49
> Nimbu pani rupees 3, Airtime rupees 1.49 ...
> ... Vegetarian or non
> What turns you on?
> Clucking potatoes with chicken genes
> Or tomatoes swimming where fish have been?
> Here come the seeds ... they're terminator seeds
> Big science watching over your food needs.
> And amma please send me to English school,
> And amma she really was no fool.[2]

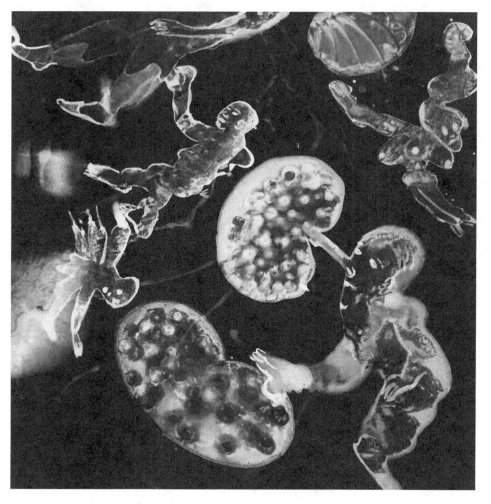

FIGURE 5A.1 Breathing placentas? Puffs of air? While visiting the Stedelijk Museum, Solomon and Yates-Doerr photographed a small section of Nalini Malini's pigmented inkjet print, *The Rebellion of the Dead Will Be the War of the Landscapes*, 2015. Photograph of the artwork reproduced with Nalini Malani's kind permission.

At a different museum the week before, Emily heard a prominent American anthropologist who was visiting Amsterdam remark that he did not want to "navel gaze." He spat the term—for him, it was an accusation. What a strange violence, Emily had found herself thinking. Navels, those small, soft places of flesh, connect us to our mothers—to those wise old *ammas* keeping us fed. What sad misogyny we live with that the gaze at the navel has become an insult. Emily's chapter, to follow, writes against this, taking as its starting point the materiality of the navel and the languages we have to speak of it. Showing how the placenta is bound up in feeding relations also shows "the individual" to be more than itself. The placenta is an organ for materializing metabolism's contradictions, being, often in the very same moment, harmful and healthy, wanted and repellent, life-giving and deadly, self and other. Ethnography of this miraculous, magical conduit—this sphere with sides—can help us to see how the person, life, and experience are not definitively located in a singular body, even as they are often done as singularities. The placenta, as such a threshold, is an organ of transgression.

Harris's chapter takes up a similar challenge through the tubes that connect the gaps between living and dying. The ventilator is a machine for life support because it delivers the basics of breath that may not otherwise be available when someone experiences traumatic injury. In injury cases, inhale and exhale—vitality and waste—do not match up. But ventilators, and the breaths people breathe on them, hardly sit on even footing in moral and economic terms. In between the intake of life support and the possibility of exhale is where ethnography can show the multiple kinds of exchange involved in feeding someone life when their own is draining away. Transgressing enclosures like tubes and lungs is the stuff of medicine, but it is also the basics of vitality.

Vada pav. Maternal bodies. Life and death. Breathing placentas. Conventions of inside and outside, with barriers and crossing them our go-to refrains.

In the museum exhibit *Transgressions*, Malani immersed us in a child's voice both thankful for and fearful of the "terminator seeds" that give us genetically modified foods, emblematic of other thunderous pressures that sustaining technologies put on lives. And in *The Rebellion of the Dead Will Be the War of the Landscapes*, we confronted an intimate diagram of the ways humans can take in and spew out life force. Sparked by Kristeva's provocation that violence and tenderness can mutually transform, we situate ourselves in and write from such transformative scenes, where food settles into fleshy material. In our chapters, too, there is a uniting theme of shadow play, set in the shadows cast by bodies of transgression.

As an analytic, transgression invites us to consider the simultaneous, inseparable gratitude and fearfulness entailed in eating. Learning to unpack the world systems that lie within the small, unexpected moments is a gift. But it comes with cords attached. The transgression of one threshold—between living and working, and between giving and taking—forces us to face what kinds of demands crossing over might entail.

NOTES

1. *Nalini Malani: Transgressions*, Stedelijk Museum, Amsterdam, Netherlands, March 18–June 17, 2017, http://www.stedelijk.nl/en/exhibitions/nalini-malan.

2. *Transgressions* (video/shadow play installation with sound), presented at *Nalini Malani: Transgressions*.

chapter six

The Placenta

AN ETHNOGRAPHIC ACCOUNT
OF FEEDING RELATIONS

EMILY YATES-DOERR

> One is too few, but two are too many.
> —DONNA J. HARAWAY, *SIMIANS, CYBORGS, AND WOMEN*

> Write your name on this line, here.
> —DIABETES CLINIC RECEPTIONIST, 2011

"YOU ARE TWO. CONGRATULATIONS," THE MIDWIFE SAID WHEN I CALLED to make an appointment. From this beginning, I was both myself and another.[1] The grammar function of my word processor doesn't like this sentence. The programmers who wrote this code did not anticipate that I would be multiplied like this. But there I was: myself, and not myself at all. Before long, another message conveying that I contained multitudes started to come from all directions: "Pregnant? Now you are eating for two!"

Anthropologists have long collected stories from remote places, bringing these stories home to make "the strange" familiar and "the familiar" strange. Yet I did not need to travel anywhere to elicit this alterity (Young 1984). I could tell my limbs to move, and they would respond. But I could not keep at bay the pains, the alternate hunger or abhorrence of foods I usually enjoyed, and the exhaustion that accompanied my transformation. The self I inhabited was increasingly unrecognizable to myself. My singularity was becoming duplicity. Or maybe it had been so all along.

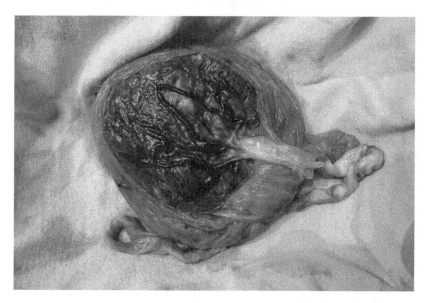

FIGURE 6.1 The placenta. Photo by Emily Yates-Doerr.

Authoring "a Body"

This chapter asks what we can learn from the placenta about relationality. By the end, it unpacks what an analysis of feeding and nourishment can teach us about the relational methods of anthropology, in which selves and others come together even while they pull apart. To get there, it enters the topic of "feeding relations" through my experience with being a multiple body in the Netherlands.[2]

When the midwife informed me that I was two, I was in the midst of a different sort of transformation. I had just moved from New York University's anthropology department, where I had received my PhD, to take a postdoctoral position in Amsterdam. As I was adjusting to life in a new part of the world, so was I adjusting to life among an interdisciplinary team of science studies scholars. And then I became pregnant.

If it had once been unusual, if not frowned upon, to find reference to an "I" in anthropological publications, this had not been the case in my training. As an undergraduate student at Stanford, I had sought out Renato Rosaldo as an adviser because of the way he had questioned the foundations of empirical objectivity by writing his experiences into scientific truth (Rosaldo 1989). I then followed him to New York University, where I studied under Emily Martin and Rayna Rapp, among others. These anthropologists helped to incite a wave of feminist anthropology challenging the self/other divide on which much positivist research—the kind of research that eschewed reference to the author—was founded (Martin 1987, 2007; Rapp 1999). Their fieldwork, and the books they produced, embraced self-narrative. Theirs was scholarship that rejected the passive voice—the voice of the "God trick" (Haraway 1988)—which rendered invisible the voice and activities of the author, replacing this with first-person narration, in which the experience of the anthropologist was evident. "Nourishment was studied" became "I studied nourishment," or even "I experienced nourishment."

In Amsterdam, however, I confronted a reaction against first-person voice coming not from the positivists but from the posthumanists. Wary of the implicitly liberal subject, members of the science studies community I had newly joined expressed concern that first-person ethnographic writing, by organizing the story in the experience and body of the narrator, risked shoring up a Western ideal of an agentive (and typically male) actor, individually responsible for his actions. These colleagues frequently used passive voice in their publications. For them, passive voice was not meant to reinforce power by dislocating it ("nourishment was studied") but was instead a means of reforming "the actor" into an actor-network, in which objects and subjects exist only as effects of coproductive relations (Asdal, Brenna, and Moser 2007, 29). *Lived experience* was likewise not a challenge to the intellectual violence wrought by positivism but an analytic that risked renaturalizing continental philosophy's valorization of (masculine, white) acting brains and their bodies. A worry was that a method that relied on experience—what Donna Haraway calls one of culture's "least innocent" products (1991, 109)—risked closing down precisely what should rather be opened up to inquiry.

As a body-in-transition—*transnational, transforming*—I was drawn to this critique and to experimental writing that seeks to undo the autonomy of the liberal subject and rework "the actor" by playing with multiplicities and passive voice (Mol 2008; Mann et al. 2011). And still I remained interested in a personally engaged anthropology whose research practice involves *being with* multispecies, multibeing others and then accounting for this experience. It was by being with pregnancy—that of mine, that of others—that my attention became focused on the placenta. In following discussions of the placenta's relationality and responsibility, I began to see a way out of the predicament that narrating *my* experience might unwittingly reproduce a shallow liberal individualism. For the placenta that I was learning about did not force me to choose between the network and the narrator. Instead, the placenta offered space for an I who is responsible *and* an I who is diffuse, an

I who is deliberate *and* an I who is not in control, an I who is one *and* an I who is many. As a barrier that is also a conduit, it helped me to understand how it is possible to be both-and while also being either-or: to be multiple and singular while feeding (with, into, on) others. The placenta taught me that I could write as an *I*—a strong, deliberate I, an *I* with boundaries—but this did not need to reinforce the (white, male, patriarchal) liberal actor. Indeed, it taught me that even as we are unevenly individualized, *we have never been individuals*. The aim of this chapter is to share this form of experience with you.

Separated Togetherness

Was I two? Like many newly pregnant people, I began to peruse local bookstores and online sites for "expecting parents," to learn about what was happening to a body that I still referred to with the possessive form as *mine*, even though the ground on which I did so began to feel increasingly unstable. Because the normative articulations of personhood—what was self and what was other, interior and foreign—were stated so explicitly in these materials, I began to take notes. Interested in what pregnant people themselves had to say, I began to carry out informal interviews with people in my new Amsterdam networks to learn more about how the placenta had figured in their experiences of pregnancy. I also became inspired to carry a pen and paper to my appointments with the midwives, the pain-preparation course I attended weekly for twenty-five weeks with roughly ten to fifteen other pregnant companions, and the courses I attended in the weeks before giving birth to learn about the skill of breastfeeding.[3] As I did so, the placenta began to develop fleshy form, both in my body and on the papers around me—a material synecdoche of feeding relations.

The markedly gendered start of the story I encountered in the pregnancy section of Amsterdam's bookstores was predictable: docile egg and remarkable, efficient sperm meet, and a blastocyst begins to form (see Martin 1991). From there, the texts shifted my attention toward the placenta—an object that did not, at least in English, have binary gender—as the primary agent of transformation. Popular literature explained that when a blastocyst buries itself into the endometrium, a new organ begins to develop: "Once firmly in place, the ball of cells undergoes the great divide—splitting into two groups. Half will become your son or daughter, while the other half will become the placenta" (Murkoff 2008, 121). The placenta was widely held to be a part of a woman's body, a provisional organ, much like the heart or liver or spleen. And yet, at the same time that it is hers, it feeds the quickly multiplying collections of cells that might become a human baby. The resources I encountered commonly depicted the placenta as an "interface" between mother and emergent life, though Haraway's (1991, 249) term *infolding* may work better, since the placenta, as a complex materialization of feedback loops, was not just a meeting of surfaces but a recursive formation of flesh. It was depicted as the site of division; it was also depicted as folding divisions together, such that the boundaries between us were never made out of neat lines (see Solomon, this volume).

Numerous sources described the placenta as a "miraculous" conduit. Through the umbilical cord, it connected a woman to the not-yet-life forming inside her, linking her own blood supply to the blood supply of the cells within her in such a way that oxygen, nutrients, and "waste materials" (carbon dioxide, for example) transfer between them, chemicals becoming human. This was not akin to Michael Reddy's (1979) famous conduit capable of moving objects, unchanged, from place to place; what is miraculous about the conduit of the placenta is that it connects through a *barrier*, containing a semipermeable layer of tissue that selectively allows substances to pass through.[4] Maternal and fetal blood come so close as to almost touch, but under typical circumstances no direct intermingling of blood will occur.

Medical literature commonly separates the placenta into two sides: the "maternal side," which is knobby with bumpy lobes and which grows from uterine tissue, and the "fetal side," which is smooth and shiny and develops from the coding material earlier found in the egg and the sperm. These look incredibly dissimilar; there is no mistaking one side for the other. Yet despite this differentiation the organ is a unity: *the* placenta. After delivery, care providers must inspect it to make sure it is intact; that it remains together through the process of childbirth is critical, as ruptured placentas can be deadly. As Elain Jones and Margarita Kay (2003, 102) note in their cultural survey of the placenta, there is not a place on earth where the delivery of the entire, complete object of the placenta is not a grave concern. That both connection and separation are necessary to survival is what makes the placenta such a compelling object for thinking through the implications of relationality. It grows from multiple beings, and its function also moves between feeding the fetus and feeding relations. It is divided and yet must remain whole. It is singular; it is also shared. It is a sphere with sides.

Non/distributed Responsibility

Into the space of ones and twos, then, I would soon come into contact with a thickening fleshy object that was, and was not, a three. When my sickness began in earnest at roughly seven weeks, midwives, literature, and other pregnant women all told me to "blame the placenta." In the beginning of pregnancy, many women find themselves tired and nauseous. A common explanation is that the woman's body is doing everything it can to develop the placenta. In the second trimester, a shift occurs, and the placenta begins to "sustain the pregnancy" (Weiss 2021). Pregnant people suffering from nausea and exhaustion are counseled to be patient and wait for this shift. "Once you hit 12 weeks, your placenta takes over the work and you are spared the tiredness," reports one user of an online pregnancy message board.[5] "Feeling quite a lot better today, hopefully that's the placenta taking over!" comments another.[6]

Both popular and scientific accounts of the placenta represent it as adaptive, adjusting itself to the pregnant person (typically referred to as a *mother*) and fetus (frequently called a *baby* and gendered as a boy).[7] As one online site targeting mothers explained: "This is where all your baby's food, oxygen and antibodies are processed, so they can be passed on to him. It's also where your baby's waste products are filtered back into your bloodstream, so that they can be broken down by your body, processed by your kidneys and excreted.... During your third trimester, the placenta becomes softer and lets more molecules from the outside world cross into the amniotic fluid that surrounds your baby. That's why your baby can start to taste the foods you eat and, according to some scientists, even detect smells."[8]

Social scientists have described the placenta as a liminal object because of its role in mediating among various political and social bonds (see Santoro 2011). As with other liminal objects, placentas are surrounded by rituals worldwide. A woman from the United States told me she was "obsessed with [her] placenta," explaining that she was more attentive to the ultrasound images of its position and size than to her fetus. An Indian mother posed with pictures of it after the birth. A woman in France ceremoniously buried it under a tree in her garden, and I heard rumors that the Vondelpark in Amsterdam was full of placental burials. (I spoke with many Americans who had wanted to bring the placenta home from the hospital but found their plans thwarted by hospital regulations, which treated it as hazardous waste and would not release it.)

Several women found the placenta to be "disturbing," "creepy," or "repulsive." Some said they could not look at it after the birth. A Dutch woman said she did not want it in the room with her. A woman in the United States said she was extremely uncomfortable when the nurse inspected her placenta: "I really didn't want her looking at it—it seemed too private for that." In the very many expressions of revulsion, disgust, or weirdness I encountered, the placenta might be understood as taking on an uncanny form, falling into "that class of the frightening which leads back to what is known of old and long familiar" (Freud 1953, 220).[9] Historian Barbara Duden (1993) refers to the classic biomedical view of the anatomy of the placenta as "atomistic," but even biomedical representations of the placenta I encountered tended to *challenge* rather than reinforce the autonomy of the subject, upending the boundaries of a solitary and unified person. As an object that makes elusive the borders between what is familiar and what is alien, it forces uncertainty about what we can know about the body that is "ours." My point is not that the placenta is inherently uncanny but, rather, that it may become uncanny for those raised in environments that celebrate individuality because of how it turns what is the same and what is different, or what is self and what is other, inside out.[10]

And yet if the placenta is involved in dissolving or blurring boundaries, it does not result in fusion. The parent does not *become* the fetus, nor does the fetus *become* the parent. The placenta may be a liminal object—a mediator of *in-betweenness*. But insofar as it upends autonomy, it does not result in egalitarian togetherness in which all beings are treated as if they are the same. It might, rather, be understood as a "thresholding object" as developed by Heather Paxson (this volume), marking both the establishment of a boundary and its transgression. It mediates between insides and outsides, selves and others, sameness and differences—crossing lines, setting limits. As it brings two beings together, so does it hold them apart.

In an interview between philosopher Luce Irigaray and biologist Hélène Rouch, Rouch suggests that although pregnancy is often understood as constituting a "successful transplant," the physiological negotiations between mother and fetus are far more complicated than those between host and transplant (1993).[11] Whereas organ transplantation depends on the suppression of immunological mechanisms that recognize a transplanted organ as foreign (the transplant must appear as self), in the case of pregnancy the growth of an embryo is possible only "if there has been a recognition, by the maternal organism, of foreign antigens" (Irigaray 1993, 41). In other words, to initiate placental hormonal reactions that are necessary for fetal development, the maternal organism must both recognize and tolerate the growth of something not-quite-self within itself. Rouch underscores that in physiological terms, pregnancy should not be understood as a condition in which parent and fetus are fused; instead, the life that comes from it depends on the recognition of constantly changing differences between self and other.

One immunologist I spoke with explained that microbial scientists today treat the placenta as having its own microbiome, which, in turn, helps to produce a separate, unique microbiome for the fetus. As it dissolves borders, refusing the terrain of either-or, it also re-creates them. It does not hold difference in place, but neither does it dissolve difference into similarity. It is, in this framing, the originary feminist object in which different kinds of differences come to matter (Ahmed 1998).

I found interest in separation evident not only in scientific literature but in conversations with women. In talking about placentas and pregnancy, women often told me that in spite of a prevailing depiction of a unity between mother and child, they were regularly reminded that the placenta—as a proxy for the fetus, or even for the eventual baby—was their responsibility. A British woman explained this, saying, "I remember thinking that the nurse can probably tell by looking at the placenta what I have been eating the entire pregnancy, what I have been breathing—bad air—and whether I have taken drugs during the pregnancy and maybe even before the pregnancy." An American woman, whose second daughter was stillborn at twenty weeks, also spoke to me of the placenta as being her responsibility when describing the death:

> When [my first daughter] was born, I remember the midwife and nurses making a big fuss about the large size of the placenta. With [my second daughter], the placenta was the issue. When I found out that she was too small, the doctor told me that the placenta was grossly oversized and that this was indicative of a chromosomal abnormality. Once she died and I gave birth to her, it was clear that the opposite was true. The placenta was under the 5th percentile for her gestational age and had failed to provide enough for her to grow and live. The placenta "failed," and this news immediately meant, in my eyes, that *I* had failed. I realized then that the news of [my first daughter's] large and healthy placenta had given me a strange sense of pride, like I was already succeeding at providing for my baby.

Evident in the woman's story of loss is that the "failure of the placenta" quickly becomes interpreted as a failure to mother. In this way, the placenta not only stands in for the fetus, as already seen, but, as a feeding organ, is also a proxy for motherhood. Though mother and daughter may be connected, there are asymmetries and even conflicts at play as women are expected to give from their own bodies to nourish the child (see Markens, Browner, and Press 1997).

This woman does not collapse her second daughter into herself, nor does the world in which she lives diffuse maternal responsibility onto the placenta. If the placenta often regulated shifting and permeable boundaries between (not quite) two people in the scientific literature, at the end of her story—where there was death and not life—it was the woman who was marked with failure. Aspirations to togetherness notwithstanding, relations are routinely forced into the form of the individual. This happens in subtle ways through doctors' admonishments or praise. It also happens in explicit ways through the denial of insurance claims or litigation that holds individual women responsible for their child's development (see Oaks 2001). "Blame the placenta" can only go so far when social institutions are primed to blame the mother.

That relationality is at times impossible—that pregnant people are routinely individualized—is not beyond the capacity of the placenta but something that the placenta can help us to see. For in the very act of facilitating connections, it establishes boundaries. It is, in this sense, an organ of "ontological choreography" (Thompson 2005), making divisions and hierarchies around beings come to matter—even as they also come to transform.[12]

Destructive Nourishment

As I learned more about the placenta from others while also feeling it grow larger inside me, it became, for me, *the* quintessential object of reproduction—an agent whose acts of agency disturb the individualizing logic of Euro-American action. The experience of pregnancy attuned me to its flesh and function, but I would also come to see its boundary-making connections as pivotal to the feeding relations out of which all beginnings, endings, and ongoingness of life take form.

At a birth-preparation class in Amsterdam, a participant asked the instructor about eating the placenta after the birth. Calling it "the only piece of meat to come from life and not death," she had heard that it was rich in nutrients that would help to ease postpartum depression and pain. Other women in the room noted that several doulas in Amsterdam offered to encapsulate placentas or blend them into smoothies immediately following birth.[13] The instructor replied that it was nice to honor the placenta in some way after birth. "But," she cautioned, "if you're looking for good nutrition after labor, there are a lot of other places to find nutrients. You must remember, your placenta does not belong to you. Your placenta belongs to the baby."

Your placenta belongs to another. These inversions of belonging happened often when people spoke of the placenta. If the placenta carries us to a world of becoming entangled, it also confronts us with disentanglement.[14] Insofar as the placenta offers a story of *belonging*, the placenta does—and does not—belong to the woman in whom it resides. It makes boundaries around the self/other—and also unsettles them: *my baby, who is not me.*

It surprised me, at first, given that the placenta is treated as a source of life, how often it was described as "treacherous," producing the baby "at the mother's expense."[15] In an article that refers to the placenta as a "turncoat" and a "very sneaky organ," the *New York Times* quotes a researcher who says that the placenta works against the interests of the mother:

> "The placenta will do everything it can to survive," Dr. Kliman said. "It's controlled by the genes of the father, and the father's goal is to make the biggest placenta and the biggest baby possible."
>
> This puts it at odds with the mother's evolutionary interests, he said. "The mother's goal is not to die during childbirth." (Rabin 2011)

Elsewhere, the placenta is described as "willfully" deceiving its host. One BBC headline reads, "Placenta 'Fools Body's Defences'" (*BBC News* 2007). An article from the Yale School of Medicine on preeclampsia depicts the placenta as deceptive: "Researchers observed how the placenta tricks the mother so she doesn't attack the trophoblasts that are trying to increase the flow of her blood into the placenta" (Peart 2011). Numerous reports suggest that the placenta does everything it can to protect the fetus. An article in *Nature*, for example, describes an experiment conducted on mice that showed that "when calories are restricted, the placenta steps up to the plate—actively sacrificing itself to protect the fetal brain from damage" (Corbyn 2011). Each of these narratives pits bodies against one another. In these descriptions the developing fetus is depicted as an invading enemy that uses the placenta to wage "all-out war with the mother" (see, e.g., Rabin 2011).

Before talking with women, I expected to find war metaphors in news reports but not in women's narratives. Mothers, I thought with the romanticism of someone who had not yet done much mothering, would surely have different ways to conceptualize their relations with their offspring than through violence. But then the women I conversed with also spoke of feeling attacked, drained, torn, and depleted by their pregnancies. I often heard iterations of the trope of the parasite: "The baby is eating me up!" Women routinely framed their relation as if through the economic logic of a limited good: given a finite amount of resources, nourishing one side of the relation comes at the cost of the other. One woman explained that when she felt weak during pregnancy, she imagined that her placenta was siphoning energy from her body to deliver it to her daughter. In the words of another woman, "Feeding it comes at a price to me."

And yet, woven into discussions of being depleted by the placenta, women also spoke of the power they derived from feeding the fetus/baby/child. If there seemed to be an economic calculus in the statement "It drains my energy," they also refused this calculus by finding the very condition of "weakness" enriching—a relation more commensal than parasitic. Indeed, most of the same women who described themselves as exhausted in their pregnancy also saw pregnancy as a source of strength. Women who described themselves as being devoured by their progeny also gained from this experience the skill and selfless virtue of motherhood (see also Paxson 2004). The way they folded strength and weakness together unraveled the mechanical model of conversion energetics, with its clearly defined self/other, inside/outside distinctions.[16] They did not seek holism, with its promise of entanglement; they often wanted separation. And yet the separations they sought were not often easy to economize into ones and twos. Placental boundaries separated self from other; these boundaries also facilitated connections. Is this a contradiction? Yes, and no. After all, the condition of nourishment is that it must be ongoing. Satisfaction is possible, and still it never lasts very long.

Experiencing "the Body," and the Problem of the "I"

I have so far suggested that the placenta may offer us an entry to conceptualize relations in such a way that temporalities, bodies, and persons loop together (*feeding back*) while also pulling apart (*feeding on*). To support this discussion of feeding relations, I have drawn on both popular and academic science as well as informal interviews with once-pregnant women. Taking inspiration from the dynamic qualities of *feeding*—which can imply giving, taking away, or something else entirely—I want to turn to write about *my* body in a way that makes apparent that this body is not only mine, nor is it a body whose "experience" is only felt inside it. The descriptions that follow experiment with using experience as a tool for accounting for that which a single body cannot contain. I hope to make evident that when we encounter the first person "I" or the possessive "my" or "mine"—we should not too quickly assume we know how many bodies or beings are involved.

THIRTY-ONE WEEKS INTO MY PREGNANCY, I SAT IN THE STARK LOBBY OF a diagnostic testing center in Amsterdam. I had recently begun to experience insatiable thirst. The feeling, which I could not locate, was entirely unfamiliar.

It would wake me up at night or catch me unawares in the middle of the day. I would drink glass after glass of water, but each sip, rather than produce relief, seemed to only incite my need for more.

I had mentioned this to the midwife, and she suggested a test for gestational diabetes: the experience of thirst was a common symptom.[17] She explained that while gestational diabetes could be serious, it was not a clear-cut disease. It results from a situation where the hormones that the placenta produces for fetal development impair insulin regulation in a woman's body. But during pregnancy it is difficult to set parameters for healthy or unhealthy insulin standards since increased insulin resistance in pregnancy is normal—and even desirable.[18] The placenta is *supposed* to create extra amounts of certain hormones since these can help to nourish the baby more efficiently, she told me. Blood sugar levels that would indicate diabetes in a nonpregnant woman might be of no concern during pregnancy.

"And the thirst?" I asked.

She responded that it was a pity I felt this, of course, "but it might be a good thing!"

The uncertainty about whether my discomfort was, indeed, undesirable was compounded by uncertainty about the consequences of gestational diabetes for the developing fetus. Scientific reports suggest that some degree of insulin resistance produces babies with a higher birth weight than they would have otherwise (Huxley 2000), but this is not a straightforward indicator of illness given that a high birth weight is often considered healthy rather than pathological. Another commonly cited effect of gestational diabetes is an increased "risk" of the development of metabolic illnesses later in the life of the offspring. Yet many with a high "risk" will never develop noticeable symptoms of disease. While it is possible that the placenta works against the interests and health of the parent, favoring the fetus, it is also possible that the condition of pregnancy will change these interests—and, with this, the conditions of health. Calculating interests may be a foundation of economic logic. It might be possible to do this here too. And still there was other accounting to be done. My suffering for the benefit of the fetus could also have a benefit for me. Its suffering for my benefit might also be good for it. What kind of grammar do we have for this mutualism?

While thirst would sometimes strike with intensity, often the feeling would go away. Was this the placenta doing its job? As it happened, when I arrived at the clinic for the gestational diabetes test, I felt no thirst at all, and because of this I was optimistic about the results (even as I was worried that the "good" timing would mask the problem). Much about this confidence changed, however, in the laboratory setting as I underwent the process of testing.

I handed my form to the receptionist, who asked if I was there for a diabetes test. She said nothing altogether inappropriate, but her question was loud enough for others in the waiting room to hear and left me feeling momentarily culpable, as though irresponsible behavior might have led me to the clinic that day. I wondered whether there was judgment in the room around me: Did others know that many women who develop gestational diabetes have no known risk factors—that there is nothing they might have done differently to prevent its onset? The feeling of responsibility I experienced was accompanied by my concrete individuation as I withdrew to the side of the room. With blame came an experience of myself as a solitary *I* that could be held at fault.

But in what way was this experience mine? It is relevant that I am no stranger to the pain and suffering of diabetes. I have conducted long-term ethnographic fieldwork in nutrition clinics in Guatemala, where diabetes was one of the main sources of concern. Through this project I lived with people suffering under the diagnosis of diabetes, encountering many stories about the struggle to manage the elusive illness—which was at times overwhelming and at others not apparent at all. I used this research to write a book illustrating varying ways that people were made responsible for metabolic illnesses—illnesses whose causes and effects, I argued, were typically not within their control (Yates-Doerr 2015). I knew that many with diabetes did not eat "unhealthy" diets and did not engage in "risky" behaviors and that "the individual" was neither at fault nor the unit through which treatment should proceed (Yates-Doerr 2017). And still I found myself wondering if *I* had done something wrong, if I had made bad decisions, and if I had somehow jeopardized my own health or the health of what was inside me. There is certainly nothing universal about this way of thinking; narratives of personal responsibility and individual accountability run deep in the United States, where I am from. But though I could trace the culturally contingent origins of the tendency to blame myself for needing to be tested, I could not think myself outside my context and, consequently, felt responsible.

Sitting in the waiting room of the clinic, I looked nervously at the paper chart in my hand. At the top, above the boxes that indicated the advised blood tests, someone had written my name in bold letters. Nearly a century ago, Marcel Mauss (1985) noted that though names and their meanings could take many forms, they constituted a basic unit of personhood. And there was the name's stark singularity. The blood they would draw was cataloged by this name, and the results of the tests would likewise be attributed to me. That I was relational was not obvious on paper; I appeared instead as distinct and bounded. This individuality was heightened when the name on the chart—my name—was called, and I was motioned into the consulting room. There was a single chair, positioned across from the desk. Had a family member or friend accompanied me, they would have waited in the lobby.

The nurse drew blood for the first sample and then had me drink a glucose-based syrup before leading me to a room at the back of the clinic. I would stay there for two hours with others undergoing the same procedure before she would return to draw a second sample of blood that would be tested to evaluate my reaction to the drink (as mediated by the placenta, the pancreas, and insulin hormones) and, from this, my degree of illness. Whereas the consultation room had individualized me, in this small backroom my relationality came rushing back. The solution I ingested was just over a cup. It didn't taste appealing, but surely I can handle this much sugar, I had encouraged myself while drinking it, as if willing my body to work. Shortly after sitting down, however, the feeling of being poisoned began. The effects of the liquid coursed through my body. My head grew numb, and my thoughts came in and out of focus—my body's evidence that it was not interested in listening to me. I clutched at my legs to keep from sliding to the floor, squeezing myself tightly, hoping that the physical pain might make me lucid. Then I felt the being inside me move and was reminded that my reaction to the sugar was not my reaction alone but was tied to the reaction of others: the placenta and the developing fetus, with cells from others still. I would not have been there, in that clinic in that poisoned position, had it not been for them.

I then recalled numerous patients I had met in Guatemala: Julia Monterrosa, who insisted over many visits to the nutrition clinic where I worked that it was not possible to eat alone; Gladis Xicara, who laughed when realizing that the recipes nutritionists had prescribed to her were single-serving portions intended for one; Carla Lopez, who was angered at how doctors had given her instructions for managing her diabetes, as if she had a choice over what and how she ate.[19] Finding myself on the patient side of the consultation, I also found myself in the company of others who had grappled with the diagnosis of diabetes. My questions—*What have I done? What should I do?* And also: *Why do you think this is something I have done? Why do you think there is anything I can do?*—had once been their questions. Along with the being that kicked from within, these Guatemalan women were there with me too.

As were other women in the Amsterdam clinic. "It's bad at first, isn't it?" one woman offered, responding to my obvious discomfort by sliding closer in case I needed help. Another also sympathized, sharing that she was there for the second time in two weeks, as her initial test had proved inconclusive. Before long, as the nausea and vertigo abated, we were speaking about foods we craved, the symptoms that had brought us there, and how strange it felt to have our flesh expand outward as our bodies became unfamiliar. We didn't learn each other's names. We didn't exchange life histories. It would not make sense to speak of us as fused. But for the two hours that we each waited for the next blood sample to be drawn, we mixed our stories together as we kept each other company—not as a totality but nonetheless connected. *Relational beings, in the act of relating.*

Surely, you might think, I did not need to narrate this experience through *my* body. Indeed, I talked with many women whose experiences, while not identical, make interesting stories, and I could easily have told a story of the partial connections of placental relations in the traditional third-person-singular style of most academic writing. But doing so would allow me to skirt a problem that must be addressed when evoking the narrative "I" in this context. For this "I" was not an independent, autonomous liberal subject. This was not *auto*ethnography as written by a conventional, *auto*nomous self. This "I" was at the same time a "we."

Feeding Relations

This chapter has mobilized the organ of the placenta to help conceptualize how relations can be simultaneously singular and shared, individualized and distributed, and nurturing and destructive. There might be a tendency to see this as a unique condition of fetal reproduction—something particular about the connection between parent and child. It is my hope, however, that the placenta offers insight into the broader relations of feeding that precondition living and dying, growing and decaying, being/having self and being/having something else.

We might be inclined to think of the placenta as a classic "boundary object" (Star and Griesemer 1989), an object that uses shared interests to facilitate exchange across differences. But in addition to being a boundary object, the placenta can also push us to rework the materiality of the boundary. In making apparent how conduits can be barriers while barriers can be porous and adaptive, the placenta can help us to see how boundaries can gain power while also changing form. In doing so, it pushes us to develop languages for articulating differences and unities in such a way as to account for the dynamism of barriers, compelling us to rethink the dualism (the binary, the separation, the division, and the border) between fusion/independence, subject/not-subject, or individual/not-individual in ways that can be otherwise. Placentas make hierarchies, even as they also undo them. They make powerful contradictions material, being, in the very same moment, harmful and healthy, wanted and repellent, life-giving and deadly, self and other.

The simultaneous "keeping while giving" of the placenta offers us the concrete lesson that we are not always autonomous individuals (Weiner 1983). And yet, because pregnant persons are still forced to be individuals in many circumstances, it also helps us to maintain awareness of the divisions that confront and shape bodies in the process of being formed. For while the placenta does not result in isolated (autonomous) beings, it is still capable of holding woman and child apart. It is not just that the placenta allows for things to be more than one and less than many; it allows for things also to be one and not one—or even one and two, or even one and many. It can handle the complexities of partial units that do not add up. It refuses unity and difference as they are conceived through the logic of liberal pluralism, helping us to see that neither is particularly good for the pregnant person. Fusion—blurring boundaries, ignoring difference, making the fetus be one with the woman that surrounds it—is not just physiologically treacherous but easily becomes a means of saddling a woman with the impossible responsibility for reproducing on her own. Yet celebrating the mutual autonomy of woman and fetus is hardly a desirable tactic either, as this can easily lead down the path of dangerous reproductive politics that pit one against another.[20] Rather than celebrate or dismiss independence, the placenta sets out to make new terms for the conversation. Feminist scholarship has taught us that "how to foster and nourish are never general questions, but relational situated ones" (Stengers 2008, 45); the feminist object of the placenta can help us to understand that the condition of "being relational" is but the beginning of the story.

And so "the story"—and how to tell it—has been a central concern of this chapter. As seen in the description of my experience with gestational diabetes, metabolic change in pregnancy can bring about embodied suffering, but this body that suffers, and the experience therein entailed, is not necessarily experienced by a discrete individual, even as this form of accounting is forced on the body. Mothers who worried about the effects that placentas had on their (individual) health also distributed their health into the bodies of others. The placentas that weakened them also gave them power. The same women who bemoaned their exhaustion also got strength from the experience of being host to their guest. In contrast to typical cost-benefit analyses, it was not feasible to sum together the drawbacks and benefits of the effects of the placenta and come out with a final score. The costs of affliction or the goods that may come of it here resist attempts at equivalency. The aspiration to balance offered by economic calculations made little sense in the everyday practice of placental boundaries; the obligation of credit or debit entailed in standard notions of reciprocity becomes hard to articulate in the space of divided connection. When I write, "I was thirsty," you might imagine an individual who experiences thirst in an independent body, whole and bounded. But as the feeding exchanges of the placenta make clear, I am never just myself.

By drawing attention to the shared singularity and distributed multiplicity of the placenta, I have suggested that there is no necessary contradiction between an embodied and distributed "I"—that these so-called contradictions are experienced by eating and feeding beings as fundamental to life. Then, in the footsteps of those who have argued for a conception of (indivi)duality that is not Cartesian and for a conception of agency that is spread across many (see Akrich and Pasveer 2004), I have suggested that the "I" of narration can be held within and distributed across bodies as well. My placenta can be mine and can also belong to another; my thirst can likewise be spread across many. Selves and experiences—*my* selves and *my* experiences—can be both embodied and shared.

Conclusion, after Birth

Marilyn Strathern has argued that "a world obsessed with ones and the multiplications and divisions of ones creates problems for the conceptualization of relationships" (2004, 53). She has gone to great lengths to illustrate the *dividuality* of social life—a term that highlights that people can appear as independent social microcosms while also reproducing "their own coded substances" in others (see McKim Marriott, cited in Strathern 1988, 348). Numerous theorists have since followed Strathern's call to situate actors (or actants) within networks of relations, but less has been made of the problem of narrating relations through the medium of written expression, where individuality reemerges through the seeming singularity of first-person authorship.

Responding to a posthuman criticism that the anthropological narrative voice risks shoring up the liberal subject's attributes of "embodiment" and "experience," in this chapter I have used the object of the placenta to consider how bodies and experiences can be objectified, singularized, while also refusing the taxonomic organization that requires the subject to be stable—such that even singularity can be done in multiple ways, and even one's experience can be spread across many. Rather than resolve the tension between writing the self and writing the other, I have instead offered the placenta as a feeding/eating organ that profusely resists resolution to show how it is possible to be both self and other, or, more radically, to rework the materiality of "the relation." For while placental relations collapse binaries, they nonetheless force us to contend with differences, distances, and separations. The women I spoke with and the journalistic and scientific representations of the placenta that I referenced illustrated a placenta that was of a woman's body and also of the bodies of others. I then narrated my experience with the placenta to make apparent that I am not, nor do I have, a body in any absolute sense. "The experience" of pregnancy helps us to see how bodies are constantly done and redone: by charts, feelings, diagnoses, tests, writing, and all their inter- and intra-actions. This is not a unique condition of pregnancy; rather, I have suggested that the placenta gives us insight into the dynamic terrain of feeding relations through which living and dying take form.

I end by drawing attention to one of the final actions of the placenta. Most pregnancy books I came across in my research consider the delivery of the placenta, not the child, as the final stage of vaginal birth. These texts routinely described the woman's body as if it were by this point in birth a willful muscle, expelling these *other*, foreign agents into the world, but I would learn, again, while giving birth that the body—my body—did not act in any solitary sense of the term. It is, after all, the suction of the newborn's mouth on the pregnant person's nipples that stimulates hormones that encourage the uterus to release the placenta. In turn, the breasts will not produce much milk so long as the placenta remains within the pregnant person's body. It is only on the placenta's exit from this body—its entry into a world it has helped to form—that the infant can begin to feast. We might think of this as a parting gift, the placenta enabling nourishment to come to the life that it has partially produced. But the pregnant person is there as well, pushing and contracting; as is the infant, also helping the process along by reaching and sucking; as is the community of partners, grandparents, siblings, and care providers and their technologies that make "the experience" possible. No one person gives a gift to another; each is instead enmeshed and intertwined even as it pulls apart, each a tenuously separate being, whose living necessarily depends on feeding relations.

ACKNOWLEDGMENTS

This chapter was drafted during frequent conversations with Rebeca Ibáñez Martín, Sebastian Abrahamsson, Filippo Bertoni, and Else Vogel, with the financial support of the European Research Council Grant #249397 for "The Eating

Body," supervised, with care, by Annemarie Mol. The Dutch Research Council Veni Grant #016.158.020 and the European Research Council Grant #759414 for "Future Health" offered me financial support during editing and rewriting. The chapter was enriched by the contributors to the European Research Council/Wenner-Gren Oslo Workshop on "Food's Entanglements with Life," generously hosted by Oslo University. Heather Paxson has been a steadfast editor, and I am also grateful to my intercalary comrades Harris Solomon and Deborah Heath for the extended conversations. I was pregnant with Orion Roper when I first wrote this chapter, and he is now ten years old. I am grateful to him and his younger brother, Saul, who continue to teach me about togetherness-in-difference.

NOTES

1. Beginnings are significant for legal and theoretical reasons, but they are not the focus of this article. I start here, with *this* beginning, because this is where someone else first articulated my pregnancy to me, drawing attention to my indivi/duality—suggesting that I was both distinguishable from others as a separate person and also twofold. For more on the complexity of describing personhood as connected to any given moment and this moment's relation to abortion politics, see especially Martin (1987), Rapp (1999), Morgan and Michaels (1999), and Halkias (2004).

2. I refer to myself here as a *multiple body* and not a body multiple to differentiate between the condition of holding various, transforming bodies *as* myself and Annemarie Mol's (2002) famous discussion of a singular body being enacted in multiple ways.

3. In line with a very strong tradition of home birth in the Netherlands, anesthesia is not a default expectation, and women are not assured of the possibility of having an epidural at birth. Because of this, there are extensive courses that coach women in techniques for pain management, and women commonly begin these at around fifteen weeks. For more on pain management and childbirth in the Netherlands, see Akrich and Pasveer (2004); and Logsdon and Smith-Morris (2017).

4. *Free Dictionary*, s.v. "placental barrier," accessed November 9, 2011, http://medical-dictionary.thefreedictionary.com/placental+barrier.

5. Posted September 20, 2011 on babyandbump.com, accessed November 9, 2011, http://www.babyandbump.com/trying-to-conceive/708482–4dpo-these-cramps-18.html.

6. Posted March 14, 2011 on babyandbump.com, accessed November 9, 2011, http://www.babyandbump.com/pregnancy-first-trimester/561201-feeling-quite-lot-better-today-hopefully-thats-placenta-taking-over.html.

7. It is common for pregnancy materials to refer to the pregnant person as a *mother* and to the developing cells (technically classified as either embryo or fetus) as a *baby* and to then give this baby a gender. In this chapter it is not my aim to encourage this way of speaking but simply to report on what was done.

For more on the difference between a pregnant person and a mother, see Davis-Floyd and Cheyney (2020).

8. "Your Placenta During Pregnancy," Ask-a-Mum, last accessed November 9, 2011, http://www.askamum.co.uk/Pregnancy/Search-Results/Health/Your-placenta-during-pregnancy/.

9. An analysis of the placenta as an "uncanny object" draws on the work of numerous feminist scholars who have analyzed pregnancy itself as an uncanny event (see especially Kristeva 1991).

10. For more on the notion of turning "the person" inside out, see the inspiring works of Emilia Sanabria (2016) and Harris Solomon (2016).

11. Influential anthropological research has considered the ways in which organ donation restructures a biomedical private, subjective sense of self (or selfhood) (e.g., Sharp 1995; Scheper-Hughes and Wacquant 2002; Waldby and Mitchell 2006). There is clearly a biomedical quality to these scientific descriptions of the placenta's hormonal flows, membrane permeability, and metabolic reactions. But under most circumstances, the placenta does not depend on laboratory life to upend notions of autonomy (but see Franklin 1995).

12. Gilles Deleuze and Félix Guattari (1987) have famously held the human organ to be a site at which subjectivity is fixed in place, but one wonders whether they have spent much time *being with* organs, since empirical examination of the placenta offers up another idea of what organs can be and do to subjectivity.

13. Rachel Vaughn (2019, 639) writes about "eating placenta" practices in the United States, noting the "paucity of research on one of the most crucial mediators of early human nutrition."

14. For more on what is gained by turning the theoretical focus on disentanglement instead of on relations, see Roberts (2017) and Candea et al. (2015).

15. The assumption made in these texts is that the pregnant woman is unquestionably the/a mother. This assumption ignores feminist scholarship that has shown how motherhood and womanhood are assembled; as a result, this association cannot be taken for granted. See, for example, Ginsburg and Rapp (1995); Franklin and Lock (2003); Thompson (2005); and Roberts (2012). For a critique of the idea that motherhood is necessarily *female*, see Strathern (2002).

16. For an insightful history of energetics as it relates to nourishment, see Landecker (2013).

17. In the Netherlands there is no routine test given for diabetes during pregnancy; the health system depends on "experience" and not routine laboratory testing for pursing the diagnosis of gestational diabetes.

18. In diabetes of the nongestational kind, the limits of "healthy" and "unhealthy" blood sugar are also far from transparent. For a discussion of how these standards are negotiated in practice, see Mol (2006).

19. All of the names are pseudonyms.

20. For a thoughtful discussion of the potential repercussions of viewing fetuses as autonomous "persons," see Morgan and Michaels (1999).

REFERENCES

Ahmed, Sara. 1998. *Differences That Matter: Feminist Theory and Postmodernism.* Cambridge: Cambridge University Press.

Akrich, Madeleine, and Bernike Pasveer. 2004. "Embodiment and Disembodiment in Childbirth Narratives." *Body and Society* 10 (2–3): 63–84.

Asdal, Kristin, Brita Brenna, and Ingunn Moser, eds. 2007. *Technoscience: The Politics of Intervention.* Oslo: Oslo Academic Press. https://www.southampton.ac.uk/~mwra1g13/msc/comp6037/pdfs/AsdalBrennaMoserTechnoscience.pdf.

BBC News. 2007. "Placenta 'Fools Body's Defences.'" November 10, 2007. http://news.bbc.co.uk/2/hi/health/7081298.stm.

Candea, Matei, Joanna Cook, Catherine Trundle, and Thomas Yarrow. 2015. *Detachment: Essays on the Limits of Relational Thinking.* Manchester: Manchester University Press.

Corbyn, Zoë. 2011. "Placenta to the Rescue." *Nature*, August 1, 2011. http://www.nature.com/news/2011/110801/full/news.2011.449.html.

Davis-Floyd, Robbie, and Melissa Cheyney. 2020. "Collaborating across Generations and Experience." *Fieldsights*, Society for Cultural Anthropology, February 6, 2020. https://culanth.org/fieldsights/collaborating-across-generations-and-experience.

Deleuze, Gilles, and Félix Guattari. 1987. *A Thousand Plateaus: Capitalism and Schizophrenia.* Translated by Brian Massumi. Minneapolis: University of Minnesota Press.

Duden, Barbara. 1993. *Disembodying Women: Perspectives on Pregnancy and the Unborn.* Cambridge, MA: Harvard University Press.

Franklin, Sarah. 1995. "Postmodern Procreation: A Cultural Account of Assisted Reproduction." In *Conceiving the New World Order: The Global Politics of Reproduction*, edited by Faye Ginsburg and Rayna Rapp, 323–45. Berkeley: University of California Press.

Franklin, Sarah, and Margaret M. Lock, eds. 2003. *Remaking Life and Death: Toward an Anthropology of the Biosciences.* Santa Fe: School of American Research Press.

Freud, Sigmund. 1953. *The Standard Edition of the Complete Psychological Works of Sigmund Freud.* Vol. 17. Edited and translated by James Strachey and Josef Breuer. London: Hogarth.

Ginsburg, Faye D., and Rayna Rapp, eds. 1995. *Conceiving the New World Order: The Global Politics of Reproduction.* Berkeley: University of California Press.

Halkias, Alexandra. 2004. *The Empty Cradle of Democracy: Sex, Abortion, and Nationalism in Modern Greece.* Durham, NC: Duke University Press.

Haraway, Donna J. 1988. "Situated Knowledges: The Science Question in Feminism and the Privilege of Partial Perspective." *Feminist Studies* 14 (3): 575–99.

Haraway, Donna J. 1991. *Simians, Cyborgs, and Women: The Reinvention of Nature.* New York: Routledge.

Huxley, Rachel R. 2000. "Nausea and Vomiting in Early Pregnancy: Its Role in Placental Development." *Obstetrics and Gynecology* 95 (5): 779–82.

Irigaray, Luce. 1993. *Je, Tu, Nous: Toward a Culture of Difference*. Translated by Alison Martin. New York: Routledge.

Jones, Elain, and Margarita Kay. 2003. *The Cultural Anthropology of the Placenta*. Walnut Creek, CA: AltaMira.

Kristeva, Julia. 1991. *Strangers to Ourselves*. New York: Columbia University Press.

Landecker, Hannah. 2013. "Postindustrial Metabolism: Fat Knowledge." *Public Culture* 25 (3): 495–522.

Logsdon, Katie, and Carolyn Smith-Morris. 2017. "An Ethnography on Perceptions of Pain in Dutch 'Natural' Childbirth." *Midwifery* 55:67–74.

Mann, Anna M., Annemarie M. Mol, Priya Satalkar, Amalinda Savirani, Nasima Selim, Malini Sur, and Emily Yates-Doerr. 2011. "Mixing Methods, Tasting Fingers: Notes on an Ethnographic Experiment." *Hau: Journal of Ethnographic Theory* 1 (1): 221–43.

Markens, Susan, C. H. Browner, and Nancy Press. 1997. "Feeding the Fetus: On Interrogating the Notion of Maternal-Fetal Conflict." *Feminist Studies* 23 (2): 351–72.

Martin, Emily. 1987. *The Woman in the Body: A Cultural Analysis of Reproduction*. Boston: Beacon.

Martin, Emily. 1991. "The Egg and the Sperm: How Science Has Constructed a Romance Based on Stereotypical Male-Female Roles." *Signs* 16 (3): 485–501.

Martin, Emily. 2007. *Bipolar Expeditions: Mania and Depression in American Culture*. Princeton, NJ: Princeton University Press.

Mauss, Marcel. 1985. "A Category of the Human Mind: The Notion of Person; the Notion of Self." In *The Category of the Person: Anthropology, Philosophy, History*, edited by Michael Carrithers, Steven Collins, and Steven Lukes, 1–25. Cambridge: Cambridge University Press.

Mol, Annemarie. 2002. *The Body Multiple: Ontology in Medical Practice*. Durham, NC: Duke University Press.

Mol, Annemarie. 2006. "Proving or Improving: On Health Care Research as a Form of Self-Reflection." *Qualitative Health Research* 16 (3): 405–14.

Mol, Annemarie. 2008. "I Eat an Apple: On Theorizing Subjectivities." *Subjectivity* 22 (1): 28–37.

Morgan, Lynn Marie, and Meredith W. Michaels. 1999. *Fetal Subjects, Feminist Positions*. Philadelphia: University of Pennsylvania Press.

Murkoff, Heidi. 2008. *What to Expect When You're Expecting*. 4th ed. New York: Workman.

Oaks, Laury. 2001. *Smoking and Pregnancy: The Politics of Fetal Protection*. New Brunswick, NJ: Rutgers University Press.

Paxson, Heather. 2004. *Making Modern Mothers: Ethics and Family Planning in Urban Greece*. Berkeley: University of California Press.

Peart, Karen. 2011. "Battle between the Placenta and Uterus Could Help Explain Preeclampsia." Yale School of Medicine, October 11, 2011. https://medicine

.yale.edu/news-article/battle-between-the-placenta-and-uterus-could-help-explain-preeclampsia/.

Rabin, Roni Caryn. 2011. "Turncoat of Placenta Is Watched for Trouble." *New York Times*, October 17, 2011. https://www.nytimes.com/2011/10/18/health/research/18birth.html.

Rapp, Rayna. 1999. *Testing Women, Testing the Fetus: The Social Impact of Amniocentesis in America*. New York: Routledge.

Reddy, Michael J. 1979. "The Conduit Metaphor: A Case of Frame Conflict in Our Language about Language." In *Metaphor and Thought*, edited by Andrew Ortony, 164–201. Cambridge: Cambridge University Press.

Roberts, Elizabeth. 2012. *God's Laboratory: Assisted Reproduction in the Andes*. Berkeley: University of California Press.

Roberts, Elizabeth. 2017. "What Gets Inside: Violent Entanglements and Toxic Boundaries in Mexico City." *Cultural Anthropology* 32 (4): 592–619.

Rosaldo, Renato. 1989. *Culture and Truth: The Remaking of Social Analysis*. Boston: Beacon.

Sanabria, Emilia. 2016. *Plastic Bodies: Sex Hormones and the Suppression of Menstruation in Bahia, Brazil*. Durham, NC: Duke University Press.

Santoro, Pablo. 2011. "Liminal Biopolitics: Towards a Political Anthropology of the Umbilical Cord and the Placenta." *Body and Society* 17 (1): 73–93.

Scheper-Hughes, Nancy, and Loic Wacquant, eds. 2002. *Commodifying Bodies*. London: Sage.

Sharp, Lesley A. 1995. "Organ Transplantation as a Transformative Experience: Anthropological Insights into the Restructuring of the Self." *Medical Anthropology Quarterly* 9 (3): 357–89.

Solomon, Harris. 2016. *Metabolic Living: Food, Fat, and the Absorption of Illness in India*. Durham, NC: Duke University Press.

Star, Susan Leigh, and James R. Griesemer. 1989. "Institutional Ecology, 'Translations' and Boundary Objects: Amateurs and Professionals in Berkeley's Museum of Vertebrate Zoology, 1907–39." *Social Studies of Science* 19 (3): 387–420.

Stengers, Isabelle. 2008. "Experimenting with Refrains: Subjectivity and the Challenge of Escaping Modern Dualism." *Subjectivity* 22 (1): 38–59.

Strathern, Marilyn. 1988. *The Gender of the Gift: Problems with Women and Problems with Society in Melanesia*. Berkeley: University of California Press.

Strathern, Marilyn. 2002. "On Space and Depth." In *Complexities: Social Studies of Knowledge Practices*, edited by John Law and Annemarie Mol, 88–115. Durham, NC: Duke University Press.

Strathern, Marilyn. 2004. *Partial Connections*. Walnut Creek, CA: AltaMira.

Thompson, Charis. 2005. *Making Parents: The Ontological Choreography of Reproductive Technologies*. Cambridge, MA: MIT Press.

Vaughn, Rachel. 2019. "Food, Blood, Nutrients: On Eating Placenta and the Limits of Edibility." *Food, Culture and Society* 22 (5): 639–56.

Waldby, Cathy, and Robert Mitchell. 2006. *Tissue Economies: Blood, Organs, and Cell Lines in Late Capitalism*. Durham, NC: Duke University Press.

Weiner, Annette B. 1983. *Women of Value, Men of Renown: New Perspectives in Trobriand Exchange*. Austin: University of Texas Press.

Weiss, Robin Elise. 2021. "Different Beliefs about the Placenta." About.com. Last modified September 13, 2021. http://pregnancy.about.com/cs/placentas/a/placenta.htm.

Yates-Doerr, Emily. 2015. *The Weight of Obesity: Hunger and Global Health in Postwar Guatemala*. Oakland: University of California Press.

Yates-Doerr, Emily. 2017. "Counting Bodies? On Future Engagements with Science Studies in Medical Anthropology." *Anthropology and Medicine* 24 (2): 142–58.

Young, Iris Marion. 1984. "Pregnant Embodiment: Subjectivity and Alienation." *Journal of Medicine and Philosophy: A Forum for Bioethics and Philosophy of Medicine* 9 (1): 45–62.

nourishment

EMILY YATES-DOERR / DEBORAH HEATH

Our chapters—one focused on the environment of pregnancy, the other on agricultural environments—share a concern with the role of nourishment in sustaining life. Both consider the thresholds beyond which organisms cease to thrive. And both recognize nourishment, as a practice of care, to be fundamentally ongoing. You don't just arrive at care and be done; it must be sustained. In eating, satiety is possible, but it never lasts for long. In our chapters and the collection overall, three overlapping terms—*care, sustainability, nourishment*—share a commitment to an ongoingness, to duration.

In Emily's chapter on the placenta, the language we have to talk about the directionality of relations fails us. One challenge presented by gestational diabetes is knowing how to parse harm from care. Even health experts hesitate to make a diagnosis because what is harmful might be good and what is good might be harmful. It would be too simple to say a parent's affliction is good for a fetus because harm to the parent extends outward, encompassing others. Health is not singular but is, as in this book's title, "beside ourselves."

Deborah's chapter on regenerative biodynamics also helps us to grasp the grounded, material implications of a relational understanding of health. The roots and rhizomes of grapevines make nourishment possible when life is under threat. The vines open up meaning's multidirectionalities, giving us a denser vocabulary to conceptualize relationalities, extending to violence as well as to care. Grapevines, like other photosynthetic plants, occupy a threshold, as entities that on the one hand derive nourishment from the sun and on the other both derive and provide nourishment beneath the soil, in the terrestrial realm. In *The Life of Plants* (2018), Emanuele Coccia refers to sun-loving plants, with their dual orientation, as ontologically amphibious. They are simultaneously one thing and another, and theirs is a central world-making role.

As plants become dependent on synthetic fertilizers, their companion soil microorganisms are disrupted and destroyed by pesticides and herbicides. Industrial chemical agriculture disrupts the cycles connecting the cosmos and our worldly domain. Forms of alternative agriculture, including biodynamics, that seek to return to interdependent networks of care reclaim something profoundly fundamental. They contest the world-destroying ethos of productivism and extractivism that utilizes resources along a linear logic, ignoring boundary-crossing networks of relations.

Deborah's discussion of biodynamics as slow science and Emily's discussion of the liminal in-betweenness of the placenta both resonate with Amy Moran-Thomas's discussion of the mechanisms of "slow care" in her *Traveling with Sugar* (2019). Under the crushing forces of racial capitalism, with its deadly impacts on the food system, people are still undertaking quiet, revolutionary acts of nourishment, as we see, too, in Ashanté Reese's discussion of delicious green tomatoes in Washington, DC (2019), or Hanna Garth's discussion of procuring rice in Santiago de Cuba (2020). Although we are mindful that just talking about pleasure and satisfaction might risk being harmful, in light of the inequities of suffering exacerbated during the present COVID-19 pandemic, there are also vital lessons to be gained from satisfaction. This is an important moment at which to reject the puritanical injunctions of capitalism that demand that we are never satisfied and to say "enough" (both that we have enough and that we have had enough).

We can, in fact, see unexpected pleasures and connections amid disruption and contagion. The social movements happening around Black Lives Matter in pandemic times have gone global, offering legitimate grounds for hope. The limits, the thresholds, that people have reached through exacerbated suffering and injustice have expanded solidarities and amplified a calling to account. Food studies scholarship remains relevant in revealing ways, from making visible the racial violence in meatpacking plants to tracking how climate change has accelerated zoonotic disease. If it was not evident before the COVID-19 pandemic that we are "eating beside ourselves," it is now. We are hopeful that this moment will lead to broader understanding of what is at stake in how we conceptualize multispecies relations and the porousness, along with the violence, of borders and boundaries, both human and more-than-human.

Emily's initial interest in the placenta was to explore how it presents us with self/other distinctions that open up questions about how to make—or unmake—family, society, and onward. Without presuming that umbilical cords and vines are the same, they do both function as transmission devices. As, of course, do viruses. Like cords and vines, viruses are thresholding objects that connect self and other, and the living and the nonliving. What impact will our new viral awareness have on clusters of social organization?

In the wine world, Deborah has heard attentive conversations during the pandemic about labor conditions for the largely Latinx vineyard workers in the U.S. who live in communities where people are typically in close proximity to one another. Folks are reconfiguring vineyard work so it can be done while maintaining physical distancing and to account for the fact that even when COVID testing is available, workers continue to circulate between work sites, complicating contact tracing. Rejuvenated attention to the importance and the (in)visibility of BIPOC stewards in vineyards, cellars, and wine commerce has challenged injustices, redistributed resources, and fostered extended kinship, all long overdue. Social media exchanges have amplified accounts of racial violence past and present, from microaggressions in the hospitality sector to Bordeaux merchants' major role, little recognized, in the transatlantic slave trade (O'Connor 2020; Brown and Gómez 2021).

Looking back from this epidemic to the near extinction a century ago of Europe's domesticated grapevines, we find a North American root louse surviving the transatlantic passage to arrive in terrains where there was no immunity. Fossil capital's accelerated pace of exchange, through steam travel, brought this critter to Europe. There are similarities here with wet markets and wherever else such transspecies exchanges occur at a pace that launches pandemics when we do not have a chance to develop a sort of interspecies familiarity to ease us into being-with one another.

In earlier discussions of COVID's origins, we heard about bats infecting humans, though of course we are not only on the receiving end of this virus but are very much part of its interspecies transmission, howsoever unevenly. The conventional US narrative sets us up to see ourselves as the protagonists of any story. Caring for children and students and growing older, in our experience, changes this: as Emily says in the previous chapter, *I* am a *we*. This is not a "we" of unity but a "we" of divisions to be honored or overcome. (As Emily writes, "Is this a contradiction? Yes, and no.") The impossibility of a fixed answer is at the heart of nourishing relations. We can help to generate nourishing relations, but "we" are not at the center of those stories because there is no center.

Reflecting on this leads us to embrace a practice of care that refuses an absolute distinction between harm and benefit and that recognizes nourishment as thresholding work that continually shifts between perils and possibilities. And that entails response-ability for staying with the trouble (thank you, Donna Haraway [2016]) within the stratified interdependencies of our multispecies entanglements.

REFERENCES

Brown, Elaine Chukan, and Tara Gómez. 2021. "What Wine Gets Wrong about Indigenous Americans." *The Four Top* (podcast), November 24, 2021. https://katherinecole.com/2021/11/24/indigenous-americans

Coccia, Emanuele. 2018. *The Life of Plants: A Metaphysics of Mixture*. Translated by Dylan J. Montanari. Cambridge: Polity.

Garth, Hanna. 2020. *Food in Cuba: The Pursuit of a Decent Meal*. Stanford, CA: Stanford University Press.

Haraway, Donna J. 2016. *Staying with the Trouble: Making Kin in the Chthulucene*. Durham, NC: Duke University Press.

Moran-Thomas, Amy. 2019. *Traveling with Sugar: Chronicles of a Global Pandemic*. Oakland: University of California Press.

O'Connor, Dinkish. 2020. "Bottles, Bones and Black Folk." *The Feiring Line*, September 3, 2020. https://thefeiringline.com/bones-bottles-and-black-folk/.

Reese, Ashanté. 2010. *Black Food Geographies: Race, Self-Reliance, and Food Access in Washington, D.C.* Chapel Hill: University of North Carolina Press.

chapter seven

Between Sky and Earth

....

BIODYNAMIC VITICULTURE'S
SLOW SCIENCE

DEBORAH HEATH

STANDING AT THE THRESHOLD BETWEEN LOCAL ROOTEDNESS AND global expansion, grapevines portend changes in our shared planetary metabolism. Deep-rooted, long-lived perennials of the genus *Vitis*, grapevines can persist in place for centuries, with some surviving specimens as much as four hundred years old. Anchored in their particular locales, grapes are touted by wine connoisseurs as exemplary emissaries of terroir, the "taste of place" (Trubek 2009), expressing the particularities of the limestone, or clay, or volcanic soil where they grow. They also actively participate in the microbial terroirs of their soil microbiomes and of the native yeasts that live on grape clusters. Biodynamic viticulture nurtures these local biologies that are threatened by conventional agriculture's chemical inputs and capitalism's enduring extractivism.

Domesticated for millennia, grapes, and the means to ferment them, have also traveled widely with their human companions, following the paths of Roman and European imperial expansion and carried forth by traders, missionaries, and settler colonists, taking root in temperate zones on either side of the equator. Grapes' noteworthy sensitivity to temperature variation has made them a proxy for and a harbinger of climate change past and future, with current climate projections indicating that as much as 73 percent of the world's principal wine regions may be unsuited for viticulture by 2050 (Le Roy Ladurie 1988; Hannah et al. 2013).

Just as the pathogens that arrived with European conquest decimated Indigenous people across the globe, the international exchange and transit of grape stock has also facilitated the spread of vine diseases like phylloxera, now endemic worldwide. In this case, the pandemic spread from North America to Europe, carried by a root louse that survived accelerated transatlantic passage on fossil capital's steamships (Malm 2015). The disease nearly wiped out Europe's vineyards in the late nineteenth century; they were saved only by interbreeding and grafting between European species and the wild grape species indigenous to North America. As the lockdowns, vaccinations, and health disparities of pandemic life in the COVID-19 moment have underscored, the boundary between contagion and multispecies conviviality is renegotiated in times of crisis, a reminder that the categories of native and invasive, companion species and pathogen, purity and danger, local and global are mutable, contestable, and coproduced.

Biodynamic and conventional wine producers share concerns about soil fertility, climate change, and persistent disease. Unlike those following a regime of agrochemical external inputs, the stewards of biodynamic vineyards, like those in Aotearoa New Zealand discussed here, use organic composting with herbal and mineral amendments, aiming to strengthen the energetic flow of the vines' immune systems and to enhance their planetary and subterranean connections. Biodynamic protocols and their more-than-human assemblages offer one approach to the "arts of living on a damaged planet" (Tsing et al. 2017), a mode of slow care (Moran-Thomas 2019) aiming to restore livability in the face of slow violence (Nixon 2013), the cumulative harm from climate change, chemical toxicities, disease, and capitalism's large-scale extractive practices.

On the autumn equinox each year, biodynamic vintners, farmers, and gardeners around the world pack cow's horns with manure and bury them to ferment until the following spring. Transformed into sweet-smelling humus over the winter, the horns' contents will be diluted and sprayed on the soil, enlivening its microbial activity and stimulating restorative humus production. This is Prep 500, one of biodynamic agriculture's nine preps, or preparations, used according to a calendar based on lunar and planetary cycles. The guidelines were first presented in 1924 by Rudolf Steiner, an Austro-Hungarian scientist, philosopher, and seer (and founder of the

Waldorf schools and Weleda natural pharmaceuticals). This series of lectures, later published as the *Agricultural Course* (Steiner [1924] 2004), was delivered to a group of farmers, landowners, and others in Koberwitz (now Kobierzyce, Poland) to address their persistent, widespread concerns about dwindling crop yields and increasing animal disease and sterility (Paull 2011a, 2011b).

The problem, according to Steiner, lay in the soil, impoverished by monoculture, the disruption of traditional nutrient cycles, and the nascent use of synthetic fertilizers that were both a response to and a symptom of intensive capitalist agriculture's much longer-standing impact on soil health and fertility. The consequences, Steiner argued, were both spiritual and material. "This is a problem of nutrition," he said. "Nutrition as it is today does not supply the strength necessary for manifesting the spirit in physical life.... Food plants no longer contain the forces people need." Therefore, he said, "The benefits of the biodynamic compost preparations should be made available as quickly as possible to the largest possible areas of the entire earth, for the earth's healing" (quoted in Pfeiffer [1956] 1993, 139). At the heart of his guidelines for rectifying this imbalance, planetary in scope with its local consequences, was his precept that the farm is an organism. Properly nurtured as a self-sufficient assemblage of plants, animals, composted manure, and living soil, the biodynamic vineyard, garden, or farm will feed itself, requiring no external inputs, with relations between sky and earth enhanced by the lively biodynamic preps in accordance with celestial temporalities.

Steiner would die a year after delivering his historic lectures but not before establishing a global network of cultivator-scientists, empirical observers constituted as the Agricultural Experimental Circle. By 1929 over eight hundred participants spread out across the globe, including followers in New Zealand and Australia. For the next decade, they would test Steiner's protocols in field and laboratory, culminating in the unveiling of this more-than-agricultural system in *Bio-Dynamic Farming and Gardening*, written by Steiner's close associate, soil scientist Ehrenfried Pfeiffer (1938, [1958] 2007).

In the intervening years since Pfeiffer's book appeared, the expansion of extractivist chemical-intensive agriculture and its attendant soil degradation has intensified. In the wine world, the post–World War II promotion of synthetic fertilizers, herbicides, and pesticides—in the name of "modernizing" viticulture through increased productivity and control—resulted in a striking decline in the vitality of valuable grapevines. Subsequently, numerous well-regarded vintners in Burgundy, the Loire, and elsewhere embraced biodynamic protocols in an effort to restore the health of their vines (see Joly 2005). In the global hierarchy of value (Herzfeld 2004), the conversion of high-status French vintners to biodynamics legitimated the use of practices otherwise marginalized as esoteric. Meanwhile, in areas where the immiseration of farmers has been most acute, such as in India, there has been a widespread embrace of biodynamics (as we note in more detail later on), this positive reception owing in part to indigenous cosmologies' alignment with Steiner's spiritual tenets linking the farm organism to the cycles of the cosmos.

In his writings and lectures that would give shape to biodynamics, Steiner paid tribute to "farmers' wisdom," *Bauernweisheit*, as a source of inspiration in his quest for alternative farming practices to counter the evident ills of European intensive capitalist agriculture.[1] Today an expanded reckoning with the roots of environmental crisis in colonialism and racialized global capitalism makes space for emerging dialogue between contemporary biodynamicists and the worldviews of Indigenous food and soil sovereignty activists, among them the collaborations with Māori and Indian farmers and activists discussed here. The "braided sciences" (Mukharji 2016) of these new and old knowledge practices present a path toward multispecies justice (Haraway 2015, 2018; Celermajer 2020; Fernando 2020; Lyons 2020; Chao, Kirksey, and Bolender 2022).

Planthroposcene Horizons

Grapevines and other photosynthetic plants play a world-making role at the threshold between celestial and terrestrial domains. Through photosynthesis, they ingest energy from the sun, transforming it to feed us twice, first by producing the oxygen essential to earthly life and then by converting sunlight into chemical energy, stored as carbohydrate molecules that generate food for other life-forms. Plants are, as agronomist and philosopher Emanuele Coccia (2018, 81) says, "ontologically amphibious" in their interstitial orientation. Able to sense and respond to both light and gravity, they maintain convivial relations below the surface of the soil with microbes and microfauna—provided that the soil is healthy and uncontaminated. While plants are phototropic above ground, swerving toward the sun, seeds, in the absence of light, are gravitropic, relying on gravity, earthly energy, as the singular cue to direct growth of both roots and shoots.

Joseph Murray, a biology professor, professional arborist, and biodynamic farmer, shares his insights on his blog and on the lecture circuit, speaking at a recent US national biodynamic conference in Portland, Oregon (2018a). In a blog post he drew on Steiner's fourth lecture from his 1924 *Agricultural Course* "to explain the importance of having an expanded awareness of subtle interactions of unseen substances, forces, and spirits to better manage one's farm" (2018b). Steiner uses his notion of "etheric vitality" to give a relational account of the connections linking plants, trees, roots, and living soil, a radical account for his day but consistent with both contemporary soil science and the perspective maintained by biodynamic and other organic farmers and gardeners who focus on sustaining the soil food web.

Murray quotes Steiner's fourth lecture, in which Steiner says that "the soil surrounding the growing plants' roots is a living entity with a vegetative life of its own, a kind of extension of plant growth into the Earth." Steiner then continues, focusing in particular on the interface between the root and its surrounding soil: "It is not at all true that life stops at the plant's perimeter. Life as such continues on, namely from the roots of the plant into the soil, and for many plants there is no sharp dividing line between the life inside them and the life in their surroundings" (quoted in Murray 2018b). This is the threshold area biologists now identify as the *rhizosphere*, a vital contact zone understood as a site of energetic encounters linking soil microbes, mycorrhizal fungi, roots, and their plants. As Murray (2018b) comments, "Beneficial bacteria which adhere to up to 40% of the root surface are involved in relationships with organisms as far out into the soil as the food web extends.... Although not well understood in 1924, today soil biologists recognize the importance of the life that occurs within, on, and near plants' roots, so much so that the rhizosphere has been called the most biodiverse and dynamic habitat on Earth." The dynamic communication between a plant's roots and its soil surround is facilitated by arbuscular mycorrhizal fungi, which exchange photosynthesized sugars with root tips, performing a range of "ecosystem services" including transporting soil minerals or water otherwise inaccessible to the plant. Now available as a commercial inoculant, these fungi are used to foster lively soil—an emerging strategy in BioAg, or biological agriculture, as an alternative to industrial chemical fertilizers, touted as a possible "middle agriculture" approach between the poles of chemical-industrial agriculture, on the one hand, and biodynamics and other holistic, organic approaches such as agroecology and permaculture, on the other (Oviatt 2020; Oviatt and Rillig 2021).

Among recent intellectual tropisms in anthropology, there has been a swerve toward plants and their multispecies soil surrounds in the midst of conceptual grappling with how to account for extractivism's anthropogenic environmental destruction while crafting spaces for a pluriverse to thrive.[2] Natasha Myers (2018) has, in playful seriousness, called this the Plant Turn, with an exhortation to envision an alternate possible future she dubs the Planthroposcene—an aspirational scene, rather than another attempt to delineate a named geological epoch to account for the planet's anthropogenic precarity (Holdrege 2014; Hartigan 2017; Puig de la Bellacasa 2017; Stoetzer 2018). Attentive to the prospects for attunements across species difference, the Planthroposcene aims to counterbalance the productionist dynamics that undergird the dominant chemically intensive objectivist worldview (Myers 2015, 2018).

Consider the contrasting temporalities of conventional agriculture and ecological care for the soil. The artificial fertility of chemically damaged soil is sustained at an accelerated pace to meet the production demands of extractivist agriculture. Biodynamicists, like the permaculture activists whom Maria Puig de la Bellacasa (2017, 170) studies, slow down the pace, aiming to remediate the blasted landscapes of chemical-industrial agriculture through what she calls "human-soil relations of care." This presents, she argues, an alter-biopolitics, which blurs the boundaries between bodies and their environments, the fraught, confounding world-making, or world-unmaking, entanglements of humans and more-than-humans at this uncertain moment.

In alliance with both long-standing and more recent conversations in feminist science and technology studies that have contemplated the intertwining of more-than-human socialities with an ethics of care, I consider how both the historical foundations and the contemporary practices of biodynamics exemplify and extend a vision of what Isabelle Stengers (2018) calls *slow science*. Along with the measured pace of biodynamic care for the soil, Steiner's slow science focused on the "arts of noticing" (Tsing 2015) or the "arts of attentiveness" (van Dooren, Kirksey, and Münster 2016), key to multispecies caregiving. Here Steiner drew inspiration from his close familiarity with the work of Johann Wolfgang von Goethe, and what Goethe called "a delicate empiricism," *eine zarte Empirie*, a participatory attunement with the natural world (Steiner [1883] 2000; Robbins 2006).

In *Thinking like a Plant*, a plant-familiarization field guide shaped directly by Goethe's work, scientist and biodynamic educator Craig Holdrege includes an enjoinder to slow down, taking the time to "dwell" with the plants, to sketch them in order to "facilitate looking," and to let "our attention spread out and wait to find what comes towards us" (2014, 49). The slow science of biodynamics nurtures plants and mycorrhizal fungi, and links celestial and terrestrial realms, through practices of engaged observation—a gentle empiricism for transforming landscapes at the edge of extinction. In the face of increasing environmental precarity, biodynamics, with its embrace of "the plant in between" (Breda 2016), offers contrasting ways of being in relation to modes of world-making, linking emergent ecologies to strategies for survival and regeneration within the present moment in capitalist world ecology (Moore 2014, 2016; Kirksey 2015; Jones 2019).

Biodynamic Cosmopolitics in Central Otago, New Zealand

Burn Cottage claims to be the first biodynamic vineyard in New Zealand's Central Otago region. The "Philosophy" page of the vineyard's website prominently displays a portrait of Rudolf Steiner and a quote from him: "All of nature begins to whisper its secrets to us through its sounds. Sounds that were previously incomprehensible to our soul now become the meaningful language of nature" (Burn Cottage, n.d.).

The daily practices of the biodynamic vintner or farmer aim for the sort of direct, experiential observation that Steiner learned to appreciate as the young editor of Goethe's scientific writings. Steiner came to embrace Goethe's dedication to a "delicate empiricism" based on close, empathic observation of dynamic natural processes, such as the transformation and variation of plants that Goethe studied closely in his *The Metamorphosis of Plants* ([1790] 2009).

As I walk through the vines with vineyard manager Shane Livingstone, he heads first thing to a compost pile, digging a hand into the dark, rich soil, amended with the special biodynamic preparations, and presents the lively earthworms within. As we continue our walk, Shane points out the cattle, which provide manure for biodynamic composts at Burn Cottage. Shane, who started out as a dairy farmer, comments that the animals bring a certain peace and soothing rhythm to the farm. He knows individual animals and plants as well, saying that he "picks up feelings" while walking through the vineyard, where, he says, he can feel the strength and resilience of the plants. Echoing Steiner's dictum that a farm is a living organism, Shane says, "It's supposed to be a whole system." Nestled in a bowl protected from winds by surrounding hills, the vineyard's ten hectares of grapevines (about twenty-five acres) are surrounded by twice as much land, dedicated to creating a self-sufficient farm system.

In the 1920s, when Steiner first framed the principles of biodynamics, nitrate-based synthetic fertilizers had just come into use, based on the discoveries of German chemist Fritz Haber. Proponents of biodynamics often set the clock on their history there. It is a longer history, however, that ties soil fertility, and its loss, to what Jason Moore (2016) calls the capitalist world ecology. The presence of animals such as cattle, sheep, and horses on biodynamic farms, coworkers in producing composts rich with microbes and earthworms, is heralded as a step toward healing the "metabolic rift" (Foster

1999; see also Landecker, chapter 2), recapturing a regenerative nutrient cycle at the level of the farm organism.

In the emerging soil science of the nineteenth century, the work of chemist Justus von Liebig led to the development of superphosphates, the first synthetic fertilizer. Though targeted by eco-activists as instrumental in the rise of agrochemicals (and thrashed by Stengers [2018] as the founder of what she calls "fast science"), Liebig and his chemical fertilizers emerged along with his harsh critique of the way in which urbanization and intensive agriculture together disrupted the nutrient cycle that traditional self-contained farming had maintained. In a scathing satirical passage, Liebig (1859) condemns the role of Britain in pillaging other parts of the world for human bones and guano, highly sought-after sources of essential soil nutrients, to replenish soil increasingly exhausted by extractive agricultural practices: "Great Britain deprives all countries of the conditions of their fertility. It has raked up the battle-fields of Leipsic, Waterloo, and the Crimea; it has consumed the bones of many generations accumulated in the catacombs of Sicily; and now annually destroys the food for a future generation of three millions and a half of people. Like a vampire it hangs on the breast of Europe, and even the world, sucking its lifeblood without any real necessity or permanent gain for itself" (quoted in Brock 1997, 178). Though Liebig, like Karl Marx and other nineteenth-century observers, correctly noted the rift in the global metabolism, his proposed agrochemical solution—and its worldwide application—has magnified and intensified the soil degradation that the slow science and slow care of biodynamics aims to address. Furthermore, the ascendance of the paradigm reducing soil to its chemical constituents (NPK: nitrogen, phosphorus, potassium), eclipsed soil biology's crucial multispecies entanglements while catalyzing and complementing transnational agriculture's expansionist logic (Marchesi 2020).

Among what Anna Tsing (2005) calls the "sticky materialities" and frictions that complicate the apparent free flow of abstract global capital, biodynamics is both locally focused and globally mobilized, while remaining entangled with the global reach of conventional agriculture. In the case of Burn Cottage, its owners, the Sauvage family, are large-scale producers of cattle, cotton, and wheat, from Oberlin, Kansas, in the United States, who launched cotton-farming operations in Australia in the 1960s. Their more recent investments include wine importing and sales as well as the recent purchase of a largely organic German winery.

Global in scope from its early days, biodynamics came to Burn Cottage under the guidance of two consultants, each with particular cosmopolitan connections. Californian biodynamic vintner Ted Lemon first trained in Burgundy, returning to California to launch one of California's first biodynamic wineries, Littorai. Littorai's website critiques conventional agriculture as "inadequate in its conception of plant growth and nutrition" and promotes "alternative agricultural paradigms" of noninterventionist viticulture, including permaculture, agroecology, and biodynamics (Littorai n.d.).

Early on, Burn Cottage also engaged New Zealand's leading biodynamic consultant, Peter Proctor (1928–2018), a soil scientist who developed a barrel compost known as *cow pat pit* (CPP), made from cow manure mixed with ground eggshell and basalt dust, inoculated with several biodynamic herbal preps. Widely used by New Zealand's biodynamic vintners, cow pat pit is an efficient way to administer several of the herbal amendments that biodynamic agriculture recommends.

Proctor taught courses on biodynamic agriculture at Taruna College, an anthroposophical training center on New Zealand's North Island, shaping the practices of a number of New Zealand's upcoming biodynamic vintners. His book on biodynamic farming and gardening, *Grasp the Nettle* ([1997] 2013), is widely read; the title is a British expression meaning "to tackle a difficult task boldly," an apt exhortation for biodynamic cultivators facing both the overwhelming dominance of chemical-industrial agriculture and the pervasive skepticism of many about biodynamics' esoteric practices.

Proctor also regularly traveled to India over a span of many years along with his partner, Rachel Pomeroy, training farmers in biodynamic agricultural practices, including the use of cow pat pit, now widely used in many parts of India by thousands of small farmers and a number of large tea plantations. Ted Lemon told me that Proctor often contrasted his widespread, enthusiastic reception in India with the effort required to persuade growers in New Zealand to move beyond conventional agriculture.

Cosmopolitical Traffic between Aotearoa and India

Proctor and Pomeroy's impressive work successfully promoting biodynamic practices in India is documented in the film *One Man, One Cow, One Planet* (Burstyn 2008). Officials from the biodynamic certifying organization Demeter report that there are nearly 100,000 Indian farmers working biodynamically, compared with 1,700 Demeter-certified farmers working in Germany. A range of factors, along with the New Zealand educators' long-term outreach efforts, contribute to biodynamics' enthusiastic reception in India.

The biodynamic model of farms as self-sustaining units free from harmful, expensive chemical inputs resonates with Indian farmers faced with widespread soil degradation, usurious seed companies, and intransigent cycles of debt. Reverence for the cow in Hindu culture ensures a positive reception for biodynamic manure-based composting. Moreover, traditional farming in India (and elsewhere) has a long history of using composted manure to enhance soil fertility. Biodynamics catalyzes the revival of soil microbial activity and the restoration of nutrient cycles through the use of cow manure compost, also central to Zero Budget Farming, a homegrown Indian organic farming movement that refers to fermented cow manure as "the nectar of life" (Münster 2018).[3]

Further, the esoteric spiritual aspects of biodynamic practices that risk dismissal in skeptical rationalistic contexts find a more receptive audience in India among farmers and agronomists alike. Sarvdaman Patel, an agronomist who teaches courses on biodynamic farming on his farm in the state of Gujarat, says, "Biodynamic stresses on spirituality and on following a calendar based on the positions of stars and the moon before planting and harvesting crops. This is something that Indians, for whom astrology is integrated into daily lives, instinctively connect with" (quoted in Kumar 2017).[4]

With decades of experience teaching about biodynamics in both India and New Zealand, Rachel Pomeroy has lectured—most recently at the 2020 International Biodynamics Conference in Switzerland—about correlations between the biodynamic calendar and both Hindu astrology and Māori star lore. Calling herself a "star lover," Pomeroy regularly participates in solstice ceremonies at Ātea a Rangi, the Māori star compass site. This large Stonehenge-like open-air structure was built in 2017 as an educational tool as part of the revival of the celestial navigation skills used by the Māori's ancestors to travel across vast expanses of open ocean waters. The fact that Austronesians' intimate knowledge of stars' daily and seasonal transits guided them from Taiwan to Polynesia and on to Aotearoa New Zealand offers to demystify star lore for the contemporary skeptic.

In Aotearoa New Zealand, the first human inhabitants, the ancestors of the Māori, arrived in the 1300s from Polynesia via a series of canoe voyages, using star maps to navigate thousands of miles of open ocean. After settling in their new locale, they charted the seasonal cycles for gardening and hunting using the positions of the stars on the horizon. Today Māori food sovereignty activists like Dr. Jessica Hutchings, who runs a biodynamic family farm, work to amplify and revitalize Māori traditions and to "elevate the mana of the soil" through an organic agriculture certification program called *hua parakore* that is based on core Māori principles like *whakapapa*, more-than-human family or heritage, the genealogy of all living things linking people to earth and sky (Hutchings et al. 2018). Hutchings has worked along with Pākehā (Euro–New Zealander) biodynamic educators, including Pomeroy, to explore shared concerns about sustainability, soil health, and social and planetary well-being, while emphasizing the role of both the afterlives of colonialism and racialized capitalism in the precarity of the contemporary food system.[5]

Celestial and Bovine Temporalities

The conversion of Central Otago vineyard Domaine Thomson was overseen by dedicated biodynamicist Su Hoskin, a British immigrant who worked at Burn Cottage and studied biodynamics at Peter Proctor's Taruna College. In 2018 she and Rachel Pomeroy hosted a biodynamic workshop at Domaine Thomson entitled "Water and Light." For several years she has moderated a biodynamic reading group that includes many of the region's prominent biodynamic vintners. Like in other biodynamic vineyards I visited in New Zealand, Proctor's influence can be seen in the shed that Su maintains with pots for barrel compost (cow pat pit) and other biodynamic preparations. The large calendar on the wall is marked with astrological constellations and their symbols, used to keep track of when different batches of compost were made and turned (see figure 7.1). Su's illuminating detailed notes, formerly housed on the winery's website, take careful note of celestial timing and of the interactions over time among animals, plants, and the cosmos.[6]

In biodynamics' slow science, cows, their horns, and their digestive processes are seen as mediators between the cosmos and the earth. Prep 500, horn manure, involves packing cow's horns with manure, which are buried in the fall and exhumed in the spring, to reveal microbially rich, sweet-smelling humus that will then be used in homeopathic dilutions for soil enhancement. Prep 501, horn silica, is made by packing cow's horns with crushed quartz; the horns are buried in the spring and dug up in the fall. Su discusses the polarities intrinsic to cows, manure, the seasons, and their environment. Writing about Prep 500, she says, "The cow reflects, in the form and substance of her horn, the living forces that are released by digestion and indeed, the whole environment from where the fodder comes and in which she lives.... The fodder is very different in quality as the seasons change. By gathering it at this culminating time of the year, we take something like a concentration from the essence of late summer ... and contain and preserve it in the horn during burial over winter."[7] The seasonal changes in the plant life that the cow eats

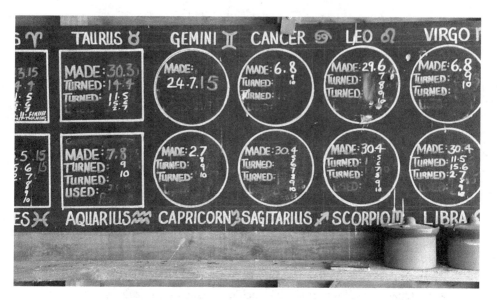

FIGURE 7.1 Su Hoskin's Biodynamic compost calendar, Domaine Thomson, Central Otago, New Zealand. Photo by Deborah Heath.

capture earthly life cycles in Prep 500, and their transformation while buried between seasons is complemented by Prep 501, in which the crushed quartz is understood to capture "crystallizing light forces." As Su says:

> One [Prep 500] is of summer origin and distributes winter forces. The other [Prep 501] is of winter origin and distributes summer forces. Homeopathy treats like with like. The resulting treatments are healing remedies for the earth and the atmosphere.
>
> It could be said that the silica is an expression of the contraction forces in nature, while the cow dung is an expression of expansion forces. One reflects the cosmos and relates to the fruit formation, colour and smell, the other is carrier of the forces that form the living structure.[8]

The biodynamic grower's direct, hands-on engagement with cows, their manure, their horns, the quartz, and other amendments used in the biodynamic compost preps, and with the seasonal cycles of transformation, invites the kind of participatory attunement across differences that Deborah Bird Rose (2011, 88) calls an "ontology of connectivity." This slow science nurtures connections among "nested metabolisms" (Landecker 2011), participatory cycles of feeding and ingestion rather than capital's subject-object relations. (Think for a moment about Alex Blanchette's endlessly partible, commodifiable hogs [chapter 3] in contrast to the integrated role of cows, their manure, and the preps on the biodynamic farm organism.)

Reflecting on the multispecies and cosmic entanglements of her biodynamic farming practices, Māori food sovereignty activist Jessica Hutchings draws on Māori *kōreros*, stories, as well as on biodynamic narratives. Both biodynamics and *hua parakore* (Māori organics) tap into what the Māori call *mauri*, life force; Hutchings remarks that "it's about vibration, it's about energy, it's about land healing" (Hutchings 2019). She draws on the Māori origin story of the primal couple, Rangi, Sky Father, and Papa, Earth Mother, to account for the dynamic role the cow and her composted manure play at the threshold between sky and earth, connecting with and revitalizing the *whenua* ("land," also "placenta"). "You think of the digestive system of the cow; it's really that middle space, that space in between that can help to bring balance when you use cow manure in a certain way on the whenua. It brings about healing, and it brings about balance. It's about that balance between Earth and Sky energy. So that's a biodynamics kōrero, but it's also a Hua Parakore kōrero, cos for me it is about mediating that relationship between Rangi and Papa, between Stars and Sky and Earth" (Hutchings 2019). The transcorporeal cycles of ingestion and feeding link cows, the grass they eat, the horn manure of Prep 500, and the other biodynamic preps to the health of living soil, crops, animals, and people. For Hutchings, this focus on elevating the *mana* (prestige, authority) of the soil is key to efforts to restore Māori land, soil, and food sovereignty. As an aspirational goal, she and her colleagues propose according personhood status to the soil, following recent legal precedent in Aotearoa New Zealand that assigned personhood to a conservation park (the Te Urewera Act of 2014) and a river (the Whanganui River Act of 2017) (Hutchings et al. 2018).

Settlers, Invaders, Healers, and Hybrids

The cows who reside at a number of the vineyards I visited graze under trees planted to enhance biodiversity on terrain that was previously used for (and denuded by) sheep grazing, part of intentional efforts that frequently include restoring "native" habitats. The presence/absence of life-forms designated as native or indigenous, and the classification of others (or the same ones) as invasive, varies with their relations and histories, and with the perspectives of those in charge of classificatory distinctions. None of the plants used in preparing the various herbal biodynamic preps are native to New Zealand, and neither, of course, are the grapevines they are being used to nourish. As Stefan Helmreich

(2009) suggests in his rich and nuanced account of such matters in Hawai'i, the very categories of nature and culture are under constant negotiation in struggles to determine where the boundaries of inclusion and exclusion, of native and invasive, lie. The distinction between threshold as limen and as limit is in flux as these boundaries shift.

Horsetail, *Equisetum arvense*, is a rhizomatic plant used to make biodynamic Prep 508, a soil treatment regarded as protecting grapevines from fungal infections such as powdery mildew that conventional viticulture treats with synthetic fungicides. Horsetail has been used in traditional Western medicine to care for wounds and to strengthen fingernails. The plant contains silica as well as calcium and potassium, and the silica is said to reduce the effects of water or humidity that can promote fungal growth. Su Hoskin says the best times to use the Prep 508 spray on the grapevine leaves are around the new and full moons. These moments in the lunar cycle, as well as periods of wet weather, have the strongest watery influences and therefore present vineyards with the greatest threat of pathological fungi. Echoing the widely held view of how Prep 508 works to combat vine diseases like powdery mildew, Su says that the function of horsetail is to bolster the plants' resistance to fungal diseases, not to kill the fungus as the widely used fungicides are intended to do.

New Zealand, like neighboring Australia, has a strict system of governance for naming and monitoring species designated as native and invasive. The national agency Biosecurity New Zealand is in charge of this task of surveilling the inclusion and exclusion of plants and animals deemed to be pests versus those that are valued or protected. Introduced in New Zealand in the 1920s, since the mid-1990s horsetail has been designated as an invasive species on New Zealand's National Pest Plant Accord, meant to prohibit its distribution and cultivation. As Su wryly notes, "On a more holistic level, this statement would seem more fitting: 'grows in abundance' due to its usefulness!"[9]

On this island nation whose only mammals were three species of bats before the arrival of its human habitants, conservation and restoration involve classificatory interventions about which life-forms are now considered deserving of protection, and which are subject to discipline or exclusion. Aotearoa New Zealand has been described as the nation with the shortest record of human habitation, beginning in the thirteenth century with the Polynesians, who would later come to be called the Māori, who brought Polynesian rats and dogs as meat sources, and crops from their homeland, including sweet potato, yam, and taro.

In the liminal nether region between wild and domestic, feral cats and dogs are on the official list of invasive species seen as threatening to native lifeforms. So are "wilding conifers," including the Douglas fir, along with plants like horsetail regarded as medicinal by biodynamic and (other) homeopathic practitioners. For vineyards and other agricultural terrain, rabbits have been seen as a particular scourge in New Zealand and Australia since their introduction by British settler colonists, with extermination efforts including the introduction of some particularly nasty viruses such as rabbit hemorrhagic disease and the mechanical ripping up of rabbit warrens and their inhabitants. Sheep, on the other hand, whose grazing habits have also been a source of significant soil erosion, have remained a protected commodity, part of the intensive large-scale agricultural practices characteristic of the New Zealand settler colony's political economy since the nineteenth century.

Viticulture in general, and biodynamic viticulture in particular, is good to think with when considering which species are considered to be at home and where the categorical boundaries of difference defining "native," "wild," and "invasive" are drawn with respect to domesticated or commercialized species of plants or animals. With no grapes native to the Antipodes, the first vines were brought to New Zealand by Marist priests, by European immigrants from regions with established traditions of wine production and consumption, and by James Busby, the Scottish immigrant designated as New Zealand's first British Official Residence in 1832, representing the British Empire in the new colony. Busby was a viticulture aficionado who had toured vineyards in France and Spain, bringing classic European vines to Australia and New Zealand (Howland 2014).

Two North American immigrants would subsequently dramatically alter the viticultural landscape in Aotearoa New Zealand, as elsewhere in the viticultural world: the destructive root louse responsible for the vine disease phylloxera and the rootstocks of grape species native to North America that are resistant to phylloxera. After phylloxera was discovered in New Zealand in 1885, many vineyards planted Franco-American hybrid varieties, a strategy followed in France before grafting European grapes onto North American rootstock became the norm. In New Zealand, hybrid grape varieties, later banned with purificatory zeal in Europe, predominated from 1900 until the 1970s.

When the country's wine industry, led by large, well-capitalized transnational enterprises, turned toward the export trade, vineyards were once again planted with Old World grapes (Overton and Murray 2014). The wine grapes that currently dominate the New Zealand wine "brand" led by these large-scale export producers are all so-called noble grapes, varieties historically associated with regions in France. Since the 1980s New Zealand has been best known for the aromatic white wine sauvignon blanc. The vintners that I visited on the cooler South Island primarily produce pinot noir and chardonnay, the famous wine grapes of Burgundy, where some of France's highest-status vintners have also embraced biodynamics.

Diagnostic Weediness and Life by Weight

East of Central Otago, in New Zealand's Canterbury region, Pyramid Valley Vineyards, which has been biodynamic since its inception in 2000, grows pinot noir and chardonnay. The late Mike Weersing and Claudia Elze, both thoughtful, philosophical committed biodynamicists, founded and ran Pyramid Valley until its recent sale in 2017, two years after my visit.[10] Mike, an American, encountered biodynamics while working on vineyards in Burgundy, Alsace, and Germany, including time collaborating overseas with brilliant, visionary California biodynamic vintner Randall Graham. In selecting a vineyard site for their Burgundian grape varieties, Mike and Claudia sought and found the combination of clay and limestone soil characteristic of Burgundy's great vineyards, which pinot noir and chardonnay are understood to prefer.

The vineyard has mostly avoided the North American interlopers that remade Europe's Old World wine terroirs and followed viticultural traffic to much of the rest of the world. Although the phylloxera pandemic reached New Zealand's first vineyards in the late nineteenth century, not long after its destructive emergence in Europe, it arrived much later on New Zealand's cooler South Island, first documented in 2002. At the entrance to Pyramid Valley is a prominent sign attached to a wine barrel:

PYRAMID VALLEY VINEYARDS
PHYLLOXERA-FREE AREA
PLEASE DO NOT TRESPASS OR ENTER
IF YOU HAVE VISITED OTHER VINEYARDS

Free of the phylloxera louse, Pyramid Valley's grapevines are mostly own-rooted, rather than grafted, a characteristic that is believed to help them express their particular terroirs. Just 3–4 percent are grafted, using Rootstock 420A, a hybrid of two North American grape species developed by French scientists at the height of the nineteenth-century phylloxera outbreak, one of many miscegenated rootstocks that now lie beneath the *Vitis vinifera* grapes of most vineyards in Europe and the rest of the world.

While in Burgundy Mike Weersing met and befriended French scientist and renowned ally of biodynamics Claude Bourgignon. A soil scientist who worked for many years in a French national research facility, Bourgignon began trials in Burgundy in the 1980s comparing biodynamic and conventional vineyard plots after demonstrating that extensive chemical inputs had left the exalted Burgundian vineyards devoid of the microbial companions essential to healthy plant-soil relations As he famously intoned in a 1992 lecture that scandalized, then galvanized, elite French vintners, the soil of Burgundy had come to have fewer microorganisms than the sands of the Sahara (Capalbo 2008). Bourgignon's field studies showed convincingly that biodynamic preparations restored the lost soil vitality, thereby persuading several premier vintners to initiate biodynamic conversion. With his partner Lydia, Claude Bourgignon now runs an independent soil analysis firm based on agroecological rather than agronomic principles, continuing to champion the power of organic and biodynamic agriculture to nourish and revitalize the microbial communities that live within healthy soil and that are essential to freeing plants from dependence on synthetic inputs (Bourgignon and Bourgignon 2015).

Following a visit to Pyramid Valley, Bourgignon pointed out that the vines planted on hybrid Rootstock 420A responded differently to the active lime in the soil. Because *Vitis vinifera* grapes are lime loving, they grow straight down. The hybrid rootstock, said Bourgignon, is merely lime tolerant, and so it grows horizontally, therefore less effectively tapping into the deeper, microbially mediated geological layers of the soil. Weersing explained, "If you're going to talk about terroir, you have to talk about microbiology," and this requires thinking about what's happening beneath the ground, since "90% of biomass is from the soil down; it's life by weight." And what Pyramid Valley is aiming to grow are *vins de terroir*, not *vins de cépage*, wines that express the terroir, not the grape varieties alone. "The grape isn't the message," he said to me; "it's the messenger."

Claudia Elze, who was born in Germany and who helped her father with his compost piles as a child, began the vineyard enterprise with Mike Weersing somewhat skeptical about the esoteric formulae of biodynamics. So she created a controlled experiment, with two compost piles, both using organic ingredients and only one containing the biodynamic preps. And she found herself amazed by the superior quality of the biodynamic compost.

Still, in the first couple of years, the struggle to remove intransigent weeds, all by hand, was arduous, and she found her commitment wavering. Finally, though, by the fourth year of working the vineyard's soil biodynamically, the weeds that had taxed them so much began to give way to other plants, different ones emerging on each of their vineyard sites. Each of their vineyard blocks has an irregular shape conforming to the outlines of particular soil types. Claudia and Mike came to see the predominant plant on each block as a fellow traveler adapted to its distinctive terroir.

Biodynamic vintners I have visited elsewhere, including Marie-Thérèse Chappaz in Switzerland, also see the naturally emerging cover crops that change over time as "diagnostic," indicative of the health of the soil and thus of the vines. This companion-species relationship, mediated by biodynamic viticulture, is captured in the labels of Pyramid Valley's estate wines, each featuring the image of its companion weed (see figures 7.2 and 7.3).

Weeds occupy an interstitial space between cultivated and wild plants, as Anna Tsing (2005) notes in the wonderful chapter, called "A History of Weediness," of her book *Friction*. Weeds are, in fact, a mutable cultural-material category, not a natural kind. They are synanthropes, undomesticated, yet living in close, often beneficial, proximity to human activity. The practices of chemical-industrial agriculture have targeted many of them for annihilation, with glyphosate, the potentially carcinogenic key ingredient in Roundup, as the normalized weapon of choice in conventional viticulture, as it is for many home gardens. Its continued widespread use in vineyards, where it is conventionally blanket-sprayed to control grass between rows, results in the "lunar landscapes" in noted viticultural areas like Champagne (Henry 2016).

A number of weeds are key ingredients in the herbal homeopathic biodynamic preps. Three of these are featured on Pyramid Valley's labels. Dandelion, used to make Prep 506, is featured on the Lion's Tooth Chardonnay, also a nod to the weedy flower's French name, *dent de lion*. Prep 506 is said to facilitate links between silicon and potassium, so that silicon can better attract cosmic forces. Yarrow is used in Prep 502, associated with reproduction and growth, and pictured on the label for Angel Flower Pinot Noir.

A third plant, presented on the Field of Fire Chardonnay, is called *twitch* or *quack* (Latin *Agropyron repens*). However revered the rhizome may be as a Deleuzian conceptual trope, this crafty rhizomatic plant is widely seen as a scourge by home gardeners and conventional cultivators. At Pyramid Valley, however, twitch has a salutary function in the particular vineyard bloc where it flourishes, where it breaks up the dense clays near the surface without interfering with the deeper layers of lime soils around the vine roots.

To display images of these particular weeds prominently on their labels hails the consumers in Pyramid Valley's wines' international distribution network with a powerful message, telling a story about both this vineyard's terroirs and its embrace of biodynamics and its lively preps. Biodynamics, according to Mike, "gives you a whole new vocabulary of observation." Paying attention to what transpires in particular times and places, at thresholds where vines and soil types, weeds and enlivened compost, meet and mingle, is central to the gentle empiricism of biodynamic practices.

Like other New Zealand biodynamic vintners I visited, Pyramid Valley uses Peter Proctor's cow pat pit, composted manure inoculated with a combination of biodynamic preps. In discussing the efficacy of the preps, Mike said that it is not about getting the plants to do something. "Preps aren't about agency. They're like catalysts to communication between soil and the cosmos." This sensibility valorizes and amplifies the world-making role that grapevines and other sun-loving plants play at the celestial-terrestrial threshold, when supported by these homeopathic amendments, crafted in attunement with seasonal cycles, and with animal allies contributing to a self-sufficient nutrient cycle.

Despite the shared passions of biodynamic vintners like Mike and Claudia and the others I have visited in Aotearoa New Zealand and elsewhere, and despite the evident efficacy of their holistic, relational practices in restoring nutrient cycles and vitiated landscapes, these remain practices at the margins of normalized chemical-industrial agriculture and of secular-rationalist technoscience. Nevertheless, the ecology of practices that comprises biodynamics' delicate empiricism remains an inspiration and a source of hope. Biodynamic arts of noticing offer to help their practitioners relocate themselves in the cosmos and recapture cosmic-terrestrial connections, at the same time that they also serve as a "technology of localization" (Grasseni 2014) that situates them in the contemporary wine world's global hierarchy of value.

Biodynamics' slow science is grounded in attentive, respectful observation and stewardship of the soil and its animal, mineral, plant, and microbial companions, along with attention to holistic local ecologies. These practices contrast with, as they also arise from, political ecologies of precarity. The rhythms of biodynamics' phenomenological-magical craft offer some sense of possibility, along with response-ability, "a praxis of care and response ... in ongoing multispecies worlding on a wounded Terra" (Haraway 2016, 105). Biodynamics' magical-empirical practices at the threshold between sky and earth provide one path to disenchant "capitalist sorcery" (Pignarre and Stengers [2005] 2011), with its attachment to, and effective imposition of, the fairy tale of progress and the promise of the technological quick fix that still guides the dominant agronomic practices in the capitalist world ecology.[11]

FIGURE 7.2 Pyramid Valley Lion's Tooth Chardonnay. Photo by Benjamin Larsen.

Donna Haraway presciently imagined that reworlding stories could catalyze a "viral response-ability," "carrying meanings and materials across kinds in order to infect processes and practices that might yet ignite epidemics of multispecies recuperation" (2016, 114). In Aotearoa New Zealand, the Māori winegrowers' collective Tuku promotes their wines along with core Māori values, among them *whakapapa*, the notion of family or heritage that "links people to all other living things, the earth and the sky, and traces the universe back to its origins" (Tuku, n.d.). The *hua parakore* Māori organics advocates also list *whakapapa* as a key concept in their soil sovereignty precepts, linking this sense of multispecies kinship to the integrity of seed stock, crops, and farming resources on self-sufficient community farms and gardens (Hutchings et al. 2012). As Bronislaw Malinowski (1954) reminded us, magic is most likely to be invoked in precarious times and circumstances. This is perhaps, then, a promising moment—at the threshold between pandemic contagion

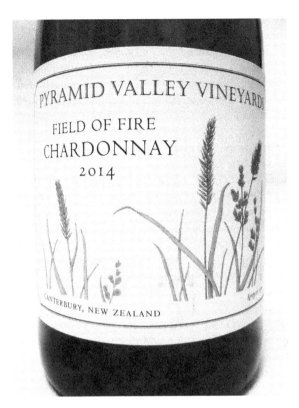

FIGURE 7.3 Pyramid Valley Field of Fire Chardonnay. Photo by Benjamin Larsen.

and the promise of multispecies conviviality—to reenchant our damaged landscapes and soil food webs in the name of both racial justice and multispecies environmental justice.

NOTES

1. Many thanks to John Paull for tracking down the original German term, sometimes rendered as "peasants' wit" in English translations of Steiner's work.

2. Anthropology's interrogations of and alternatives to the Anthropocene, drawing attention to racialized capital and colonialism, the plantation economy, and multispecies assemblages, range from the Capitalocene, Plantationocene, and Chthulucene to the pluriverse (Moore 2014, 2016; Haraway 2015; Todd 2016; Davis and Todd 2017; de la Cadena and Blaser 2018).

3. On a cautionary note worthy of further discussion, Daniel Münster (2018) also points to the links between Zero Budget Farming's return to traditional agricultural

practices and the rise of nativist Hindu nationalism. See Subramaniam (2019) for a subtle, comprehensive exploration of the intertwining of science, religion, and Hindu nationalist efforts to link an idealized past with present-day technoscience.

4. Vintners I met with in Central Otago report that their vineyard crews from the largely agrarian Polynesian nation of Vanuatu were receptive to biodynamic precepts and practices. See Bailey (2014) on the generally well-regarded government-managed program that brings ni-Vanuatu agricultural workers to Aotearoa New Zealand. Also see Brendbekken (2002) on the positive reception of biodynamics and its spiritual precepts among cultivators at the border between Haiti and the Dominican Republic.

5. See Kathryn Yusoff's (2019) *A Billion Black Anthropocenes or None*, a powerful indictment of the color lines of the Anthropocene's extractive histories of colonialism and slavery.

6. I am grateful for Su Hoskin's generous permission to cite the passages from her notes included in this chapter.

7. Su Hoskin, notes, Domain Thomson website, accessed May 17, 2018 (no longer available); cited with Su Hoskin's permission.

8. Hoskin, notes.

9. Hoskin, notes.

10. Mike passed away in 2020; his vision and contributions are widely noted across the wine world. British scientist and wine writer Jamie Goode's (2020) obituary offers a glimpse of the depth and complexity of Mike's perspective on viticultural naturecultures. Pyramid Valley was purchased in November 2017 by US billionaire Brian Sheth, an entrepreneur and conservationist from Austin, Texas. Sheth is committed to retaining the biodynamic practices integral to the label (Hutching 2007).

11. Stengers has long used the Weberian notion of disenchantment to refer to the violence following from capitalist logic, along with offering a call to embrace reenchantment, seen in both activist interventions and Indigenous knowledges (the latter, for example, in a recent lecture Stengers held with Starhawk, May 31, 2021, at École Polytechnique Fédérale de Lausanne (EPFL), Switzerland, https://www.epfl.ch/campus/art-culture/museum-exhibitions/archizoom/starhawk-and-isabelle-stengers/).

REFERENCES

Bailey, Rochelle. 2014. "Working the Vines: ni-Vanuatu Labour, Central Otago Pinot, and Economic Development in Vanuatu." In *Social, Cultural and Economic Impacts of Wine in New Zealand*, edited by Peter J. Howland, 71–85. New York: Routledge.

Bourgignon, Claude, and Lydia Bourgignon. 2015. *Le sol, la terre et les champs: Pour retrouver une agriculture saine*. Paris: Éditions Sang de la Terre.

Breda, Nadia. 2016. "The Plant In Between: Analogism and Entanglement in an Italian Community of Anthroposophists." *Anuac* 5 (2): 131–57.

Brendbekken, Marit. 2002. "Beyond Vodou and Anthroposophy in the Dominican-Haitian Borderlands." *Social Analysis* 46 (3): 31–74.

Brock, William Hodson. 1997. *Justus von Liebig: The Chemical Gatekeeper*. Cambridge: Cambridge University Press.

Burn Cottage. n.d. "Philosophy." Accessed August 24, 2021. https://burncottage.com/pages/philosophy.

Burstyn, Thomas, dir. 2008. *One Cow, One Man, One Planet*. Written by Barbara Sumner-Burstyn. Stonington, CT: Green Planet Films.

Capalbo, Carla. 2008. "Claude and Lydia Bourguignon: Famous Chateau Secrets." *Decanter*, June 4. https://www.decanter.com/features/claude-and-lydia-bourguignon-famous-chateau-secrets-247201/.

Celermajer, Danielle. 2020. "Multispecies Justice: Theories, Challenges, and a Research Agenda for Environmental Politics." *Environmental Politics* 30 (1–2): 119–40.

Chao, Sophie, Eben Kirksey, and Karin Bolender, eds. 2022. *The Promise of Multispecies Justice*. Durham, NC: Duke University Press.

Coccia, Emanuele. 2018. *The Life of Plants: A Metaphysics of Mixture*. Cambridge: Polity.

Davis, Heather, and Zoe Todd. 2017. "On the Importance of a Date, or Decolonizing the Anthropocene." *ACME* 16 (4): 761–80.

de la Cadena, Marisol, and Mario Blaser, eds. 2018. *A World of Many Worlds*. Durham, NC: Duke University Press.

Fernando, Jude. 2020. "From the Virocene to the Lovecene Epoch: Multispecies Justice as Critical Praxis for Virocene Disruptions and Vulnerabilities." *Journal of Political Ecology* 27 (1): 685–731. https://journals.uair.arizona.edu/index.php/JPE/article/view/23816/0.

Foster, John Bellamy. 1999. "Marx's Theory of Metabolic Rift: Classical Foundations for Environmental Sociology." *American Journal of Sociology* 105 (2): 366–405.

Goethe, Johann Wolfgang von. (1790) 2009. *The Metamorphosis of Plants*. Translated by Douglas Miller. Introduction by Gordon Miller. Cambridge, MA: MIT Press.

Goode, Jamie. 2020. "Remembering Mike Weersing, an American Who Brought Something Special to New Zealand's Fine Wine Dimension." *Wine Anokrak*, November 12, 2020. https://wineanorak.com/2020/11/12/remembering-mike-weersing-an-american-who-brought-something-special-to-new-zealands-fine-wine-dimension/.

Grasseni, Cristina. 2014. "Re-localizing Milk and Cheese." *Gastronomica* 14 (4): 34–43.

Hannah, Lee, Patrick R. Roehrdanz, Makihiko Ikegami, Anderson V. Shepard, M. Rebecca Shaw, Gary Tabord, Lu Zhie, Pablo A. Marquet, and Robert J. Hijmans. 2013. "Climate Change, Wine, and Conservation." *Proceedings of the National Academy of Sciences* 110 (17): 6907–12.

Haraway, Donna J. 2015. "Anthropocene, Capitalocene, Plantationocene, Chthulucene: Making Kin." *Environmental Humanities* 6 (1): 159–65.

Haraway, Donna J. 2016. *Staying with the Trouble: Making Kin in the Cthulucene*. Durham, NC: Duke University Press.

Haraway, Donna J. 2018. "Staying with the Trouble for Multispecies Environmental Justice." *Dialogues in Human Geography* 8 (1): 102–5.

Hartigan, John, Jr. 2017. *Care of the Species: Races of Corn and the Science of Plant Biodiversity*. Minneapolis: University of Minnesota Press.

Helmreich, Stefan. 2009. *Alien Ocean: Anthropological Voyages in Microbial Seas*. Berkeley: University of California Press.

Henry, Caroline. 2016. "France in a Flap over Bidding Adieu to Vine Herbicide." Wine-Searcher, July 8, 2016. http://www.wine-searcher.com/m/2016/07/france-in-a-flap-over-bidding-adieu-to-vine-herbicide.

Herzfeld, Michael. 2004. *The Body Impolitic: Artisans and Artifice in the Global Hierarchy of Value*. Chicago: University of Chicago Press.

Holdrege, Craig. 2014. *Thinking like a Plant: A Living Science for Life*. Great Barrington, MA: Lindisfarne Books.

Howland, Peter J. 2014. "From 'Civilizing' Māori to Fruit-Driven Exuberance: An Introduction to Wine in New Zealand." In *Social, Cultural and Economic Impacts of Wine in New Zealand*, edited by Peter J. Howland, 1–22. New York: Routledge.

Hutching, Chris. 2017. "US Billionaire Brian Sheth Buys North Canterbury Vineyard." Stuff, November 13, 2017. https://www.stuff.co.nz/business/98817839/north-canterbury-wineyard-bought-by-us-billionaire.

Hutchings, Jessica. 2019. "Jessica Hutchings." Interview by Philip McKibbin. *He Ika Haehae Kupenga*, December 2019. https://www.heikahaehaekupenga.com/jessicahutchings.html.

Hutchings, Jessica, Jo Smith, and Garth Harmsworth. 2018. "Elevating the Mana of Soil through the Hua Parakore Framework." *Mai Journal* 7 (1): 92–102.

Hutchings, Jessica, Percy Tipene, Gretta Carney, Angeline Greensill, Pounamu Skelton, and Mahinarangi Baker. 2012. "Hua Parakore: An Indigenous Food Sovereignty Initiative and Hallmark of Excellence for Food and Product Production." *Mai Journal* 1 (2): 131–45.

Joly, Nicolas. 2005. *Wine from Sky to Earth: Growing and Appreciating Biodynamic Wine*. 2nd ed. Greeley, CO: Acres, USA.

Jones, Bradley M. 2019. "(Com)Post-capitalism: Cultivating a More-than-Human Economy in the Appalachian Anthropocene." *Environmental Humanities* 11 (1): 3–26.

Kirksey, Eben. 2015. *Emergent Ecologies*. Durham, NC: Duke University Press.

Kumar, Sunaina. 2017. "Can Biodynamic Farming Solve India's Agricultural Woes?" *Deutsche Welle*, November 23, 2017. https://www.dw.com/en/can-biodynamic-farming-solve-indias-agricultural-woes/a-41498853.

Landecker, Hannah. 2011. "Food as Exposure: Nutritional Epigenetics and the New Metabolism." *BioSocieties* 6 (2): 167–94.

Le Roy Ladurie, Emmanuel. 1988. *Times of Feast, Times of Famine: A History of Climate since the Year 1000*. New York: Farrar, Straus and Giroux.

Liebig, Justus von. 1859. *Letters on Modern Agriculture*. London: Walton and Maberly.

Littorai. n.d. "Generative Agriculture." Accessed May 18, 2020. http://www.littorai.com/generative-agriculture.

Lyons, Kristina. 2020. *Vital Decomposition: Soil Practitioners and Life Politics.* Durham, NC: Duke University Press.

Malinowski, Bronislaw. 1954. *Magic, Science, and Religion and Other Essays.* New York: Anchor Books.

Malm, Andreas. 2015. *Fossil Capital: The Rise of Steam Power and the Roots of Global Warming.* New York: Verso.

Moore, Jason W. 2017. "The Capitalocene, Part I: On the Nature and Origins of Our Ecological Crisis." *Journal of Peasant Studies* 44 (3): 594–630. https://doi.org/10.1080/03066150.2016.1235036.

Moore, Jason W., ed. 2016. *Anthropocene or Capitalocene? Nature, History, and the Crisis of Capitalism.* Oakland, CA: PM Press.

Moran-Thomas, Amy. 2019. *Traveling with Sugar: Chronicles of a Global Epidemic.* Oakland: University of California Press

Mukharji, Projit B. 2016. *Doctoring Traditions: Ayurveda, Small Technologies, and Braided Sciences.* Chicago: University of Chicago Press.

Münster, Daniel. 2018. "Performing Alternative Agriculture: Critique and Recuperation in Zero Budget Natural Farming, South India." *Journal of Political Ecology* 25 (1): 748–64.

Muru-Lanning, Charlotte. 2020. "A World beyond Our Feet: Rethinking Our Relationship with Where We Grow Our Kai." The Spinoff, October 20, 2020. https://thespinoff.co.nz/food/20-10-2020/a-world-beyond-our-feet-rethinking-our-relationship-with-where-we-grow-our-kai/.

Murray, Joseph. 2018a. "A Biodynamic Understanding of Trees." Paper delivered at the Biodynamic Conference "Transforming the Heart of Agriculture: Soil. Justice. Regeneration," November 17, 2018, Portland, OR.

Murray, Joseph. 2018b. "How Rudolf Steiner's Agriculture Lectures Can Help Us See the Forest for the Trees." *7 Acre Wood Farm* (blog), January 13, 2018. https://7acrewoodfarm.com/how-rudolf-steiners-agriculture-lectures-can-help-us-see-the-forest-for-the-trees/.

Myers, Natasha. 2015. "Conversations on Plant Sensing: Notes from the Field." *NatureCulture*, 3:35–66.

Myers, Natasha. 2018. "How to Grow Livable Worlds: Ten Not-So-Easy Steps." In *The World to Come: Art in the Age of the Anthropocene*, edited by Kerry Oliver Smith, 53–63. Gainesville, FL: Samuel P. Harn Museum of Art.

Nixon, Rob 2013. *Slow Violence and the Environmentalism of the Poor.* Cambridge, MA: Harvard University Press.

Overton, John, and Warwick Murray. 2014. "Boutiques and Behemoths: The Transformation of the New Zealand Wine Industry, 1990–2012." In *Social, Cultural and Economic Impacts of Wine in New Zealand*, edited by Peter J. Howland, 25–40. New York: Routledge.

Oviatt, Peter. 2020. "Soil Drugs of the Future: The Sustainability of BioAg and the Repair of Arable Land." *Environment and Planning E: Nature* and Space. First published online, July 29, 2020. https://doi.org/10.1177/2514848620943894.

Oviatt, Peter, and Matthias C. Rillig. 2021. "Mycorrhizal Technologies for an Agriculture of the Middle." *Plants, People, Planet* 3 (5): 454–61.

Paull, John. 2011a. "Attending the First Organic Agriculture Course: Rudolf Steiner's Agriculture Course at Koberwitz, 1924." *European Journal of Social Sciences* 21 (1): 64–70.

Paull, John. 2011b. "Biodynamic Agriculture: The Journey from Koberwitz to the World, 1924–1938." *Journal of Organic Systems* 6 (1): 27–41.

Pfeiffer, Ehrenfried. 1938. *Bio-Dynamic Farming and Gardening: Soil Fertility Renewal and Preservation*. Translated by F. Henkel. New York: Anthroposophic Press.

Pfeiffer, Ehrenfried. (1956) 1993. "New Directions in Agriculture." In *A Man before Others: Rudolf Steiner Remembered*, edited by Rudolf Steiner Press, 137–47. Bristol: Rudolf Steiner Press.

Pfeiffer, Ehrenfried. (1958) 2007. Preface to *Rudolf Steiner, Agricultural Course*. Rudolf Steiner Archive. http://wn.rsarchive.org/Lectures/GA327/English/BDA1958/Ag1958_preface.html.

Pignarre, Philippe, and Isabelle Stengers. (2005) 2011. *Capitalist Sorcery: Breaking the Spell*. Translated by Andrew Goffey. London: Palgrave Macmillan.

Proctor, Peter. (1997) 2013. *Grasp the Nettle: Making Biodynamic Farming and Gardening Work*. Rev. ed. Great Barrington, MA: SteinerBooks.

Puig de la Bellacasa, Maria. 2017. *Matters of Care: Speculative Ethics in More Than Human Worlds*. Minneapolis: University of Minnesota Press.

Robbins, Brent Dean. 2006. "The Delicate Empiricism of Goethe: Phenomenology as a Rigorous Science of Nature." *Indo-Pacific Journal of Phenomenology* 6 (s1): 1–13.

Rose, Deborah Bird. 2011. *Wild Dog Dreaming: Love and Extinction*. Charlottesville: University of Virginia Press.

Steiner, Rudolf. (1883) 2000. *Nature's Open Secret: Introductions to Goethe's Scientific Works*. Translated by John Barnes and Mado Spiegler. Great Barrington, MA: Anthroposophic Press.

Steiner, Rudolf. (1924) 2004. *Agricultural Course: The Birth of the Biodynamic Method*. Dulles, VA: SteinerBooks.

Stengers, Isabelle. 2018. *Another Science Is Possible: A Manifesto for Slow Science*. Cambridge: Polity.

Stoetzer, Bettina. 2018. "Ruderal Ecologies: Rethinking Nature, Migration, and the Urban Landscape in Berlin." *Cultural Anthropology* 33 (2): 295–323.

Subramaniam, Banu. 2019. *Holy Science: The Biopolitics of Hindu Nationalism*. Seattle: University of Washington Press.

Todd, Zoe. 2016. "An Indigenous Feminist's Take on the Ontological Turn: 'Ontology' Is Just Another Word for Colonialism." *Journal of Historical Sociology* 29 (1): 4–22.

Trubek, Amy. 2009. *The Taste of Place: A Cultural Journey into* Terroir. Berkeley: University of California Press.

Tsing, Anna. 2005. *Friction: An Ethnography of Global Connection*. Princeton, NJ: Princeton University Press.

Tsing, Anna. 2015. *The Mushroom at the End of the World: On the Possibility of Life in Capitalist Ruins*. Princeton, NJ: Princeton University Press.

Tsing, Anna Lowenhaupt, Nils Bubandt, Elaine Gan, and Heather Anne Swanson, eds. 2017. *Arts of Living on a Damaged Planet: Ghosts and Monsters of the Anthropocene*. Minneapolis: University of Minnesota Press.

Tuku. n.d. "We Stand for Unity." Accessed May 15, 2020. https://tuku.nz/unity.

van Dooren, Thomas, Eben Kirksey, and Ursula Münster. 2016. "Multispecies Studies: Cultivating Arts of Attentiveness." *Environmental Humanities* 8 (1): 1–23.

Yusoff, Kathryn. 2019. *A Billion Black Anthropocenes or None*. Minneapolis: University of Minnesota Press.

contributors

ALEX BLANCHETTE is associate professor of anthropology and environmental studies at Tufts University. He is the coeditor of *How Nature Works: Rethinking Labor on a Troubled Planet* (2019) and the author of *Porkopolis: American Animality, Standardized Life, and the Factory Farm* (2020), published by Duke University Press.

DEBORAH HEATH is an independent scholar in Portland, Oregon, USA. She is currently researching multispecies relations in wine and food production, regenerative agriculture, and soil sovereignty movements. Her earlier work in anthropology, science and technology studies, and gender studies focused on Senegalese gender politics and genetic knowledge production. Her publications include the coedited volume *Genetic Nature/Culture: Anthropology and Science beyond the Two-Culture Divide* (2003).

HANNAH LANDECKER holds a joint appointment across the life and social sciences at the University of California, Los Angeles, where she is a professor in the Institute for Society and Genetics and the Department of Sociology. A historian and sociologist of the life sciences, her research concerns the social shaping of the biological world through processes of biotechnology and industrialization.

MARIANNE ELISABETH LIEN is a professor in the Department of Social Anthropology at the University of Oslo, Norway. She has worked ethnographically in the Nordic Arctic for decades and has published widely on domestication, human-animal relations, food and eating, and, more recently, colonization in the North. She is the author of *Becoming Salmon: Aquaculture and the Domestication of a Fish* (2015).

AMY MORAN-THOMAS is associate professor of anthropology at the Massachusetts Institute of Technology. Her work often focuses on the social lives of medical objects, exploring the human and material entanglements that shape health in practice. She is the author of *Traveling with Sugar: Chronicles of a Global Epidemic* (2019).

HEATHER PAXSON is William R. Kenan, Jr. Professor of Anthropology at the Massachusetts Institute of Technology. She is the author of *Making Modern Mothers: Ethics and Family Planning in Urban Greece* (2004) and *The Life of Cheese: Crafting Food and Value in America* (2013). More recently, she has written about the labor of importing perishable foods.

HARRIS SOLOMON is the Fred W. Shaffer Associate Professor of Cultural Anthropology and Global Health at Duke University. He studies the connections between bodies and environments in India and social medicine in the United States. He is the author of *Metabolic Living: Food, Fat, and the Absorption of Illness in India* (2016) and *Lifelines: The Traffic of Trauma* (2022), both published by Duke University Press.

WIM VAN DAELE is associate professor of anthropology in the Department of Nutrition and Public Health at the University of Agder, Norway. His research on food, cooking, and eating in Sri Lanka has been published widely in anthropology and food studies journals.

EMILY YATES-DOERR is associate professor of anthropology at Oregon State University and the University of Amsterdam, where she is the principal investigator on a European Research Council–funded project to study the production of "future health" through maternal nutrition interventions. She is the author of *The Weight of Obesity: Hunger and Global Health in Postwar Guatemala* (2015).

index

absorption, 4, 10, 15–16, 37, 140–41
abstraction, ix–x, 34–35, 198
access, accessibility, 5, 46, 95–97, 105, 107n12, 117–20, 130–31, 137–38
accountability, 175
accounting, 63, 178–79
actors, actants, 120, 165–66, 179. *See also* networks
AFB International, 101
affect, 94–95, 100, 154
affinity. *See* belonging
Agard-Jones, Vanessa, 34
agent, agency, ix–x, 3, 6–7, 13, 20, 60, 65–66, 76, 92–93, 100, 105, 131, 165–67, 171, 179–80, 209
agribusiness, 90–92, 102–3, 107n16, 112. *See also* agriculture
Agricultural Experimental Cycle, 193. *See also* biodynamics
agriculture: alternative, 188, 192–94, 198–99, 209; animal, 56–79, 96–97, 103–5; and biology, 91–92, 102, 104–5, 195; chemical, 17, 33–36, 40–41, 60–63, 67–70, 89–92, 94–97, 188, 191–98, 208–9; ecologies of, 3, 12–13; extractivist, 188, 191–96, 198; geopolitical considerations of, 72; histories of, 32–33, 35–36, 40–41, 45, 58, 60–64, 68–70, 72–79, 79n1, 80n4, 192–94, 198; industrial, 12–14, 29–30, 33, 35–36, 39–41, 57–59, 61–64, 67–70, 86–88, 89–93, 96–99, 102–5, 188, 195–96, 208–9; intensification of, 72–74, 80n4; regenerative, 187, 192–94, 196–99. *See also* agribusiness; biodynamics;

metabolism; monocultures, monoculturing; viticulture
allergies, 16
ambivalence, x, 19–21
American Cyanamid, 74
amputation, 44–45, 48n3. *See also* diabetes
Amsterdam, 158–61, 164–67, 171, 173–74, 176–77
ancestors, 36–37, 44, 200–201
anesthesia, 97–98, 145–48, 181n3
animals: as consumers, 63–64, 73–74, 100–101; and conversion, 60–64; and domestication, 10–14; and humans, ix–x, 4–5; husbandry, 13–14, 68–69, 73–74, 78–79, 80n4, 133n6; labor of, 99–100; life, 59; livestock, 4–5, 11–12, 74–75, 106n7; and pleasure, 94–95, 99–101; and reproduction, 91–92; and sensation, 86, 89–95, 99–102, 104–5, 106nn7–8, 107n14. *See also* eating; food; pets; vermin; *and* individual animals by name
Anthropocene, 211n2, 212n5. *See also* climate, climate change
anthropocentrism, 92, 104–5
anthropology, ix–x, 3–4, 11–12, 86, 111–12, 115, 211n2; and air, 153–54; and colonialism, 36; feminist, 163–65; and interspecies writing, 49n5; of living, 141; and monocultures, 102–3; and personal experience, 164–65, 179–80; and plants, 195–96; and reduction, 92–93; and selfhood, 182n11; and thresholds, 48n4; and travel, 163.

anthropology (Continued)
    See also ethnographic writing; food studies; science and technology studies; thresholds
antibiotics, 73–77. *See also* medicated feed
Aotearoa New Zealand, 197–203, 208–9; and biodynamics, 210–11; history of viticulture, 205–7; National Pest Plant Accord, 204; negotiation of indigeneity, 203–5. *See also* biodynamics; Māori; viticulture
Appadurai, Arjun, 7, 158–59
appetite, 4, 7, 13–14, 76–77, 92–93, 100–101, 111–12
aquaculture, 3, 15–16, 37–38
Armsby, Henry Prentiss, 60–61, 79n2
arsenicals, 72–77, 78–79. *See also* antibiotics; medicated feed; vitamins
assemblage, 12–13, 114–15, 130, 132, 132n1, 192–93, 211n2
autoimmune diseases, 16
autonomy, 8–9, 97–98, 165–66, 168–69, 177, 178, 182n11, 182n20

Barbados, 48n3
barriers, 6–7, 16, 161, 165–66, 167, 177–78. *See also* boundaries; thresholds
Beckles, Hilary, 45, 48n3
Belize, 5–6, 9–10, 30–33; and climate change, 38–39; and diabetes, 32, 34–35, 38–39, 44–46; and existential thresholds of healing, 36–37; harmed ecologies of, 39–41; and legacy of sugar, 36; and pesticide runoff, 33–34. *See also* diabetes; sugar
belonging, 112, 118–19, 120, 134n11, 171–72. *See also* relations
Bertoni, Filippo, 2
Besky, Sarah, 102
biodynamics, 187–88, 191–211; and care, 196; daily practices of, 197; and food sovereignty, 200–201, 203; in India, 199–200; and indigenous practices, 210–11, 212n4; local and global relations of, 198–99; preps, 192–93, 201–2, 204, 208–9; and relationality, 194–95, 196–98, 209; remediating soil, 196, 207–8; restoring native habitats, 203–5; slow science of, 188, 196–98, 201–3, 209; spiritual tenets of, 193–94, 200–202, 212n4; and weeds, 207–9. *See also* agriculture; Aotearoa New Zealand; viticulture
bioethics. *See under* ethics; *also* euthanasia
biofilm (microbial mat), 12
biomedicine. *See under* medicine
biopolitics, 58–59, 102, 141, 143–44; alterbiopolitics, 196; (micro)biopolitics, 7, 11–12
Black Lives Matter, 188
Blanchette, Alex, 202–3
blood sugar, 9–10, 30–31, 38, 174; thresholds of, 38–40. *See also* diabetes
body, ix; and air, 153–54; animal, 60, 96–97; boundaries of, 37; embeddedness of, 3–4; and exchange, 137; and injury, 142–43; and knowing, 142, 158, 178–79; and machines, 147; and metabolism, 66; and multiplicity, 163–67, 173–74, 179–80, 181n2; new sites of labor and value within, 90–91; and politics, 1–2; and processes of resuscitation, 140–41; regulatory functions of, 7–8; and relations, 44–47, 159–60, 176–80; thresholds of, 5–8, 38, 139, 166–67, 169–71; in transition, 168, 172–73
Bond, David, 38–39
borders, border crossing, 5, 18. *See also* boundaries
boundaries, ix–x, 18; and body, 37; crossing, 159; dissolving, 168–71; between inside and outside, 131; materiality of, 177–78; multispecies, 192; between native and invasive species, 203–5; negotiating, 115; and relations, x; between self and other, 166–73
boundary object, 177–78
Bourgignon, Claude, 207
breastfeeding, 166

222 · INDEX

breath, breathing, 139–49, 158; in anthropology, 153–54. *See also* ventilator, ventilation
Brillat-Savarin, Jean Anthelme, 105
Brown, Vincent, 45–46
Burn Cottage, 197–99, 201
Burroughs, Wise, 75–76
by-production, 90–92, 103, 105n3. *See also* agriculture; waste

calories, 8–9, 45–46, 60, 77–78, 103–4, 113, 146, 172
Canguilhem, Georges, 38–39
capitalism, 7, 86; and agriculture, 192–94; ecologies of, 58–59, 197–98; extractivist, 191–96, 212n5; global, 198; logistics of, 105n2; as process, 102–3; racial, 30–31, 47n1, 188, 200–201; and sensory experiences, 97–99; subject-object relations of, 202–3; transcorporeal, 103
carbohydrate, 8–9, 35, 37, 45, 66, 146, 194
care, 1, 16, 154, 187, 189, 196; and life, 141–42; multispecies, 196, 209; slow, 188, 192, 198; work of, 47
Caribbean Community and Common Market (CARICOM), 45, 49n5
Caribbean: and colonialism, 33; and environmental violence, 34, 45–46; and sugar, 33, 35, 45–46, 48n3. *See also* Belize
CARICOM. *See* Caribbean Community and Common Market
cats, 89–95, 99–101, 104–5, 106n7. *See also* animals
chains, 2, 11, 18–19, 31, 59, 87–88, 101, 126. *See also* webs
cheese, 12–15, 17, 21n2. *See also* cows; milk
chickens, 56–57, 70, 72–73, 75, 77–79, 86–87, 89, 98–99, 103–4, 159. *See also* animals
class, 1–2, 17–18, 30, 130; and consumption, 45–46
classifications, 9, 48n4, 111, 122–23, 126–28, 129–30, 181n7, 203–4

climate, climate change, 35–39, 42–43, 45–46, 188, 191–92. *See also* Anthropocene
cloudberries, 116, 118–20
Coccia, Emanuele, 187, 194
Cohen, Lawrence, 137–39
colonialism, 5–6, 119–20, 159–60, 200–201, 212n5; and anthropology, 36; and global consumption, 48n3; and postcolonialism, 143–44; settler, 35–36, 47n1, 205; and sugar economies, 33
commensality, ix, 3–11, 124–25, 173. *See also* relations, relationality
Commercial Solvents Corporation (CSC), 67–68
commodity, commodification, 31, 47, 69, 88, 91, 93–95, 103, 106n8, 202–3, 205
compost, 20, 192–93, 197–203, 207–9. *See also* biodynamics; cow pat pit; manure
conduit, 59, 69–70, 160–61, 165–67, 177–78. *See also* barrier; placenta
Cone, Richard, 16
consumption, 4–5, 17–18, 31, 34–35, 37–38, 45–46, 48n3, 90–91, 111–13, 126, 128–31, 134n9, 154; animal, 59, 60, 63–65, 68, 75–76, 86–87, 94–97, 100–101, 103–5; overconsumption, 3, 10. *See also* eating; edibility; food; palatants
conversion, 172–73. *See also under* animals
conviviality, 192, 194, 210–11. *See also* relations, relationality
coral reefs, 31–32, 36–41
cosmopolitanism, cosmopolitics, 197–201. *See also* global; local; planetary; worlds, world-making
COVID-19 pandemic, 2–3, 188–89, 192. *See also* pandemics
cows, 11–14, 17, 56, 64–65, 70, 76–78, 106n8, 192–93, 197–204. *See also* animals
cow pat pit (CPP), 199, 201, 209. *See also* biodynamics; compost; manure

CPP. *See* cow pat pit
Crowell, Mary, 77–78
cruise ships, 41
culture (human), 3–4, 7, 99, 102–3, 120, 165, 200, 203–4
culture (microbial), 66–67, 70. *See also* fermentation; microbes

Das, Veena, 144–45
DDT, 42–43. *See also* pesticides; toxins, toxicants
death, dying, 38–39, 144–45; dignity of, 151–52; and exhalation, 145–46; expiration, 144; industrialized, 89–92; and life, 115–16, 122–23, 138–41, 143–44; normalization of, 46, 142–43; relations of, 115–16, 138–39, 153–54. *See also* life, living
DeLanda, Manuel, ix
diabetes, 5–6, 9–10, 30–35, 182n18; and diagnostic technologies, 48n2; and exposure to pesticide runoff, 34, 42–43; gestational, 174–76, 182n17; as global health epidemic, 3, 38–39; among Indigenous peoples, 35–36; and legacy of settler colonialism, 35–36, 45, 48n3; and loss, 44–46; pathology of, 38; thresholds of, 38–39. *See also* Belize; sugar
diet: animal, 13–14, 87, 103–4; and health, 8–9, 64, 66, 70, 175; modern, 4, 34–35, 59; moral nature of, 64, 175; and overconsumption, 3. *See also* eating; food
diethylstilbestrol (DES), 75–77
difference, 1–3, 100–101, 114, 117–19, 131–32, 134n9, 168–70, 177–80, 194–95, 202–3, 205
digestion, 1, 4–5, 11–14, 17–18, 111–13, 129, 132, 201–3. *See also* eating; edibility; fermentation
digests, 93–94, 106n6. *See also* palatants; pet food
digital, digitalization, 2, 146–47
dioxins. *See* pollution, pollutants; toxins, toxicants
disability, 1–2

disenchantment, 209–11, 212n11
disgust, 2, 122–23, 127–28, 168–69. *See also* edibility
dividuality, 179. *See also* individual, individualism
Domaine Thomson vineyard, 201
dogs, 86–87, 93, 100, 103–5, 106n7, 204–5. *See also* animals
domesticity, domestication, 4–5, 7–8, 10–14, 16, 56, 58, 89–91, 94–95, 100, 107n15, 144–45, 191–92, 205, 208. *See also* animals; pets
Dow Chemical, 70, 76–77
Duden, Barbara, 168–69
Dunn, Elizabeth, 7–8
DuPuis, E. Melanie, 64
duration, 101, 187. *See also* time, temporality

eating, ix–x, 1–4, 6–7; boundaries of, 114; as embodied performance of appetite, 128–31, 134n9; and health, 8–9; and justice, 17–18; materiality of, 57–58; and nonhuman animals, x, 2, 12–14, 103–4; politics and ethics of, 92; relations of, 1–4, 105, 114–15, 130–31, 134n11, 172–73; as thresholding project, 7–9, 18; as transgression, 161; webs or chains of, 87–88. *See also* culture (human); digestion; edibility; food
ecology, 3–7, 12–13, 15–16, 31, 33, 35–41, 58, 77–78, 96–97, 102, 195–97, 209. *See also* agriculture; monocultures, monoculturing
economy, 57–58, 60–61, 80n4, 96–97, 172–73; colonial, 33, 211n2; and culture, 97–99, 133n6; global, 7–9; and growth, 75–78, 90–91; political, x, 92, 102–3, 143–44, 153–54, 205; and value, 137–38; waste, 62. *See also* capitalism; industrialization
edibility, 6, 86–87, 121–25, 131–32, 134n10; economies of, 137–38; as embodied performance, 128–31, 134n9; inedibility, 111–13; thresholds of, 114–16, 125–31; and waste, 112–13. *See also* eating

224 · INDEX

efficiency, 57, 61–65, 70, 72–77, 90–91, 94–95, 199
Elze, Claudia, 207–8
embodiment, 128–31, 134n9, 140–41, 158, 178–79; disembodiment, 48n3, 86–87. *See also* body
enable, enabler, 4–5, 58–59, 74–75, 94–95, 117–18, 146–47
enactment, ix–x, 2, 6–8, 12, 100–101, 115–32, 134n9, 134n11, 140–41, 181n2. *See also* edibility; embodiment
enchantment. *See* disenchantment
energy, energetics, 11, 56–61, 173, 182n16, 194–95, 203; "energy balance theory," 8–9. *See also* calories; metabolism
entanglement, ix–x, 6–7, 103–5, 120, 189, 196; disentanglement, 171–73, 182n14; global, 29–32; multispecies, 189, 196, 198, 203. *See also* relations, relationality
environment, 3–18, 37–39, 41–42, 56, 90–91, 96–97, 193–97, 201–202, 210–11. *See also* biodynamics; ecology; metabolism; monocultures, monoculturing
Environmental Protection Agency (EPA), 41
epidemics, 3, 38–39, 48n3, 189, 210–11. *See also* COVID-19 pandemic; diabetes; pandemics
epigenetics, 3–4, 11, 32–33
ethics, 17, 18, 91–93, 102–5, 137–39, 141, 152–54, 196; bioethics, 155n1. *See also* care; euthanasia
ethnographic writing, 165–66. *See also* anthropology
eugenics, 91–92
euthanasia, 143–44, 149–50, 155n1. *See also* life support; ventilator, ventilation
exchange, 8–9, 33, 115–17, 137–38, 161, 178–79, 189, 195
experience, 3–4, 44, 97–99, 115, 158, 160–61, 164–66, 171, 173–80, 182nn17–18, 197; animal, 89–90, 94–95, 103–5, 106n8. *See also* pregnancy; taste, tasting

expertise, 32, 39, 63–64, 99–101
exposure, 5–6, 15–16, 34–39, 42–43, 97
extract, extraction, extractivism, 21n1, 33, 36, 58, 65, 69–70, 74, 96–97, 188, 191–98, 212n5. *See also* capitalism; colonialism; palatants; vitamins

factories, 29–31, 45–47, 69–70; and animals, 89–96, 101–5, 105n2, 106nn6–7, 107n12. *See also* agribusiness; monocultures, monoculturing
farming: and animals, 13–14, 17, 60–64, 79n2, 89–95, 101–5, 107n12, 112–13; and climate change, 42; industrial, 3–4, 89–95, 101–5, 107n12; organic, 192–95, 197–201, 210–11. *See also* biodynamics; factories; monocultures, monoculturing
Fassin, Didier, 141
fat, 89, 91, 104, 130
feeding, 1–2, 8–9, 11–12, 15–16; ancestors, 36–37, 47; animal, 57, 59, 60–64, 73–74, 77–79, 79n2, 86, 94–95, 103–5; and biodynamics, 202–3; and life support, 140–42, 146–49, 154, 158; and pregnancy, 164–67, 170–73, 177–79; scientific, 60–63. *See also* eating; food; nutrition; pregnancy
feminism, 158–61, 164–65, 170, 178, 182n9, 182n15, 196. *See also* gender; science and technology studies
fermentation, 2–5, 11–13, 67–68, 59, 65, 74, 79n1, 191–93, 200; industrialization of, 67–68. *See also* culture (microbial); microbes
fertilizer, 33, 61–62, 90–91, 188; runoff, 39–41; synthetic, 68, 188, 193–98. *See also* compost; manure
fetus, 167–80, 181n7, 182n20, 187. *See also* mothers, motherhood, mothering; placenta; pregnancy
Finnmark (Norway), 112–13, 116–17, 124, 131–32. *See also* Sámi
fish, 15–16, 41–43, 62, 68–70, 112–13, 116–19, 127–28, 133nn3–4, 134n10, 159–60. *See also* animals

flavor, 9, 12–14, 17, 33–35, 56, 86–87, 89–90, 93–94, 96, 98–102, 106n7. *See also* eating; food; palatant; sensation; taste, tasting
Food and Drug Administration (FDA), 72–73, 76
food studies, ix–x, 1, 92, 105n3, 115. *See also* anthropocentrism; anthropology
food, 2–3, 11; additives in, 9, 69, 76–77; animal, 7, 13–14, 56–59, 61–65, 68–70, 72–77, 86, 89–95, 99–105, 106n6, 106n8, 107n15; as care, 154; as cultural construction, 3–4; and edibility, 9, 15–16, 111–13, 121–22, 124–32, 134nn9–10; "ethnic," 21n1; as gift, 117–19, 124–26, 131–32, 137–38; and global economy, 7–8; and identity, 119–20; and injury, 142; and labor, 92–93; and life, 154; as media, 139; and medicine, 31; and modernity, 58–59, 79; and pleasure, 94–95; and power, 58; and practice of coming into being, 115, 125–26, 130–32; processed, 86–87; production, 3–4, 7–8, 17–18; relations of, ix–x, 7, 10–11, 114–15, 117–20, 122–26, 131–32, 154, 164; and resuscitation acts, 140–41; safety, 7–8; and sensation, 97–99; and sovereignty, 6, 200–201, 203; and subsistence practices, 120; thresholds of, 18, 114–15, 122–26, 131–32; and value, 128–31, 137–38. *See also* animals; eating; feeding; medicated feed; pet food; taboos; thresholds
Foster, John Bellamy, 58
Foucault, Michel, 43
fragility, ix–x, 91–92, 104–5, 139
France, 193–94, 205–6. *See also* viticulture
fungi, 2, 4–5, 11–12, 17–18, 64–65, 70, 195–97, 204

Garifuna, 36–37, 44–45. *See also* Belize
Garth, Hanna, 6, 188
gastronomy, 4–8
gastro-politics, 7–8

gender, 1, 118–19, 133n3, 144–45, 166–67, 181n7. *See also* feminism; mothers, motherhood, mothering
Gennep, Arnold van, 6, 48n4
geography, 48n2, 101–4
gifts, giving, 117–19, 124–26, 131–32, 137–39
global, 7–8, 30–31, 36, 43, 45–46, 48n3, 96–97, 102, 191–94, 198–99, 209. *See also* capitalism; local; planetary; worlds, world-making
glucose, glucometer, 7, 9–10, 32, 34–35, 38. *See also* diabetes; sugar
goats, 12–13, 17–18. *See also* animals
Goethe, Johann Wolfgang von, 196–97
grapevines. *See* plants; viticulture
Green, Amanda, 130
growth, 13–14, 56, 58–59, 61–64, 69–70, 72–79. *See also* antibiotics; capitalism; vitamins
Guatemala, 9, 175–76

Haber, Fritz, 197
Haraway, Donna, 4–5, 38–39, 165–67, 210
Hardin, Jessica, 9–10
harm, 4–5, 16, 31, 41–43, 46, 92, 121, 160–61, 177–78, 187–89, 192, 200
Hartman, Saidiya, 35–36
healing, 36–37, 44, 193, 197–98, 202–3. *See also* biodynamics
health, ix–x, 3–4, 6, 8–10, 15–17, 30–33, 36–39, 43, 182n18; animal, 56–59, 64, 73, 77–79; individual, 160–61, 174–75, 177–78, 187; soil, 193–94, 200–201, 203, 207–8. *See also* diabetes; epidemics; medicated feed; metabolism; nutrition; vitamins
Helmreich, Stefan, 203–4
heterogeneity, x, 111, 114–15, 132. *See also* multiplicity
Hinduism, 200, 211n3
history, 29–31, 35–37, 47, 64, 86
Hobart, Hi'ilei Julia, 4
Hoffman-La Roche, 69–70
hogs, 7, 87, 89–97, 101, 102–4, 106n10, 107n11, 111–12, 202–3. *See also* animals

Holdrege, Craig, 196–97
hope, 47, 144, 153–54, 188, 209
hormones, 17, 42–43, 61, 65–66, 73–77, 79, 174, 176, 180, 182n11. *See also* antibiotics; growth
Hoskin, Su, 201, 204
hospitals, 36–38, 138, 140–54, 155n1. *See also* life support; ventilator, ventilation
human: body, 3–4, 8–9, 15–16, 60, 154; relation with nonhuman, ix–x, 2–5, 7, 10–14, 31, 36–37, 40–44, 56–59, 64–67, 77–78, 86–87, 91–95, 97–98, 103–5, 111–13, 120–21, 131, 191–92, 196, 200–201; and social, 17–18, 196; subject, 92–93, 97–98, 111–13, 179–80, 182n12. *See also* animals; body; self, selfhood
Hutchings, Jessica, 200–201, 203
hygiene, 3–4, 12, 16. *See also* safety

Ibáñez Martín, Rebeca, 2
identity, 6, 97–98, 112, 116, 119–24, 128, 131. *See also* self, selfhood
illness, 1–2, 6, 8–10, 48n2, 152, 174–76. *See also* health; metabolism
imperialism, 4, 21n1. *See also* colonialism
incorporation, x, 3–4, 6–7, 14–18, 91–92, 125, 159–60
India, 10–12, 144–45; and biodynamics, 193–94, 199–200; and euthanasia, 149–50, 155n1
indigeneity, Indigenous people, 192, 203–4; and culinary imperialism, 4, 35–36; and food sovereignty, 6, 193–94, 200–201, 203, 210–11; knowledges of, 125, 193–94, 200, 212n11; of northern Norway, 116, 130. *See also* Māori; native; Sámi
individual, individualism, 164–66, 168–69, 171, 175–79, 182n11. *See also* body; relations; self, selfhood
industrialization, 57, 92; and metabolic relations, 86–87; processes, 86–88; and waste, 62, 79n3, 86, 89–91. *See also* by-production; waste
infolding, 166–67
infrastructure, 9–10, 46, 48n3, 62, 68–70
ingestion, 1–3, 8–10, 15–18, 202–3; animal, 92, 94–95, 103–5, 106n8. *See also* digestion; eating; feeding
injury, 141–43, 161. *See also* trauma
intensification, 6, 65, 68–69, 72, 79n2, 91, 93–95, 102, 193–94, 198
intermediary, 66–67
intimacy, ix–x, 7, 35, 98–99, 141, 161
intubation, 140–42, 147–49, 152. *See also* life support; resuscitation; ventilator, ventilation
invasive, 192, 203–5. *See also* native
Irigaray, Luce, 169–70

Jones, Elain, 167
Jones, Hans, 37
judgment, 2, 100, 130. *See also* taste, tasting
Jung, Yuson, 7–8
justice: injustice, 45, 188–89; multispecies, 20, 194, 210–11; racial, 210–11

Kay, Margarita, 167
kinship, 121, 144–45, 148–49, 189, 210–11. *See also* relations, relationality
knives, 7, 121–24
knowledge: Indigenous, 125, 194, 200, 212n11; normative, 158; scientific, 61, 73–74, 77–78, 86, 91, 102–4
Korsmeyer, Carolyn, 6
Kristeva, Julia, 158–59, 161

labor, 92–93; agricultural, 72; animal, 93–94, 99–100; conditions of, 189; and death, 91–92
Landecker, Hannah, 2, 37
language, 32, 60, 87–88, 90–91, 116, 119–20, 131–32, 143–44, 159–61, 177–78
Latin America, 34, 48n3. *See also* Belize; Caribbean
Liebig, Justus von, 198
Lien, Marianne Elisabeth, 104–5

life, living, ix–x, 64–67, 72–73, 152, 154, 158–61, 187, 203; animal, 90–92, 96–97; and colonialism, 29–33; and death, 115–16, 122–23, 138–41, 143–44; and ecology, 40–43; plant, 194–95, 201–2; and pregnancy, 166–67, 169–70, 171–72; relations of, 57–59, 96–97; thresholds of, 6, 38–39, 43, 115–16, 120, 121–26, 137–39, 140–42, 149. *See also* death, dying; ventilator, ventilation

lifeline, 142–43

life support, 140–44, 150–54, 161. *See also* ventilator, ventilation

limen, liminality, 1, 6, 48n4, 168–69, 188, 204–5. *See also* thresholds

Lingis, Alphonso, 138–39, 151–52

Littorai winery, 198–99

livestock. *See under* animals

local, 43–44, 62, 98–99, 116, 118–19, 130, 132, 133n6, 191–93, 198, 209. *See also* global

Lock, Margaret, 147

logistics, 89–90, 92–94, 96–97, 99–101, 104–105, 105n2

London, 29–31, 45–47

loss, 37–39, 44–45, 159–60, 170–71

machines, 34, 36, 45–46, 60–61, 67, 143–44, 147–49, 153–54. *See also* glucose, glucometer; ventilator, ventilation

Malani, Nalini, 158–61

Malinowski, Bronislaw, 36, 210–11

Mansfield, Becky, 15–16

manure, 106n5, 192–93, 197, 199–203. *See also* biodynamics; compost; cow pat pit (CPP)

Māori, 194, 200–201, 203, 210–11. *See also* indigeneity, Indigenous people

Maroney, Stephanie, 4

Martin, Emily, 16, 164–65

Marx, Karl, 40–41, 58, 79n1, 198

Masco, Joseph, 43

Mauss, Marcel, 116–17, 175

McCay, Clive, 77–78

McCollum, Siobhan, 40

meahcci, 120, 125–26, 131–32, 133nn5–6. *See also* Sámi

meat, 64, 72, 74–75, 77–78, 87–88, 90–92, 103–5, 112, 115–16, 122–28, 137–38, 142, 171. *See also* animals

meatpacking plants, 90–91, 96, 188

media, mediation, 7–9, 16, 18, 34–35, 139, 152, 168–69, 176, 201–3, 207–8. *See also* thresholds

medicated feed, 7, 13–14, 56–59, 61–65, 68–70, 72–77. *See also* food; vitamins

medicine, 13–14, 31–33, 39, 48n4, 56, 58–59, 65–66, 69, 144, 149, 161, 204–5; biomedicine, 5–6, 20, 48n2, 48n4, 168–69, 182n11

Meigs, Anna, 3

Menu Foods recall, 93, 106n6

Merck, 69–70

metabolic rift, 58, 197–98

metabolism, 1, 3–4, 8–9, 11, 57, 79n1; and acceleration, 59; and capitalism, 40–41; contradictions of, 160–61; and conversion, 59–64; and efficiency, 72–76; and environment, 37; and health, 57–58; history of, 79n1; and hormones, 75; industrialization of, 57–65, 77–79, 87–88; and legacy of colonial anthropology, 36; microbial, 65–67, 70, 73–74; "nested," 3, 202; relations of, 64–65, 86–87; and scale, 59; and vitamins, 65–67

Mexico City, 16

microbes, 3–4, 11–13, 64–65; and body, 4, 170–71; industrialization of, 67–70; and soil health, 191, 195, 207; and vitamins, 66–70. *See also* cheese; metabolism; microbiome; vitamins

microbiome, 4, 13, 170, 191

migration, ix, 13–14, 116, 133n6, 137–38, 143

milk: dairy, 12–15, 17, 21n2, 62–64, 72; human, 180; sow, 94–95. *See also* cheese

Mintz, Sidney, 29–31, 35, 47, 47n1

modernity, modernization, 4, 58–59, 62–63, 72, 79, 90, 97–98, 102, 193–94

Mol, Annemarie, ix, 2, 4, 17, 142, 181n2
monocultures, monoculturing, 33, 90–94, 97, 102–3, 104–5. *See also* agriculture; factories; farming
Moore, Jason, 58, 197
Moran-Thomas, Amy, 5–6, 9–10, 115, 188
mothers, motherhood, mothering, 144–45, 160–61, 166–73, 181n7. *See also* gender; kinship; pregnancy
movement, 40–41, 57, 79, 120, 143–44, 149–50, 152–54
multiplicity, x, 138, 154, 163–67, 179, 181n2
Mumbai (India), 138–54
Münster, Daniel, 11, 211n3
Murray, Joseph, 194–95
mutualism, mutuality, 3–7, 11, 111, 115, 126, 132, 161, 174–75. *See also* relations
mycorrhizae, 4–5, 20, 195–97. *See also* fungi
Myers, Natasha, 195–96

narration, narrative, 97–99, 152, 172–73, 175, 179; first-person, 164–65, 177, 179
native, 11–12, 191–92, 203–5. *See also* invasive
navel, 160–61
Nestle, Marion, 93
Netherlands, 164, 181n3, 182n17. *See also* Amsterdam
networks, 2, 73–74, 99–101, 117–18, 165–66, 179, 188, 193. *See also* actors, actants; chains; webs
New Zealand. *See* Aotearoa New Zealand
nonhumans, ix–x, 2, 11, 86, 92–94, 102–5, 120, 131. *See also* relations
normal, normality, 1–2, 9–10, 38–39, 46, 91, 174, 208–9
Norway, 112–13, 116, 119–20; Norwegianization, 116. *See also* Finnmark; Sámi
nourishment, 1–2, 4–6, 114, 164–65, 171–73, 180, 182n16, 187–89
nutrition (science), 3, 8–10; animal, 103–4; of biodynamics, 193; and deficiency, 65–67; of extractivist

agriculture, 197–98; feeding trauma patients, 146; and growth, 77–78; and "human motor," 60; and nonfoods, 9; of interrelated bodies, 36–37

ontology, 2, 92–93, 99, 111–13, 127–28, 129–31, 187, 194, 202–3. *See also* edibility; meat
organic farming. *See* biodynamics
organism, 6–8, 10–11, 14–16, 20, 187–88; farm as, 90, 101, 193–94, 197–98, 210–11; as machines, 60–61, 64–65; maternal, 169–70; and metabolism, 57–58, 64–65, 67, 79n1, 87–88; and modernity, 58–59
organs, 90–91, 96–97, 101, 103–5, 106n10, 107n11, 111, 124–25, 166–67
Overstreet, Katy, 13–14, 106n8
ownership, 121, 133nn6–7, 171–72

pain, 38–39, 138–39, 148, 152–53, 163, 166, 171, 175–76, 181n3
palatants, 89–95, 99–100, 102–3, 106nn6–8; and consistency, 97, 100–101. *See also* pets; pet food
pandemics, 188–89, 192, 206–7, 210–11. *See also* COVID-19 pandemic; epidemics
parasites, parasitism, 4–5, 8–9, 64–65, 72, 172–73. *See also* commensality; mutualism, mutuality; relations, relationality
passive voice, 164–65. *See also* narration, narrative
Patel, Sarvdaman, 200
Paxson, Heather, 91, 169
permaculture, 195–99. *See also* biodynamics
personhood, 115, 131, 165–66, 181n1, 182n20; more-than-human conception of, 203; and naming, 175–76. *See also* self, selfhood
pesticides, 9, 15–16, 33–34, 42–43, 188, 193–94. *See also* toxins, toxicants
Peters, Rudolph, 66
Petryna, Adriana, 38–39

pets, 4–5, 86–87, 90–95, 99, 100–101, 102–5, 106n6. *See also* animals
pet food, 7, 86, 89–95, 99–105, 106n6, 106n8, 107n15. *See also* food; palatants
Pfeiffer, Ehrenfried, 193
Pfizer, 68–70
pharmaceuticals, 3–4, 38, 67–68. *See also* antibiotics; medicated feed
placenta, 158, 160–61, 164–66, 171, 182n11, 182n13, 203; asymmetries of, 170–75, 178–79; atomistic view of, 168–69; as conduit, 167; as liminal object, 168–71; as provisional organ, 166–67; relations of, 167, 177–80; and subjectivity, 182n12; sustaining, 168; uncanniness of, 182n9. *See also* fetus; mothers, motherhood, mothering; pregnancy
planetary, 5, 20, 43, 46, 191–93, 200–201. *See also* climate, climate change; global; local; worlds, world-making
plantations: ecological legacies of, 35–36, 39–41; sugar, 29–30, 32–33, 45
Planthroposcene, 195–96
plants, 2, 4–5, 11, 32–33, 57–61, 64–67, 70, 87, 187–88, 194–97, 201–2, 204–5, 207–9
plastics, plasticity, 15–16, 31–32, 36–37, 41, 76
pleasure, 21n1, 35, 90–92, 94–95, 100–102, 140, 188
plurality, x, 2, 17–18. *See also* multiplicity
Pollan, Michael, 105
pollution, pollutants, 14–15, 33–34, 39–41. *See also* toxins, toxicants
Pomeroy, Rachel, 199–201
porosity, 2, 7–8, 15–16, 31, 177–78, 188. *See also* barriers; boundaries; relations, relationality; thresholds
posthumanism, 165, 179–80
post-Pasteurian, 12
power, 17–18, 58, 60, 112, 144–45, 154, 159, 165, 177–78
precarity, precariousness, ix–x, 117, 195–97, 200–201, 209–11
preeclampsia, 172

pregnancy, 163–66, 168, 174; and difference, 168–70; and gender, 181n7, 182n15; and parasitism, 172–73; relations of, 179–80, 181n1. *See also* fetus; gender; mothers, motherhood, mothering
Probyn, Elspeth, 15
process, 86–88, 115; of gestation, 168; of monoculturing, 102; processed foods, 4, 9, 31, 86–87, 99; of resuscitation, 141–42, 147–48; thresholding, 111–12
Proctor, Peter, 198–99, 201
profit, 61–63, 73–74, 87, 90–91
protein, 42, 60–65, 68–70, 93–95, 112, 146
public health, 9, 30–31, 36–37
Puig de la Bellacasa, Maria, 196
Pyramid Valley Vineyards, 206–9, 212n10

quality, qualities (material), 13, 86–87, 129, 201

rabbits, 205. *See also* animals
race, 1–2, 17–18, 21n1, 30–31, 35–36, 47n1, 48n3, 188–89, 194, 200–201, 210–11, 211n2. *See also* capitalism; indigeneity, Indigenous people; plantations; slavery
Raffaetà, Roberta, 12–13
Rapp, Rayna, 164–65
reciprocity, 117–19, 178–79
Reddy, Michael, 167
reenchantment. *See* disenchantment
Reese, Ashanté, 188
regionalism, 98–99
reindeer, 14, 112–13, 115–16, 121–26, 128, 130–32, 133nn6–7, 137–39. *See also* animals; Sámi
relations, relationality, ix–x, 7, 130–32, 134n11, 144–45, 164–66, 172–73, 179–80; bodily, 159–60, 167; coproductive, 165; impossibility of, 171; of individual to more than itself, 160–61, 175–77, 188–89; and industrialization, 64–65; and interrelation, 47, 202–3; between

life and death, 115–16, 122–23, 161; metabolic, 86–87; multidirectionalities of, 187; multispecies, ix–x, 10–11, 94–95, 100, 102–3, 112–15, 165–66, 188–89, 194–95, 208, 210–11; scale of, 57; social, ix–x, 117–19, 124–26, 130, 179. *See also* commensality; kinship; media, mediation; mutualism, mutuality; pregnancy

reproduction, 17–18, 21n1, 91–92, 165–66, 171, 177–79, 208. *See also* fetus; mothers, motherhood, mothering; placenta; pregnancy

respiration, 61, 147. *See also* ventilator, ventilation

responsibility, 165–66, 170–71, 175–78

resuscitation, 140–42, 149, 154; circuit of, 146–47; as movement, 143–44. *See also* ventilator, ventilation

revulsion, 16, 168–69

rhizosphere, 194–95. *See also* soil

ritual, ix, 6, 44, 48n4, 168, 192–93

Roach, Mary, 95, 100, 106n8

Roberts, Elizabeth, 16, 18

Rosaldo, Renato, 164–65

Rose, Deborah Bird, 202–3

Rosenberg, Gabriel, 91–92

Rotman, Brian, 2

Rouch, Hélène, 169–70

safety (food), 6–8, 12, 14–16. *See also* hygiene

Sámi, 116, 119–20, 123–32, 133nn5–6, 133n8, 134n10, 137–38. *See also* indigeneity, Indigenous people; Norway; reindeer

Samoa, 9–10

sanitation. *See* hygiene; safety

Saraiva, Tiago, 58

satisfaction, 100–101, 173, 188. *See also* pleasure

scale, ix–x, 35, 40–41; of animal agriculture, 56, 90–91; of capitalism, 58–59; of global consumption, 45–46; metabolic, 59, 73–74, planetary, 43; quantitative, 97. *See also* growth

Schor, Juliet, 6

science and technology studies (STS), 3, 164–65, 196. *See also* anthropology; food studies

science, slow, 196–98, 201–3

self, selfhood, 2, 131, 182n11; and autoimmune diseases, 16; digital, 2; and multiplicity, 160–61, 163–66, 168–73, 175, 177–80, 181n2, 188–89; narrating, 164–66. *See also* body; individual, individualism

self-sufficiency, 193, 197, 209–11. *See also* biodynamics

sensation, 86, 89–91, 93–94, 97–100, 106nn8–9, 107n14. *See also* palatants; taste, tasting

sentinel, 41–42

Seremetakis, C. Nadia, 97–98

Sharpe, Christina, 35

sheep, 12–14, 17–18, 197–98, 203–5. *See also* animals

Shorb, Mary, 69

Simpson, Audra, 35

slaughter, slaughterhouses, 89–91, 115–16, 121–26

slavery, 45, 47n1, 48n3, 189, 212n5. *See also* colonialism; race

Smil, Vaclav, 58

social, society, ix–x, 1–2, 6–11, 57–59, 96–99, 111–13, 114–18, 129–32, 133n6, 141–42, 179, 188–89, 196. *See also* individual, individualism; relations, relationality

soil, 191–93; degradation, 193–94, 196, 198; enhancement, 201–2, 207; fertility, 197–200; and indigenous sovereignty, 194, 210–11; multispecies relationality of, 195–96; vitality of, 194–95. *See also* biodynamics; indigeneity, Indigenous people

solidarity, 97–98, 188

Solomon, Harris, 10, 37

sovereignty, 6, 200–201, 203. *See also* indigeneity, Indigenous people

Steiner, Rudolf, 192–97

Stengers, Isabelle, 196, 212n11

Strathern, Marilyn, x, 179
subject, subjectivity, 97–98, 115, 131, 165–66, 168–69, 177–80, 182n11, 202–3. *See also* self, selfhood
substance, 2–6, 15–16, 79n1, 89–91, 93–94, 111–13, 114–15, 139, 140–41, 147–48, 153–54
sugar, 9–10, 29–30; and biology, 34–35; and chronic conditions, 32, 35; contradictory meanings of, 35, 44–45; and ecology, 33–34; history of, 29–30, 45; and interrelation, 47; and legacy of racial capitalism, 35–36, 45, 48n3. *See also* Belize; capitalism; diabetes; plantations
survival, 5–6, 38–39, 68–69, 159–60, 167, 196–97
sustainability, 6, 17–18, 187, 200–201. *See also* biodynamics
systems, 5, 18, 32–36, 57–59, 73–74, 86–88, 94–95, 105, 133n6, 188, 193, 197; analysis of, 58, 161; bodily, 15, 149–50, 154. *See also* networks

taboos, 111–12
TallBear, Kim, 43
taste, tasting, 1, 4, 29–30, 106n9, 124–26, 128–31; animal, 13–14, 89–95, 99–100, 104–5, 106nn7–8, 107n14; ethics of, 17–18; and industrial capitalism, 97–99; judgments, 128–31; transcorporeal, 13–14. *See also* experience; palatants; sensation
Taussig, Michael, 35
taxonomies, 2, 115, 127–28, 179–80, 208. *See also* classifications; edibility; food
terroir, 13–15, 191, 206–9. *See also* viticulture
thresholds, ix–x, 2, 4–6, 48n4; bodily, 37–38, 139, 160–61, 169–71; between celestial and terrestrial domains, 194; between conditions or states of being, 8–10; of edibility, 6, 112–16, 129–30; ethical, 18; and ex/change, 158; of healing, 36–37; and intensification, 6, 38–39; and limits, 6; between living and dying, 115–16, 122–23, 125–26, 137–39, 140–41, 149; between local and global, 191; and nourishment, 187, 189; between organism and environment, 14–18; and processes, 87–88; relations of, 114–15, 130–31; among species, 10–14; and world-making, 6–7. *See also* anthropology; barriers; borders; boundaries; edibility; food
thresholding objects, 7 169, 188–89
thresholding projects, 5, 18, 111–12
time, temporality, 2, 11, 31–32, 35–36, 43–44, 59, 62, 78–79, 117, 138–39, 144–47, 152–54, 173, 193, 196, 201–3. *See also* duration
tolerance, 16–17, 38–39. *See also* thresholds
total mixed rations (TMR), 13–14
toxins, toxicants, 5–6, 8–9, 11, 15–16, 37–43, 57, 192. *See also* pollution, pollutants
Tracy, Megan, 11
transcorporeality, 3, 14, 91–92, 94–95, 103, 203
transformation, x, 1–2, 6–8, 10–12, 48n4, 64–65, 86, 89–90, 101, 103, 111–13, 114–16, 121, 124–28, 158–59, 165–67, 181n2, 196–97, 201–3
transgression, 8, 20–21, 158–61, 169
transmission, 11, 133n6, 139, 158, 188–89
transnationalism, 90–91, 96–97, 165–66, 198. *See also* global; planetary
transplantation, 35–36, 147, 169–70
trauma, 2, 48n3, 140–49
Tsing, Anna, 198, 208
Turner, Victor, 6, 48n4

uncanny, 168–69, 182n9
uniformity, 13, 93–94, 97, 101, 103–5

value, 12–13, 90–93, 102–3, 107n15, 129–31, 134n9, 193–94, 204, 209–11
Varanger. *See* Norway
ventilator, ventilation, 7, 138–44; economy of, 143–44, 153–54, 161;

and extubation, 146–47; as feeding, 146–47, 151, 154; and intubation, 147–48; materiality of, 148–49; narrative of, 152; technology of, 147–49; as threshold, 149; and weaning, 149–53. *See also* breath, breathing
vermin, 4–5. *See also* animals
Vialles, Noëlie, 115–16
violence: environmental, 34; histories of, 32–33; materiality of, 159, 161; racial, 188; slow, 192
viruses, 188–89
vitality, 92–93, 143, 148–49, 161, 194–95, 207. *See also* soil
vitamins, 64–67; and growth, 72–73, 77–78; industrial production of, 67–70. *See also* growth; medicated feed
viticulture: biodynamic, 192–94, 198–99, 201, 203–8; and climate change, 191–92; history of, 205–6; and Latinx workers, 189; and pandemics, 189, 192, 205–7; thresholds of, 191; and transatlantic slave trade, 189; and weed management, 207–9; world-making role of, 194. *See also* biodynamics; soil
Vogel, Sarah, 41

Walker, Kara, 36
waste, 10–11, 14–16, 33, 41–43, 58, 60–63, 73–74, 79n3, 86–87, 90–91, 112–13, 124–26, 161, 167–68. *See also* by-production
weaning. *See under* ventilator, ventilation
webs, 2, 18–19, 31, 57, 87–88, 194–95, 210–11. *See also* chains
weeds, 113, 206–9
Weiss, Brad, 106n9, 107n13
well-being, ix–x, 92, 200–201. *See also* health
Wells, Jonathan, 58
West, Harry, 12
Weston, Kath, 43
Whitmarsh, Ian, 35
wine. *See* viticulture
World Health Organization, 38–39
worlds, world-making, 3–4, 6–7, 17–18, 34, 58–59, 79, 97–98, 111–13, 115, 118–19, 131–32, 139, 187–88, 194–97, 209–11. *See also* global; planetary
Wrye, Jen, 90–91

Yates-Doerr, Emily, 9, 127–28, 142

Zero Budget Farming, 200, 211n3